Instructor's Manual

Psychology

Second Edition

Instructor's Manual

GLEITMAN

Psychology

Second Edition

Henry Gleitman
UNIVERSITY OF PENNSYLVANIA

Christine Massey
UNIVERSITY OF PENNSYLVANIA

Hilary Schmidt
UNIVERSITY OF PENNSYLVANIA

Alan Silberberg
THE AMERICAN UNIVERSITY

with *A Guide to Audiovisual Materials*

James B. Maas
CORNELL UNIVERSITY

W • W • NORTON & COMPANY • NEW YORK • LONDON

ISBN 0-393-95384-X

W. W. Norton & Company, Inc., 500 Fifth Avenue, New York, N.Y. 10110
W. W. Norton & Company, Ltd., 37 Great Russell Street, London WC1B 3NU

1 2 3 4 5 6 7 8 9 0

Contents

Introduction   1

Chapter 1   **Introduction**   19

Chapter 2   **Biological Bases of Behavior**   23

Chapter 3   **Motivation**   31

Chapter 4   **Learning**   41

Chapter 5   **Sensory Processes**   57

Chapter 6   **Perception**   71

Chapter 7   **Memory**   81

Chapter 8   **Thinking**   93

Chapter 9   **Language**   111

Chapter 10   **The Biological Basis of Social Behavior**   119

Chapter 11   **Social Psychology**   129

Chapter 12   **The Individual and Society: The Contributions of Sigmund Freud**   139

Chapter 13   **General Issues in Development**   147

Chapter 14   **Cognitive Development: Thought**   159

Chapter 15   **Cognitive Development: Language**   175

Chapter 16   **Social Development**   185

Chapter 17   **Intelligence: Its Nature and Measurement**   195

Chapter 18   **Personality Assessment**   203

Chapter 19   **Psychopathology**   209

Chapter 20   **Treatment of Psychopathology**   227

A Guide to Audiovisual Materials   233

　　Some Recommended Films for Introductory Psychology   234

　　Catalogs   258

　　Film Series   259

　　Slide Sets and Overhead Transparencies   264

　　Audio Catalogs and Programs   265

　　Addresses of Distributors   266

　　Index of Abbreviations   269

　　Computer Simulations   270

Instructor's Manual

Psychology

Second Edition

Introduction

This manual is intended to be a guide to the second edition of Henry Gleitman's *Psychology.* It begins with a discussion of the book as a whole, starting out with the author's approach to teaching, followed by a few summary comments about the book's organization and content. It then proceeds chapter by chapter, following the text. Each chapter of the manual begins with an "Overview" in which the major organizational themes of the chapter are set forth, followed by a "Summary of Main Topics." After this, there are two sections called "Discussion Topics" and "Demonstrations" which provide a number of suggestions for supplementing lectures. Each manual chapter concludes with an annotated list of selected readings.

The final section of the manual is devoted to a film and media guide prepared by James B. Maas of Cornell University. This guide offers suggestions on how to use films, slides, computer simulations, and so on, and where to get them.

Approach to Teaching

Any author who writes an introductory textbook presumably has some underlying educational philosophy—about teaching in general and teaching the introductory course in particular. This philosophy cannot help but shape the way his book is written. To indicate the educational philosophy adopted by the author of *Psychology,* we here reprint a speech he gave about the introductory course in psychology a few years ago.*

*This speech was originally presented as the American Psychological Foundation's Distinguished Teaching Award address at the meeting of the American Psychological Association in Anaheim, California, in August, 1983. It was reprinted by the *American Psychologist* under the title "Introducing Psychology" (1984, 39: 421–27) and is here reproduced in a slightly abbreviated form.

Introducing Psychology

I would like to share some of my ideas about the introductory psychology course, a course I've taught for many years. But please don't get me wrong; I don't mean to advise anyone on how to teach it. Teaching is an exceedingly personal activity, and anyone who presumes to advise anyone else on how to go about it does so at his or her own risk. One of the first who tried was Socrates, and everyone knows that he did not come to the best of all possible ends. (Of course, it's just possible that his end had more to do with the fact that he did not publish than his teaching, but that is another story.)

What I want to do is relate what I think about this course; how I came to conclusions about it; to what audience the course is addressed (or at least to whom *I* address it); what I hope this audience gets out of it and how; and finally, what it is that I personally get out of this enterprise of academic introduction. . . .

I still remember my first lecture. I was terrified. I looked at the students uncertainly. There were so many of them, and so few of me. I then realized that the first thing you need is a *beginning*. But what kind of beginning is the right one?

For that first, dreadful lecture I used what I now call the *confused beginning*. The students looked hostile, and I shuffled, paused, and said that "Psychology is the Study of Behavior." And I felt that the atmosphere had become more hostile. So I smiled uncertainly, and added, "It is also the study of consciousness," and the atmosphere got even more hostile.

Since then, I tried a number of different approaches. The second semester I taught the course, I used the *no-nonsense beginning*. I just came in and said, "Psychology is a science," and looked at them defiantly. Surprisingly enough it worked. Another year I thought up the *historical beginning,* but I never had the courage to use it, then or since. It went like this: "In 1879, Wundt said: 'Let there be psychology.' And behold—there was darkness!"

The beginning I finally settled on, the one that minimizes the recurrent anxiety and stage fright I always have at the very start, is the *bureaucratic beginning,* which goes as follows: "The name of this course is Introductory Psychology. My name is Henry Gleitman. There will be two midterms and a final." I regard the bureaucratic beginning as one of my major contributions to the theory and practice of teaching the introductory course. I've memorized it until I can recite it in my sleep. It gives me my opening line and gets me over my nervousness.

Alright, so I got the beginning. Once I got that, I realized that there were one or two further questions I had to ask myself, such as "What is psychology about?" and "How do I tell beginning students about it?" These questions have occupied my thoughts for the last 30 years. Oddly enough, I discovered that my attempts to answer these questions were not unrelated to some of my own personal characteristics, including the fact that I have a strong interest in the theater.

WHO IS THE AUDIENCE?

The first question I asked myself was "Who is the audience?" The initial step was to discover who that audience is not. I now realize that, when I first started, I addressed an imaginary audience made up of my professors in graduate school. I must have wanted to impress Edward Chace Tolman and Warner Brown, my own great teachers who were not even there to hear me. I still wanted to prove that I was oh so smart and clever and could win any argument, whatever its pros and cons. It was a catastrophe, and I hereby apologize to all my early Psych 1 students who were exposed to this foolishness and vanity. Instead of teaching them, I tried to impress them, and I failed at both.

So, I recognized that the proper audience is *not* composed of the persons who taught *me*. Well then, who is it? A widely held view is that the primary audience is made up of those students who will go on and take further courses. Or, in fact, that it should be that subset of this group who will become majors and eventually go to graduate school. I personally took a different tack, for I decided that an audience that is even more important is just those students who will *not* go on. After all, God must have loved Psych 1 students, for He made so many of them. The large majority of them will *not* go on to become psychology majors. At my own institution, a half or two-thirds of them do not go on to take any further courses in the field. Should we just forget these students and treat them as some species of eductional cannon fodder while concentrating all our efforts on the ones who do go on? We could go all the way and focus just on those who'll go to graduate school and get a Ph.D., who will presumably teach Psych 1 in their turn and focus on those students who go on to get their Ph.D., who will then teach Psych 1 in their turn . . . and so on until the end of time. It doesn't make sense.

There is another reason for my concern for the people who don't go on to take another course in psychology. Whatever mistakes the instructor makes in teaching them are forever. There is no way to rectify them. On the other hand, if an instructor somehow misteaches the misguided creatures who do take a further course, let alone become psychology majors, other colleagues who teach those later courses can fix the errors. Needless to say, I'm overstating my case. The students who do go on must obviously get a foundation for what they'll learn later. So the students who never take another course are surely not the *only* audience. But they are a vital audience, and they are so often ignored.

What can be done for this audience that will never again set foot in a psychology lecture hall? My own attempts are based on the belief that psychology is part of their training in the liberal arts. Actually, *training* is the wrong word. Training is what golf pros provide. Golf pros don't teach; they train, and that's exactly what they should do. I don't want my golf pro to tell me his philosophy of life, or the relationship between golf and democracy, or golf and spinal reflexes, or golf and reductionism. I want him to tell me about golf so that I can swing the club properly. Period. In short, I want him to *train* me, not to teach me. But in the introductory course, I see myself as a teacher, not a trainer. I want the students who take Psych 1 to see something about psychology that makes it worthy to be taught in a college or a university. I believe that this course has to be taught so that it becomes relevant to the artistic and intellectual achievements that are part of our human heritage. If so, it will be of genuine value to the students who will never go further. But it will also help students who do go on. They will first have learned something about psychology as part of a broad human cultural enterprise that includes chemistry and English novels and Gregorian chants before they become professionals and narrow their vision and scope.

WHAT I TRY TO AVOID IN TEACHING

I've said a bit about who the course is for. But what should it teach and how? I'll begin with a few of my prejudices about what should not be stressed.

Emphasizing What's Backstage Rather Than Out Front. After some early mistakes, I made a resolution. To use theatrical terms, I decided not to take the students backstage. For the trouble is that in psychology the sheer quantity of backstage apparatus is awesome. In fact, it can be argued that we have more stuff offstage than onstage—methodology piled upon methodology, arguments about definitions, technical philosophical discussions, and so on. Personally, I try to avoid such matters whenever I can. Thus, I prefer not to get into methodology as such, and I will not present an early lecture on dependent and independent variables, statistical methods, or the nature of causation. These are things students would have to know if they wanted to become professionals themselves, but these topics are not appropriate for beginning students. It's different if the methodology grows out of the particular subject matter itself. Then the methodology must be taught, but the students will understand why. If the instructor is talking about IQ, heredity, and environment, then the instructor obviously has to bring up correlation coefficients and what they do and do not mean. But now the instructor can say, quite truthfully, "Look, if you want to understand this topic, you have to understand another subject first."

I have rather similar feelings about lengthy discussions of why psychology is a science. As I mentioned, I sometimes began the course by asserting that "psychology is a science," and then I felt obliged to go to the blackboard and tell the class what a science is and parade about with second-hand comments about the philosophy of science. . . . But by now, I've come to the conclusion that psychologists shouldn't make that much of a fuss about whether psychology is or is not a science. Currently, I simply say that psychology is a science and quickly add that it doesn't wear a white coat, but that's all. It's my job to show students that psychology is a science, not to badger them with assertions. To show them the areas of solid accomplishment—as in visual perception and language. Or work that's truly elegant—as in certain reaction time studies of memory search. Or efforts of great potential social value—such as attempts to relate psychopathologies to neurochemistry or learning theory, or both. But the point has to be made by actual demonstration. A physicist can get away with simply saying that physics is a science, but a psychologist has to show them. I try to do this, but I don't want to overemphasize psychology's methods. After all, there are so many areas of psychology in which there are such huge mountains of methodology and such little mounds of results.

Emphasizing What's Wrong Rather Than What's Right.   Another thing I try to avoid, especially in the introductory course, is to convey an attitude of disrespect for positions I don't agree with. I never want students to sneer. Therefore, I try very hard (here, too, atoning for past sins) to present all views in such a way that they appear to be reasonable positions that men and women of good will and fine intellect may once have held and may still hold, despite the fact that I may be personally quite certain that these views are wrong. Although in graduate school many students (myself included) were rewarded for proving that some other person was wrong and silly, it doesn't work in the classroom, at least not for me. I think it's too easy for a lecturer to deride others, even major thinkers of the past or present because *they* can't appear in the classroom and defend themselves. Then the real losers are the students.

For somewhat similar reasons, I also try to avoid spending a long time in building up a position, only to tear it down subsequently. It makes the students feel tremendously frustrated and dissatisfied. As an example, what can be done with someone like Freud? I believe that 90 percent of Freud's theorizing can be attacked on grounds of looseness, circularity, or methodological naivety, or because it's just plain false. If someone wants to make a case that Freud's work was all just a monstrous hoax and illusion, he or she certainly can. But what is the point? Freud is obviously someone the students *want* to know about. And he is someone they *should* know about because he is so clearly a gigantic figure. I usually introduce him by saying that he represents something of a paradox. He should probably not be regarded as a great scientist, but I tell the students that he was something else—he was a genuinely great man, one of those people who changed the thinking of not just one generation, but a whole century. I believe that he, like many others, has to be taught with respect, so that students can understand his position and see the sense in which it is so important in nineteenth- and twentieth-century thought.

WHAT I DO TRY TO ACCOMPLISH

Thus far, I've talked about things I try *not* to do. What I do attempt has two aspects: one intellectual, the other emotional.

The Intellectual Aspect.   Intellectually, one of the most important things I try to achieve is to tie the course together, to integrate it so that the subject is not seen as a set of unrelated topics and so that the student's mind does not become a mirror of so many of psychology's research activities—fragmented into ever smaller pieces. . . .

The trick is to create organic links within the subject. I've tried to do this, but it only works up to a point. The trouble is that psychology is not a neatly organized field, but a kind of Hapsburg Empire of the sciences that's always threatening to fall apart. I've tried to forge some links by presenting different topics within overarching conceptual categories that help the student organize the material. In recent times, I tried to present the field as a few major ways of understanding "mind." One broad topic was "mind as a reflex machine," a general category that allowed me to talk about Descartes, neurophysiology, and conditioning, so that students could see that behavior theories relate to the field as a whole and don't just float off by themselves. Another broad topic was "mind as knower," which let me treat the fields of sensation, perception, memory, thinking, and language under one common, conceptual umbrella, linked by a common set of questions and by the nature–nurture issue that runs through all of them despite enormous differences in their substantive particulars. . . .

Thus far, I've talked about establishing links within the subject, but there are links between psychology and other disciplines that are no less important. As a teacher, I want the students to see some relationships between the different fields that are represented in a college curriculum. They may be listed on different pages of the school catalog and may be offered by different departments, but if they stay forever walled off in different compartments of the student's mind, there is something wrong with his or her education. I think that psychology is unusually suited to counteract this. The linkages are there in the subject matter of psychology and all the instructor has to do is to point them out. Suppose I'm talking about sensation or perception. The natural starting point is to begin with the questions that John Locke and those who followed him asked themselves: "Where does human knowledge come from? What is its nature? How does it ever get into the head?" Before I know it, I'm into the nature–nurture controversy. There is an intimate relation between some of the problems debated by philosophers and those that theorists of perception try to settle in the laboratory. Students seem to be enormously pleased when they can connect something they hear in one field with what they've learned in another. They tell me: "Now I finally understand what went on in my philosophy class." I certainly hope that they tell their philosophy instructor: "Now at last I understand what's been going on in my psychology class." It's not that psychologists can explain such things better than their colleagues in philosophy, but that it helps to bring up topics in a new and different context.

Much the same is true of other areas—biology, the social sciences, linguistics, and the arts. Consider perception. A student's appreciation of this area will become deeper if he or she understands that, apart from its roots in philosophy, the study of perception began with the Renaissance painters who tried to

represent a three-dimensional world on a two-dimensional canvas. Such linkages
help students learn the subject matter, for they give them a framework within
which their knowledge can be organized. However, I think that these linkages
are a good thing in and of themselves because they are what a liberal arts education is all about. . . . Psychologists live at the intersection of a large number of
intellectual trade routes. As a result, they can shed plenty of light on just about
everything (as well as plenty of darkness).

There's still another kind of intellectual linkage that I care about, and that
concerns the relation between various aspects of the field to intellectual and
socioeconomic history. Consider John Locke and the idea that all knowledge
comes through the senses, which is the starting point for a psychologist's concern
with sensation and perception. I believe that students should know that John
Locke was a spokesman of the English merchant class that had just rid itself of
absolute monarchy and the last Stuart king. They should understand why
Locke's opposition to built-in ideas can also be an argument against built-in ideas
of the divine right of kings and ultimately against hereditary privilege. If all
human beings enter life with a *tabula rasa*, then all distinctions between them
must be due entirely to a difference in their environments. I want the students
to see how this idea is incorporated in the Declaration of Independence, with its
self-evident truth that "all men are created equal"; how it underlies the American belief that men and women are almost infinitely perfectable by proper
changes in their environment, especially through education; and how it finds its
modern expression in American behaviorism and its insistence on the paramount
importance of learning and the near-limitless plasticity of animals and human
beings. Once students understand this, they start to recognize that views about
the nature of the human mind tend to have social and political consequences.

All this time I've discussed my attempts to connect the subject matter
(sensory mechanisms, animal learning, social behavior, etc.) to other areas within
the field of psychology, to other disciplines, or to social and intellectual history.
Yet I've found that there's a danger here because I have to make sure that in my
concern for the forest I don't lose the trees. Of course, the specifics of the subject matter must be taught. There are so many facts to be learned—lateral inhibition, variable-interval schedules, attribution theory, and so on. (After all,
how else could I examine the students with multiple-choice questions?) In fact,
it turns out that the students are more likely to learn and remember these
specifics of the subject if they are embedded in the larger contexts I have tried
to sketch. This may be because these contexts provide organizing frameworks
for memory retrieval; because they help motivate the students by adding another
perspective on the material that interests them; or because they give me a
different slant on the subject, which then motivates *me*. Whatever the reason, I
found that providing such general contexts helps the student learn the subject's
particulars.

There's still another danger in any attempt to present an organized account of the subject matter. The links provided may be fragile; the conceptual umbrellas may have holes in them. How serious is this? I believe that as a teacher I have to make a choice. In any science, and certainly in psychology, we can't hope for theoretical formulations that truly organize more than a fraction of the data. There are always discrepancies and counterexamples, so that it's a virtual certainty that whatever framework I have chosen doesn't really fit all of the known facts. But I believe that without such a framework the students will understand nothing at all. Suppose I try to present the real truth to the best of my knowledge (and of course I don't even remotely know all the facts, for no one could possibly read even a tenth of the available literature and still find time to eat and sleep). Suppose I do try to present the scientific truth of 1983, all of the truth, and nothing but the truth. If so, I'll be forced to present just a catalog of the data, with perhaps a list of footnotes about the many theories that failed. At best, my students will demonstrate that, if sufficiently motivated, they can memorize this catalog, just as they can memorize dozens of nonsense syllables.

So I've decided to present links, umbrellas, and frameworks, despite the fact that they are wanting. Suppose I discuss language. I know that the so-called standard theory of syntax has enormous problems, but can I possibly present those problems and provide any kind of coherent picture? I think not, and so I present a very simplified version of this old standard theory, and I am very pleased if the students understand even that. Consider memory, which I usually discuss in terms of the standard stage theory. I know that this theory is beset by difficulties on every side, such as the different levels of processing, the question of whether short-term memory is best described as activated long-term memory, and contradictory results from human amnesic patients. I again make a choice and present the material as organized by the old theory: The conceptual framework is some years out of date, but I honestly believe that it's better than no framework at all.

Is this approach reasonable? I've said that any framework I present must be wanting and that there is simply no way in which I can present anything remotely like the whole truth (even if I knew it). However, suppose the framework I have chosen is utterly false; suppose I've decided to organize the material in terms of some psychological equivalent of phlogiston theory. What then? I can only hope that I'm a good enough psychologist to avoid such errors, but who can be sure? Teaching is always a tightrope act. In order to teach, an instructor must oversimplify and must present a coherence that is not really there. The instructor presents a caricature and hopes that it captures the essence. But if it doesn't, if the links given turn out not to be genuine, they will still have served some purpose, at least for those students who do go on. For these links provide a scaffolding for the knowledge these students are asked to acquire, even if this scaffold has to be dismantled later on.

In sum, all the science of psychology gives us is small islands of coherence in a vast sea of chaos. As a teacher, I want my students to concentrate on the islands even though I want them to know that the sea is there.

The Emotional Aspects.   Thus far, I've talked primarily about the intellectual aspects of teaching the introductory course. However, I believe that teaching is not just an intellectual process; it is also an emotional one. This point brings me back to the relationship between the psychology of the teacher and that of the actor. When giving a lecture, the teacher's job is not just a matter of getting the students to understand the subject, no more than the actor's task is merely to have an audience follow the playwright's lines. It's also a personal business of bringing it across. I believe that, to accomplish this, the teacher has to show his or her own personal involvement. I give a lecture, and out there are 300 freshmen and sophomores sitting on uncomfortable seats, in a hall that on most days is badly ventilated and is not too well lit. They're there because Psych 1 fulfills a distribution requirement or because they need an extra elective credit. If it's a nice spring day (and even if it isn't), these eighteen- and nineteen-year-olds might prefer to do all sorts of things other than listen to a lecture on the ins and outs of dissonance theory. How can I make them listen? I am sure of one thing. They won't care, if they don't feel that *I* care. Somehow my caring has to be part of the course, and the odd thing is that it cannot be faked. It has to be for real. But worse, it must be for real every time I teach the course. It's easy enough to convey the excitement I feel about a topic the very first time I talk about it. But what about the next semester and the semester after that? I've discovered that the way I try to keep the subject fresh is similar to what actors do in a long-run show. To keep from going stale, they try to revive the emotion they felt on opening night and during rehearsal. I see my job as much the same. I have to recreate my original excitement as a lecturer. The only way I can manage—and I'm afraid, I don't always succeed—is by thinking about the subject again before a lecture, no matter how often I've lectured on the subject previously. By now, I've taught fifty-four semesters of introductory psychology, but even so, I wouldn't think of *not* preparing a lecture. The fact that I've given a particular lecture before doesn't matter; I still need another couple of hours just to freshen my mind, to give it a new emotional sense.

To speak more broadly, I believe that teaching is, in part, a sort of libidinal enterprise. It conveys some passion, and this helps to involve the student. Again, the analogy to the actor may be relevant. Actors want an audience to become involved. If the actors are good, they will not be too narcissistic. They will want the involvement to be not so much with them as through them with the play and the characters they portray. I think that much the same goes on in teaching. Somehow, the teacher must get the students interested in him or her. Here too, the narcissistic temptations have to be resisted. The trick is (and I don't know how it's done) to somehow stand off to the side so that whatever emotion was directed at the teacher ends up where it belongs—with psychology.

I said that I want the students to become involved with psychology, but I want to amend that statement. What I really want is for students to become involved with the intellectual life, with the process of learning. Personally, I don't really care whether they end up loving psychology, philosophy, or biology. I want them to love learning. If it turns out that this love is for psychology, then fine. If it's for some other discipline, that's fine, too.

WHAT DO I GET OUT OF TEACHING THIS COURSE?

I've talked about some of my ideas about the introductory course—to whom I direct it and what I want students to gain from it. There's one thing I haven't mentioned: what *I* receive from teaching it. Why do I keep on teaching Psych 1 after all these years? There are several reasons.

One is that it is exciting for me intellectually. I've found that when I am teaching these people who are new to the field, I have to be at my sharpest as a psychologist. Surprisingly enough, people can generally fool their colleagues. They can always throw out clouds of obfuscation that will let them get away with presuppositions that they've never really examined, because colleagues are often too polite or preoccupied to press on. But Psych 1 students are different. They are like the little boy and the emperor's clothes. They say: "I don't understand why." And the teacher can't answer, "Because it is more objective," or "Because it's a science," since they'll just ask the same question again. They may ask, "Why should I care about color vision when I really want to know how people think and feel?" or "What's the point of studying rats and pigeons?" So, teachers are forced back to basics and have to question themselves honestly and without evasion. . . .

From teaching this course I also gain as a social being. What I get from a good lecture is what an actor gets from a good performance: an emotional high, a peak experience. (There are one or two experiences that are in the same ballpark, but they tend to occur in more private settings.) This doesn't mean that lecturing doesn't have its negative side. If I give a bad Psych 1 lecture, I become depressed and drag myself around for an hour or more afterwards. When that happens, what I really want to do is to give that same lecture again, to undo it. For a while, I taught two Psych 1 courses—each one and a half hours long—back to back. Teaching three hours in a row was physically killing, but it was gratifying even so. When one of the two lectures didn't go well, I remembered the other that did. (Of course, when *both* went badly, I wanted to shoot myself.)

So, by teaching Psych 1, I gain as a psychologist: It enhances my understanding. I also gain as a social being: It gratifies my vanity. But over and above that, I gain in still another, simpler, human way—as a moral being. What I get is a sense of day-by-day fulfillment. Research does not give me that. In research, the issue is not whether the investigator is well-intentioned, smart, or hard-working: What ultimately matters is whether he or she is *right*. Unfortunately, that is not up to the individual but to nature or, if you wish, to God. There's every reason to believe that God doesn't like psychologists because He almost always proves them wrong. So, research may be fun, but on a day-to-day basis it's so often frustrating. However, when I teach these young sophomores and freshmen in Psych 1, I get an immediate feeling of fulfillment, a sense that in a small way I'm affecting people's lives and that I have earned my daily bread. Emotionally, teaching is my daily bread and butter; research is the cake.

To teach is to affect young people of all sorts. I've been blessed with some wonderful students, and several that I taught in Psych 1 have gone on to become psychologists and are now among our finest scholars. Some of them originally wanted to enter other areas, such as physics or political science, but after taking my course, they decided on a career in psychology. Should I congratulate myself? Should I pat myself on the back and say: "How wonderful that I have influenced these marvelous people to go into psychology?" I'm not sure. Of course, I'm pleased and proud—who wouldn't be? But let's face it. I might just as well say that I've robbed physics or political science, for these brilliant people would surely have become first-rate in whatever they chose. There's no way of stopping the very best students: They'll go on to be top-notch whether in one field or in another. So with them, I'm not sure whether I've really done something for the world, although I believe I did achieve something for psychology.

What about the poorer students? There's one I'll always remember. I gave him an F for plagiarism. This was in the days when I was young enough to act on my educational convictions and assign term papers (to a class of 200). I read his paper, and it had some wonderful sections, with brilliant and provocative prose. As I read on, I gradually realized that it was the brilliant and provocative prose of Edna Heidbreder. I checked, and indeed, the pages were taken *verbatim* from her *Seven Psychologies.* In due course, the student came into my office. He looked like a born loser, with flushed face and shaking voice, but he finally convinced me—and it took some convincing—that he had *not* been plagiarizing. He was only quoting, he really didn't know that he was supposed to indicate quotations with quotation marks. He was not dishonest; he was only stupid. So I said, "Okay, here's your D. Now go, with my blessing." Well, he went off, but I saw him again and again because he decided to become a psychology major, D or no D. I had him repeatedly, in various later courses, in which he struggled and worked hard and always did mediocre work. Finally, in his senior year, he reached the pinnacle of his intellectual capacity and earned a B-. When he graduated he came up to me in his cap and gown, shook my hand sheepishly, and thanked me because I made him see what a wonderful thing it is to read a book. At least to me, he no longer looked like a loser. I felt that this was someone I had really done something for and that in the grand scheme of things it may have been just as valuable as convincing a potential top-notch physicist to become a top-notch psychologist instead.

In the last analysis, I believe that the academic business is not just a profession or a trade; it comes down to being a calling. The calling is to perpetuate knowledge, and add to it, and hold it dear, and transmit it to others. Teaching the introductory course is just one of the ways in which that calling is practiced.

Because of this, I can say to myself on any given day: "My experiments are going badly; I just lost my research grant; a paper of mine was rejected; my daughter has the measles; and I had an argument with my wife. But—I gave a great Psych 1 lecture, and so all is well."

The Organization of *Psychology*

The preceding section described the author's general approach to teaching the introductory course. Some aspects of this approach—in particular the concern with providing an organizing framework—are reflected in the general organization of the book.

The book is organized around five main questions: How do humans (and, where relevant, animals) act? How do they know? How do they interact with each other? How do they develop? How do they differ among themselves? The five main parts of the book—Action, Cognition, Social Behavior, Development, and Individual Differences—describe psychology's attempts to answer these questions. In brief outline, the topics are dealt with as follows:

Chapter 1 "Introduction" serves as an introduction to the field as a whole. Its main theme is that psychological phenomena can be regarded from various perspectives—as mental events, as overt behaviors, as reflections of underlying physiological processes, as social interactions, as manifestations of development, and so on. To illustrate this point, the chapter takes up one phenomenon, dreaming, and then shows how this can be considered from each of the various perspectives.

PART I   ACTION

This part focuses on overt behavior and its physiological basis.

Chapter 2 ("Biological Bases of Behavior") concerns the biological underpinning of human and animal action and presents a discussion of the nervous system and its operation.

Chapter 3 ("Motivation") deals with directed, motivated behavior and asks about the biological basis of such acts. The topics include self-regulatory motives like thirst and hunger, the emergency reactions of strong fear and rage, and various states of arousal as well as arousal's opposite, sleep.

Chapter 4 ("Learning") shows how the action-oriented perspective described in Chapters 2 and 3 has been applied to describe how organisms learn to behave in new ways. Its topics include classical and instrumental (that is, operant) conditioning and a general approach to these areas that goes under the umbrella-title "behavior theory." The chapter continues with a description of some applications of behavior theory and concludes with a discussion of certain limitations of this general approach.

PART II   COGNITION

This part is concerned with what humans know, how they come to know it, and how this knowledge is retrieved in memory, transformed through thinking, and communicated by language.

Chapter 5 ("Sensory Processes") asks how the senses can provide us with information about the world outside. After a brief discussion of psychophysics and an introduction to the basic ideas of signal detection, the chapter takes a brief tour through all the senses, and then focuses on one sense modality, vision. It takes up such topics as visual receptor action, sensory interaction, and color vision.

Chapter 6 ("Perception") is concerned with the organization and interpretation of sensory information which leads to the perception of objects and events. The chapter considers certain aspects of perceptual organization, including form, depth, and movement, and asks how they might arise in light of the nature-nurture controversy.

Chapter 7 ("Memory") deals with the way knowledge is stored in memory, is maintained over time, and is retrieved when called for later. Among its topics are the distinctions between various memory systems, such as short-term and long-term memory, the contrast between associative and organizational theories of memory, and various aspects of memory search and retrieval.

Chapter 8 ("Thinking") deals with the way knowledge is reorganized through thinking. After a discussion of the hierarchical structure of directed thinking in adults, and of attempts to simulate such mental activities in computers, the chapter turns to a discussion of deductive and inductive reasoning, decision making, and some characteristic errors in thinking produced by various heuristics.

Chapter 9 ("Language"), written by Lila and Henry Gleitman, concerns language, a crucial component of the human cognitive system and the primary means of communicating knowledge. The chapter describes language as a hierarchically organized, rule-governed, and interpersonal system. It then deals with modern approaches to the study of language comprehension, language production, and attempts to determine whether language is a uniquely human accomplishment.

PART III   SOCIAL BEHAVIOR

The preceding parts focused upon the individual as an isolated organism, abstracted from the social world in which it lives. Part III changes this emphasis and deals with behavior as it occurs in a social context, not merely as action but as interaction. The succeeding chapters ask what the factors are that determine such social behavior.

Chapter 10 ("The Biological Basis of Social Behavior") considers factors that derive from our long-gone, genetic past and are rooted in our biological heritage. It begins with an old question that is yet another variant of the nature-nurture controversy: What is the basic social nature of Man? To answer this question, the chapter draws on the findings provided by both psychologists and ethologists and looks at various social tendencies in animals that evidently have a built-in basis, such as patterns of aggression, of sexual behavior, of parent-child interaction, and of various communicative displays. A major question throughout is whether similar conclusions apply to humans. The chapter concludes that while human social behavior is obviously enormously shaped by cultural factors, it does exhibit certain built-in bases that in some respects resemble those found in certain animals.

Chapter 11 ("Social Psychology") describes social processes in humans that are vastly more complex than those found in animals and that depend heavily on various cognitive processes. The chapter focuses on the way in which people interpret the social world so that it makes sense to them, in the perception both of others and of themselves. This subject includes such topics as attitudes and attitude change, attribution processes, attraction to others, and the perception of various aspects of the self such as the way in which we experience emotions. A final section considers blind obedience and some apparent failures of rationality, as in various forms of crowd behavior.

Chapter 12 ("The Individual and Society: The Contributions of Sigmund Freud") turns to another factor that presumably helps to determine how we act toward others and how we feel about them: our childhood rearing. The chapter describes an early and extremely influential conception of how this childhood rearing channels and modifies many of the built-in social patterns that are part of our biological makeup—the psychoanalytic approach of Sigmund Freud. It describes his conceptions of unconscious conflict, of human personality development, and the way many of these are expressed in such cultural products as myths and literature. The chapter then turns to a reexamination of Freud's views, in the light of clinical, experimental, and anthropological evidence.

PART IV   DEVELOPMENT*

Freud's theories provide a convenient bridge to a section on human development. The preceding chapters stress two approaches to the explanation of psychological phenomena. One focuses on mechanism—it tries to explain how something works. The second emphasizes function—it tries to explain what something is good for. The chapters in this new section (Chapters 13, 14, 15, and 16) supply yet another perspective on psychological phenomena—they try to explain how they came into being, how they developed.

Chapter 13 ("General Issues in Development") sketches the historical background of developmental psychology, lays out some of the major issues that run throughout much of the field, and then tries to exemplify these issues by discussing physical and motor development.

Chapter 14 ("Cognitive Development: Thought") considers the child's mental growth. It begins by using Jean Piaget's theories of mental development as an organizing framework. It then takes up a number of newer and quite different approaches, including some influenced by the Gibsons' approach to perception that grant the infant much more in the way of built-in rudiments of adult cognition than Piaget had assumed, and others that have been affected by an information-processing analysis.

*This entire section is new to this edition, though a number of its components were drawn from discussions that were formerly distributed throughout the first edition of the book.

Chapter 15 ("Cognitive Development: Language") written by Lila and Henry Gleitman, takes up language acquisition. The problem of language learning is posed by the fact that language use is creative, for words and sentences that are learned in one context can be applied in entirely novel contexts by the young language learner. The chapter asks how the young child picks up the rules or principles that allow this creative use, and it discusses the way in which this complex activity is based both on innate predispositions and environmental supports.

Chapter 16 ("Social Development") discusses social growth and development, including such topics as attachment, early socialization, effects of different kinds of child rearing, the development of moral action and moral reasoning, sex roles, sexual orientation, and development in adulthood.

PART V   INDIVIDUAL DIFFERENCES

Whereas the concern in previous chapters was with the nature of humankind in general, the four next chapters focus on the ways in which humans differ from each other.

Chapter 17 ("Intelligence: Its Nature and Measurement") deals with mental testing in general and intelligence testing in particular. It considers both practical and theoretical issues that grow out of the use of these tests, such as some conceptions of intelligence based on factor analysis. The chapter then turns to the nature-nurture controversy as it crops up in this context, where the debate concerns the relative role of heredity and environment in determining differences in test performance within a given population.

Chapter 18 ("Personality Assessment") concerns attempts to describe and assess personality. It begins by considering several approaches to assessment (e.g., personality inventories and projective techniques), turns to some central theoretical issues in the field (e.g., whether behavior is determined by traits, by the situation, or by some interaction between the two), and finally deals with some attempts to provide a taxonomy according to which personality differences can be described (e.g., by factor-analytic means, by reference to biological factors).

Chapter 19 ("Psychopathology") discusses certain differences in human personality that go beyond the range of normal functioning and take on the appearance of psychopathology. The chapter takes up the major categories of psychopathology, adopting the diagnostic nomenclature of DSM-III—schizophrenia, affective disorders, anxiety disorders, conversions and dissociative disorders, psychophysiological disorders, and sociopathy—and describes current views of their immediate psychological and/or physiological causes as well as beliefs about more remote causes like hereditary predispositions, environmental precipitants, and childhood experience. The chapter then turns to recent sociological critiques of the entire concept of psychopathology as exemplified by labeling theory.

Chapter 20 ("Treatment of Psychopathology") describes attempts to provide treatment for psychopathological conditions. It considers current somatic therapies, describes the major kinds of psychotherapy (including psychoanalysis, behavior therapy, and humanistic therapies), and discusses some problems in evaluating therapeutic outcome.

Epilogue. A brief final section takes a backward look at the entire book and asks what we have learned.

Appendix—"Statistics: The Collection, Organization, and Interpretation of Data." This appendix presents some general methods for gathering and analyzing psychological data. It considers how data are described by different scales (e.g., interval scales), considers the major techniques for collecting the data (e.g., the experiment), discusses selection problems posed by the difference between sample and population, and then outlines the way the data are organized by descriptive statistics (e.g., measures of central tendency and variability, correlation). Finally, it introduces some of the ideas of inferential statistics (e.g., confidence intervals, testing statistical hypotheses).

The *Study Guide*

The *Study Guide* was written by John Jonides of the University of Michigan and Paul Rozin of the University of Pennsylvania, and is designed to help the student understand and apply the material presented in the text. Each chapter in it corresponds to one in the textbook. There are four sections in each Study Guide chapter: Learning Objectives, Programmed Exercises, Self Test, and Investigating Psychological Phenomena.

LEARNING OBJECTIVES

The authors have provided an outline of the key issues discussed in each chapter. Each entry in the outline refers to a basic fact, theory, or relationship that the student should have learned from the chapter. These entries are listed in the order in which they occurred in the chapter, arranged under the same headings used there. Reading the learning objectives before reading a given chapter may help to orient the students to the major issues, to see the "big picture" of the chapter and not lose the forest for the trees.

PROGRAMMED EXERCISES

For each chapter of the text, the authors have provided fill-in-the-blank questions that test basic knowledge of the key terms and concepts. These questions are very straightforward and can be looked up and verified in the text. All answers appear on the right side of the page. To facilitate locating the answers in the text, the programmed exercises are arranged under the major headings of the chapter and follow the order of presentation in the text. This allows the student to see which fact or theory pertains to which major point of the chapter.

SELF TEST

For each chapter in the text, there is a self test composed of multiple-choice questions, again following the order of the text. In general, these questions are more difficult than the fill-ins, though both types of questions cover the range of materials presented in the text. The multiple choices sometimes highlight subtle distinctions, ask for some amount of integration, or test the student's ability to apply some of the material in the text. Answers and page references are provided.

Since multiple-choice questions are commonly used in examinations, the authors have devoted an entire section in *To the Student* to describing and illustrating the kinds of multiple-choice questions that students are likely to encounter (see *Study Guide*, pp. vii–ix).

INVESTIGATING PSYCHOLOGICAL PHENOMENA

For each chapter of the text, the *Study Guide* provides one or two activities or experiments that build upon concepts or theories presented in the chapter and extend and deepen the student's understanding and appreciation of them.

There are a variety of activities. Some emphasize the generation or testing of theories, others focus on data collection or analysis. The authors cover the major methods of data collection used by psychologists: the experiment, the questionnaire, direct observation, and the interview. Some instructors may wish to include these activities as part of the course. Report (data) sheet pages for most experiments are located at the end of the *Study Guide* in Appendix B, and you can have the student tear them out and hand them in. The following activities or experiments can be found in the *Study Guide:*

The consistency of dreams

Speed of the nerve impulse: The use of reaction time in the measurement of a psychological process

Effects of mental process on autonomic activity

Maze learning

Learned taste aversions

Measuring brightness contrast

The effect of mental set

The effect of imagery instructions in memory

The Stroop effect

Measuring lexical retrieval time

Personal space: Behavior in elevators

Person perception: The effect of context or set on first impressions

Analysis of dream content

Conservation of number

Implicit learning

Sex differences

"Intelligence tests"

Constructing a personality inventory

Depression and negative experiences

Demonstration of role playing

Applications of statistical concepts

Each of these were class tested in the authors' courses. In many cases actual data from the authors' studies with their students are include to provide a base for comparison with the data collected by your students.

The Test-Item File

Test questions are available for all chapters in *Psychology,* including the appendix on statistics. They are contained in a booklet from which questions can be copied on a machine. The test-item file is also available on computer tape.

The questions are in multiple-choice form. There are two types: some stress factual knowledge; others (the majority) focus on understanding the material. The questions are indicated as to type. Also, some questions from the *Study Guide* are included, and are again indicated as such.

Other Resources for the Instructor

Various books and articles have been written offering general suggestions on how to teach the introductory course. The following is a list of recommended readings on this topic that the instructor may wish to consult:

Daniel, R. S., ed. *Teaching of psychology.* Published quarterly. Department of Psychology, University of Missouri, Columbia, Mo. 65201. A journal that contains articles on all aspects of teaching of psychology, from new demonstrations to discussions of teaching evaluation procedures, to comparisons of different forms of testing students.

Gleitman, H. 1984. Introducing psychology. *American Psychologist* 39: 421–27. Reproduced in this manual in a slightly abbreviated form.

Lowman, J. 1984. *Mastering the techniques of teaching.* San Francisco: Jossey-Bass. A well-written book on virtually all aspects of undergraduate teaching by an author who obviously can teach and cares about teaching.

MacLeod, R. B. 1971. The teaching of psychology. *American Psychologist* 26: 245–49. MacLeod was a highly reputed teacher in a prior generation, and his insights are still worth reading about.

McKeachie, W. J. 1978. *Teaching tips: A guidebook for the beginning college teacher*, 7th ed. Lexington, Mass.: Heath. Tips from an acknowledged master teacher.

Walker, E. L., and McKeachie, W. J. 1967. *Some thoughts about teaching the beginning course in psychology.* Belmont, Calif.: Brooks/Cole.

CHAPTER 1

Introduction

Overview

This chapter was written to introduce the student to the field of psychology, a field that he probably has not formally encountered in his prior schooling and about which he may well have quite a number of false preconceptions. The chapter spends little time in attempting a formal definition but begins with a brief tour of the field that stresses concrete examples. It tries to make two points:

First, psychology is a science of unusually broad scope, for the phenomena which it takes as its province cover an enormous range, stretching from the borders of biology to those of the social sciences. To illustrate this, the chapter takes a quick look at a number of concrete phenomena: blood flow in the brain during different mental activities, perceptual and linguistic ambiguities, automatization of reading (the Stroop effect), depth perception in infancy (the visual cliff), courting behavior in birds, and panic behavior in crowds.

Second, psychology is a science of many faces that approaches its subject matter from several perspectives, each of which is valid in its own right. The chapter takes up one concrete example—dreams, a topic that is obviously of interest in its own right but that is also a fine demonstration of the point. The section shows how dreams can be regarded as mental experiences (dream images that are reevocations of previously experienced sights and sounds), as overt behaviors (among other things, there are rapid eye movements during dreams), as reflections of underlying biological events (EEG patterns during "active sleep" when dreams occur), as aspects of cognition (the relationship between waking imagery and knowledge and dream experience), as reflections of social interactions and culture, as indications of social patterns through expressions of internalized conflict, as indicators of cognitive development (adults understand that dreams are "not real" but young children do not), and as manifestations of individual differences (for example, dreams in different groups of mentally disordered patients). The discussion shows how these different perspectives are complementary rather than competing, for psychology is a science of many faces, and to see it fully, one must see them all. This theme of multiple perspectives serves as a general framework for the rest of the book.

The chapter concludes by emphasizing that psychology is a science, and therefore seeks general principles underlying human behavior. Unlike art and literature, psychology focuses on unique characteristics of individuals and events only in so far as they offer insight into these general principles.

Organizational Note

The methods of psychology, such as the experiment, correlational studies, and case studies, are discussed, not in the first chapter, but rather appear in the appendix on statistics and in chapters where they are relevant—e.g., correlations in Chapter 17 ("Intelligence: Its Nature and Measurement"). The reason is that in the author's view, a discussion of methods is premature if it comes before a consideration of the contents to which these methods are to be applied. Students can get very interested in learning how to find out something after they understand what it is one wants to find out and why. It is harder to motivate them to learn points of methodology beforehand.

Demonstration

Recalling dreams.   Many people say that they dream only rarely. But as we know from the chapter, this flatly contradicts the evidence provided by sleep laboratories. All persons go through several episodes of REM sleep every night. If awakened in the middle of one such episode they generally report a dream. Under the circumstances, the best guess is that people who think they do not dream are in error; it's not that they do not dream, but rather that they *don't remember* their dreams. One reason for this may be the fact that dreams are rather fragile mental events that, at least on the surface, seem generally unconnected with the events of waking life so that they are hard to recall. This failure to remember dreams is all the more pronounced because of the many activities that are interposed between the dream and the attempt to recall it. The alarm clock wakes us, and we then perform the various rituals that go with getting up: we go to the bathroom, shower, brush our teeth, and dress. By this time, the dream can no longer be retrieved from memory.

To demonstrate this effect, ask the students to start a dream diary for a number of days. The students should be divided into two groups. Group I is made up of all the students whose birthdays fall on odd days of the month; Group II consists of the students whose birthdays fall on even days. Group I's job is simple: They should write down as much as they can remember of the dream (or dreams) they had the night before *immediately* after they wake up. Group II's task is a bit more complicated. The *first thing* they should do upon waking is to call the local weather station and jot down the expected high temperature for the day. *Then* they should write down as much as they can remember of the dream (or dreams) they had the night before. (If your area does not have such a phone service, substitute some other brief task that requires the student to attend to something other than their dreams in the first minute or so after they wake up.)

After three or so successive days of this procedure, ask the students to report the total number of dreams they wrote down during this period and compile the numbers in class. Group I should report more dreams (and more detail per dream) because they did not experience a delay during which they were distracted with irrelevant information. (After Cohen, D. B., and Wolfe, G. 1973. Dream recall and repression: Evidence for an alternative hypothesis. *Journal of Consulting and Clinical Psychology* 41: 349–55.)

There are a number of other demonstrations in this manual that deal with dreams and could be combined with the one just described. One is Demonstration 4 in Chapter 3 ("Motivation"), which tries to show the considerable variation from one person to the other in number of dreams recalled. Another is Demonstration 5 in Chapter 12 ("The Contributions of Sigmund Freud"), which also features a dream diary and deals with day residues, dream themes as they relate to current emotional preoccupations, and a possible increase in number of dreams recalled over the period of time the diary is kept, which suggest that people learn to rehearse their dreams if there is some special reason for doing so (for example, if they are patients in psychoanalytic therapy).

CHAPTER 2

Biological Bases of Behavior

Overview

This chapter on the nervous system starts with a discussion of the historical background of the field. It begins by considering the question posed by Descartes and other pioneers, "What makes humans and animals move?" and the hypothesis that such movements are governed by the same laws that rule the motions of physical objects. This hypothesis led to the view that the organism can be regarded as a machine, a view that underlies much of the pioneering work on the neurological underpinnings of behavior. Without an appreciation of this background, a student may very well learn about neurons, reflexes, and various brain structures, without ever knowing why he should care. A discussion of the historical bases of the study of nervous function—for example, the story of Descartes's development of the reflex concept—places this information in a context that instructs the student why it is important to know this and why it is a part of psychology.

Having placed the study of neural processes in its proper context, the chapter proceeds to a discussion of what we know about such matters today. This discussion goes from the simple to the complex. It begins with a description of the smallest functional unit of the nervous system (neuron), turns to the ways in which individual neurons excite and inhibit each other (reflex, synapse, and neurotransmitters), and then considers the function of large aggregates of neurons (the structures of the basic central nervous system). An important emphasis throughout is on hierarchical organization within the central nervous system, as highlighted by disruptions of this organization in transection studies and in certain cases of cortical lesion, for example, aphasia. This principle of hierarchical organization will be encountered in other chapters, for example, those on thinking and language (Chapters 8 and 9).

Summary of the Main Topics

THE ORGANISM AS MACHINE

This chapter is not a mere catalog of the neurophysiological bases of behavior. Instead, it traces the history of an idea—that behavior can be best understood

23

mechanistically. This conception stems from Descartes's mechanical metaphor for action. It led to two insights that in one form or another are still with us: (1) at least some actions can be interpreted mechanically in terms of a reflex arc, and (2) nervous function can be understood in terms of a tripartite classification —the reception of stimulus input; the conduction, integration, and interpretation of this stimulus by the nervous system; and the reaction of muscles and glands, which represents the end of the action sequence.

This tripartite classification defines the sequence of action in the nervous system. The beginning (i.e., the stimulus) and the end (i.e., the response) of this sequence are often observable from the outside; what falls in between is the action sequence played out in the nervous system: *stimulus* → (receptors → afferent nerves → interneurons → efferent nerves) → *response*.

NERVE CELL AND NERVE IMPULSE

The next topic is the role of the neuron in the action sequence. The discussion centers on the neuron's structural properties (it is composed of dendrites, cell body, and axon), its functional and anatomical characteristics (there are receptor cells, sensory neurons, motoneurons, interneurons), and its electrical and chemical properties (resting vs. action potential). Once these characteristics of the neuron are elaborated, it should be easy for the student to understand why a neuron behaves as it does—that is, why it fires on an all-or-none basis, why it has a fixed impulse velocity, and so on.

INTERACTION AMONG NERVE CELLS

While the neuron serves as the building block for characterizing nervous function, the action of a single neuron is seldom sufficient to account for even simple action. For this to occur, there must be an interaction among neurons—a fact inherent in Descartes's conception of the reflex arc. This discussion introduces the notion of the synapse. It begins with a brief discussion of Sherrington's classic behavioral work by means of which the synapse was inferred. It then moves to more recent anatomical and neurophysiological studies that document this inference and have begun to show how the synapse actually works, including a discussion of the action of neurotransmitters and endorphins.

INTERACTION THROUGH THE BLOODSTREAM:
THE ENDOCRINE SYSTEM

This section discusses the role of the endocrine system as an instrument of communication complementing the nervous system. Though its properties are somewhat different, the endocrine system, like the nervous system, carries out a critical integration function by means of chemical messengers.

THE MAIN STRUCTURES OF THE NERVOUS SYSTEM

The complexity of neural interactions increases dramatically as the ganglion replaces the neuron as the functional anatomical unit. The story told is that of evolution—how eons of Darwinian selection caused interneurons to clump together into ganglia that relay information between receptors and muscles; how, in some species, ganglia evolved into regional centers for the control of body function; and how this evolutionary tendency led to the formation of a master clump of ganglia—the brain. Next, the brain itself is sketched out anatomically in terms of its major components: the hindbrain (including medulla and cerebellum), the midbrain (including the reticular formation, and the forebrain (including thalamus, hypothalamus, cerebral hemispheres, and cerebral cortex).

THE CEREBRAL CORTEX

The last sections of the chapter focus on the functions of different regions of the cerebral cortex, the structure generally believed to underlie the most complex aspects of behavior. After a consideration of the sensory and motor projection areas, which serve as receiving stations for sensory impulses and as dispatching centers for motor commands, the discussion turns to the cortical association areas. Their function concerns such higher mental processes as planning, remembering, the organization of the sensory world, and thinking and language, as shown by the effects of various lesions in these areas which produce apraxias, agnosias, or different kinds of aphasia. A final section deals with lateralization, the differences between the functions of the two hemispheres.

Organizational Notes

1. A number of biopsychological topics have not been dealt with or are discussed only in passing. Those that pertain to the biological underpinning of motivation, arousal, and some aspects of emotion are discussed in Chapter 3 ("Motivation").

2. Other topics sometimes included in a chapter on the biological bases of behavior are (*a*) genetics and (*b*) built-in, complex behavior patterns of the kind studied by ethologists and sometimes called "instincts." These are dealt with in chapters where they are most pertinent. The biology of genetics is thus presented in the first chapter that deals with development, Chapter 13 ("General Issues in Development"). Instinctive behavior patterns are discussed in Chapter 10 ("The Biological Basis of Social Behavior"), where the findings of ethologists are taken up.

Discussion Topics

1. *Machine-model metaphors.* Before explaining any behavior in psychology, one must address the problem of what constitutes understanding. This is a diffi-

cult philosophical problem, but many psychologists have opted for a simple solution: if you can make a machine that behaves in ways comparable to the behavior of the organism, then you have explained that behavior. The classic example comes from Descartes. If you can construct a machine that withdraws from heat, then the blueprints of that machine explain why one withdraws one's hand from fire. Descartes's model was the hydraulic action of various statuaries, which in principle could be modified to produce motion when exposed to heat.

Examples of the use of machine-model metaphors certainly extend beyond those of Descartes. For example, telephone switchboards were once popular as mechanical models of cognitive processes in humans. This tradition lasted only until the advent of another machine, the computer. Now many psychologists use computer terminology, and computer methods, language, and logic in order to interpret information processing in humans.

2. *The problem of choice.* Descartes found it necessary to postulate the conarium, the point where the soul intervenes to direct the flow of animal spirits toward one or another muscle group. He was forced to make some such assumption to explain why the same stimulus sometimes leads to one response, sometimes to another. Among many other troubles, this explanation begs the question, for one now has to explain why the soul makes its choice between the various response alternatives. In modern psychophysiological thinking, the conarium has been replaced by intermediary devices within the nervous system. At a molecular level, this intermediary is the synapse where various excitatory and inhibitory impulses summate to determine whether a given neuron will or will not fire. At a more complex level, the choice system is not one synapse but a great number of interlocking synapses in various structures of the brain. Does this solve the problem of choice? Is it a step toward a solution?

3. *An early approach to brain function—phrenology.* The modern history of the problem of the localization of brain function has a bizarre origin: the rise and fall of *phrenology.* This doctrine was developed around 1800 when Franz Joseph Gall, a respected Viennese anatomist, thought that he could detect a correlation between the mental attributes of some of his acquaintances and the shapes of their heads. He theorized that various mental "faculties" (e.g., firmness, hope, acquisitiveness—thirty-seven of them all told) were localized in different regions of the brain: the larger a given region, the more prominent that faculty in the individual so endowed. The further assumption that the relative size of these various subcomponents of the brain can be accurately gauged from the exterior conformation of the skull that encases it, led to a ready-made instrument for mental diagnosis: by the shape of their skull shall ye know them. What started as a novel (and, as it turned out, quite misconceived) hypothesis about cerebral localization soon became a widely accepted practical guide to matters of daily living, especially in America, where the movement found a fertile soil. There the Fowler brothers published manuals for self-diagnosis, counseled on hiring job applicants (Horace Greeley had suggested in 1852 that rail-

road workers to be selected by the shape of their heads), and found countless other ways to turn phrenology into a family fortune—a massive saga of human gullibility that did not end until shortly before World War I.

Introductory treatments often make fun of the phrenologists, and no doubt they were in egregious error. But for us—150 or more years later—it is more important to understand why they asserted what they did (and of course to note just why it is utterly wrong) than to spend much time in self-congratulations about our own greater knowledge.

Why phrenology found such a ready acceptance, especially in America, is a fascinating question. Belief in its teachings was not limited to the uneducated; men like Edgar Allan Poe and Walt Whitman were among its adherents. One reason for phrenology's widespread appeal may have been the very reason that it was so vehemently denounced by various churchmen and moralists on both sides of the Atlantic who saw the new doctrine as subversive of religion and free will, "reducing all mind to the mere accidental shape of the head." However wrong in its particular assumptions, phrenology was a step toward a modern point of view. Man's attributes were a product of his cerebral endowment, and any mental or moral defect was thus a disease, no less organically based than kidney trouble. Small wonder then that its opponents saw it as "French materialism . . . that reduce(s) man to a mere machine . . ." But this materialist bias, this concrete orientation, is exactly what would appeal to that practical common sense that many observers have always associated with the American character. Under the circumstances, we can understand why, at least in its earlier years, phrenology was often associated with various reform movements of the time: phrenologists espoused a more humane treatment of the insane, generally opposed slavery, advocated prison reforms—all under the banner of an enlightened, scientific point of view. (A brief history of phrenology can be found in Chapter 2 of Fancher, R. E. 1979. *Pioneers of psychology.* New York: Norton. Quotations are from Davies, J. D. 1955. *Phrenology: Fad and science.* New Haven, Conn.: Yale U. Press, p. 68.)

Demonstrations

1. *Calculation of conduction time in the sensory axons of the arm.* Have the students hold hands to form a chain and then close their eyes. Instruct the student at one end to squeeze his companion's hand immediately after you touch his free hand. Each student in turn will then squeeze his neighbor's hand immediately after his own hand has been squeezed. When the last person in the chain has his hand squeezed, he raises his free hand. The experimenter's job is to time the interval between his touching the hand of the student at one end of the chain and the student at the other end raising his hand. Have your students repeat this exercise until there is no substantial improvement in performance.

Divide the elapsed time on the last trial by the number of students in the chain and write the time on the blackboard.

Now repeat the procedure with one change: the students will now squeeze their neighbor's shoulder instead of their hand. The time now required for the "squeeze" to pass through the chain should be less than before, because neural conduction will now pass through one arm only. If you divide the group time by the number of students and subtract this number from the number on the blackboard, you should have a rough figure for the conduction time for the sensory axons of one arm. (Rozin, P., and Jonides, J. 1977. Mass reaction time: Measurement of the speed of the nerve impulse and the duration of mental processes in class. *Teaching of Psychology* 4:91-94.)

2. *A demonstration of a spinal reflex.* Let a student stand up, with eyes closed and one arm extended, palm up. Have another student place a textbook on the first student's open hand. While the student is supporting the text with his hand, place a second textbook on top of the first. The student's hand should drop a little and then rapidly return to its original position. This illustrates a simple spinal reflex. Stretching the extensors in the arm by the added weight of the second book is signaled by afferent nerves from the muscle, which produce an automatic and reflexive readjustment that compensates for the added weight.

Selected Readings

GENERAL WORKS

Blakemore, C. B. 1977. *Mechanics of mind.* New York: Cambridge University Press. A beautifully illustrated, well-written, popularized overview of the field based on a series of popular lectures over the British Broadcasting System.

Fancher, R. E. 1979. *Pioneers of psychology.* New York: Norton. See especially Chapters 1 and 2 for a good discussion of some of the great figures and their explorations.

Robinson, D. N. 1980. *The enlightened machine.* New York: Columbia University Press. A remarkable short paperback that is a highly readable introduction to neuropsychology written from a historical perspective and with a broad point of view.

Valenstein, E. 1973. *Brain control.* New York: Wiley. This readable book reviews the history of psychosurgery and brain stimulation and directly addresses the popular social implications of these brain-control techniques.

CLASSICS

Luria, A. R. 1966. *Higher cortical functions in man.* New York: Basic Books. A discussion of the effects of various cortical lesions in humans, and of the theoretical implications of these effects.

Sherrington, C. S. 1906. *The integrative action of the nervous system*, 2nd ed. New Haven, Conn.: Yale University Press, 1947. The classic account of Sherrington's studies of reflex action.

REFERENCE WORKS
Carlson, N. R. 1981. *Physiology of behavior*, 2nd ed. Newton, Mass.: Allyn and Bacon. A good, well-written, undergraduate text.

Fearing, F. 1930. *Reflex action: A study in the history of physiological psychology*. Baltimore: Williams and Wilkins. A more advanced historical introduction for someone who really wants to dig into the historical background.

Gallistel, C. R. 1980. *The organization of action*. Hillsdale, N.J.: Erlbaum. An important but rather advanced exposition of the way in which certain elementary units of behavior, such as the reflex and the negative feedback system (which will be taken up in Chapter 3) interact to produce complex action. It emphasizes the hierarchical structure of the nervous system, and it reprints some classic papers by Sherrington and other pioneers in neuropsychology.

Rosenzweig, M. R., and Leiman, A. L. 1982. *Physiological psychology*. Lexington, Mass.: Heath. An excellent undergraduate text that is remarkably comprehensive, well conceived and organized, with good illustrations. Particularly good for discussions of the physiology of learning, memory, language, and cognition.

Teitelbaum, P. 1967. *Physiological psychology*. Englewood Cliffs, N.J.: Prentice-Hall. A short paperback that focuses on the key issues—what are the behaviors whose physiological underpinning we want to understand?

CHAPTER 3

Motivation

Overview

Whereas Chapter 2 began with the question "What makes animals act?" the present chapter asks why their actions are often directed. Its main concern is with actions that are directed toward some future end—the general topic of motivation. The emphasis is on motives based on biological patterns of self-regulation (e.g., temperature maintenance, hunger, thirst), self-defense (e.g., the sympathetic emergency system in cases of flight or counterattack), and self-restoration (e.g., rest and sleep).

One important issue is how one can reconcile the view that the organism is a machine with the fact that this organism is capable of directed action and has goals and motives. The chapter discusses one important solution: the concept of negative feedback systems. It shows how neural-control systems based on negative feedback underlie various forms of directed action, whether simple motives directed toward environmental stimuli or self-regulatory motives such as hunger directed toward future goals (e.g., food).

A second theme concerns arousal. Motives direct behavior, but they also have another function: they arouse the organism and make it act more vigorously. This state of arousal (and its opposite, quiescence) is discussed in two contexts. One pertains to the arousal of the body and the utilization of its energy resources as it responds to the tug-of-war between the sympathetic and the parasympathetic branches of the autonomic nervous system (with maximum activation effected by the sympathetic emergency reaction and its behavioral concomitants, flight or fight). Another aspect of activation concerns the arousal (or lack of arousal) of the brain as reflected by the action of the reticular activating system and its effects on wakefulness and sleep.

A third theme that runs through the entire discussion was already encountered in the preceding chapter, the concept of antagonistic control. There we saw that excitatory and inhibitory processes oppose each other at many synapses. This reciprocal antagonism, which is so apparent at the level of individual neurons, is seen again at a higher level, where integrated nervous action occurs. For example, in this chapter, we see antagonistic systems in the sympathetic and parasym-

31

pathetic divisions of the autonomic nervous system, in the reticular activating
system and the brain stem of the arousal system, in the lateral hypothalamus and
ventromedial nuclei of the hypothalamus in the food-regulation system, and,
more generally, in the opponent-process theory of motivation. The ubiquity
of process antagonisms demonstrates what must be viewed as a central property
of the biopsychological organization of animals.

Summary of the Main Topics

MOTIVATION AS DIRECTION

Motives are inferred whenever we see goal-directed behavior. While goal-
directed acts might seem a violation of the mechanical metaphor developed in
the preceding chapter, this is not the case. Engineers have developed servomechanisms that can continuously monitor their behavior through negative feedback.
For example, there are machines that make spot welds on automobiles moving
down an assempbly line which automatically adjust to changes in the automobile's position and movement. The point of negative feedback systems in
industry is to maintain some process in a steady state. Negative feedback systems
play a similar role in maintaining the "wisdom of the body," which we here call
homeostasis.

SELF-REGULATION

In this section, the text elaborates on homeostatic mechanisms in animals. An
example of this is temperature regulation. When exposed to temperature challenge, humans and other warm-blooded animals can respond in two ways: by automatic internal adjustments such as vasodilatation or vasoconstriction, or by behavioral
adjustments such as taking off a shirt or putting on a sweater. The internal adjustments that occur are largely controlled by the autonomic nervous system, which is
composed of two antagonistic subdivisions—the sympathetic division, which tends to
energize the system (e.g., increasing the heart rate), and the parasympathetic division,
which does the opposite (e.g., decreasing the heart rate). In turn, the higher-level
neural control of the various regulatory systems is located in the hypothalamus of
the brain. Thus a direct alteration of the temperature of the hypothalamus leads to
autonomic changes (e.g., vasodilatation or vasoconstriction) and behavioral changes
(bar pressing for heat or a water shower), even if there has been no change in the
temperature of the rest of the animal's body.

THIRST

What holds for temperature holds for most other homeostatic regulations as
well. An example is thirst. The section first considers how the organism is informed about its water balance by volume receptors, which monitor the total

volume of its body fluids, and by osmoreceptors, which react to the concentration of various minerals dissolved in these fluids. It then considers how water loss is made up for. One means is by reflexive mechanisms including the secretion of the antidiuretic hormone (ADH), which instructs the kidneys to reabsorb more of the water that passes through them. Another is through behavior—drinking.

HUNGER

The next section considers the biological motive that has been studied in most detail—hunger. The first question concerns the stimuli that control the onset and cessation of feeding. Some of these come from the internal environment: the nutrient levels in the bloodstream and metabolic processes in the liver. Other stimuli that control feeding are external. An important example is the palatability of the food.

According to several authors, the central control for feeding lies in two antagonistic centers of the hypothalamus, one located in the lateral hypothalamus (LV), the other in the ventromedial hypothalamus (VMH). Since lesions in the LV region produce aphagia, a complete refusal to eat, it is regarded as the hunger center. In contrast, lesions in the VMH lead to hyperphagia, a vast increase in food intake, which suggests that the VMH is a satiety center.

While homeostatic factors determine *that* an animal feeds, they have less of an effect on *what* it feeds on. Food selection is determined by a number of factors, including built-in preferences and various modes of learning.

The section concludes with a discussion of obesity. It considers the externality hypothesis, which holds that overweight persons are disproportionately sensitive to external rather than internal cues for eating, and then it takes up some recent alternative views. One of these is the set-point hypothesis, which holds that overweight people have a higher set-point for body weight.

FEAR AND RAGE

In contrast to thirst and hunger, which are largely based on homeostatic factors from within, a number of motives are instigated from outside. An important example is the organism's reaction to intense threat. Its biological underpinnings include the operations of the two antagonistic branches of the autonomic nervous system, the sympathetic and the parasympathetic systems. While the parasympathetic branch serves the vegetative functions of everyday life, such as digestion and reproduction, the sympathetic branch activates the body and mobilizes its resources. It increases available metabolic fuels and accelerates their utilization by increasing the heart rate and respiration. Intense sympathetic activity can be regarded as an emergency reaction, which underlies the overt reactions of fight or flight and their usual emotional concomitants, rage and fear.

The sympathetic emergency reaction is not always biologically adaptive. It can be exceedingly disruptive, as in psychophysiologically produced disorders and certain cases of "sudden death."

SLEEPING AND WAKING

While the autonomic nervous system regulates activation of visceral function, the reticular activating system (RAS) controls arousal in the brain. RAS stimulation can occur in two ways: from sensory stimulation and from the cortex itself. The effect of sensory stimulation is by an indirect pathway from the RAS to the cortex, as shown by the fact that sleeping cats will awaken to sound even if the direct auditory pathway to the cortex has been severed. As for cortical stimulation, the RAS evidently amplifies it as if it were transforming a weak stimulus into a stronger one.

The next topic is sleep. Just prior to sleep, electroencephalograms (EEGs) are characterized by the alpha rhythm. As sleep begins, the EEG patterns change; they become more random at first (light sleep) and are then replaced by patterns with higher voltages and lower frequencies (deep sleep).

During sleep, we oscillate between two kinds of sleep. One is quiet sleep, characterized by the various EEG patterns already described. The other is active sleep, in which cortical activity is considerable and rather similar to waking. In addition, there are rapid eye movements, or REMs. Active sleep is the period during which dreams occur. Just why they do is still unknown; nor is it clear what, if any, function they serve.

WHAT DIFFERENT MOTIVES HAVE IN COMMON

The chapter ends with a discussion of what (if anything) different motives have in common. One theory is drive reduction which asserts that all built-in motives act to reduce stimulation and arousal. This position is rarely held today, given the evidence that both humans and animals often seek stimulation rather than trying to avoid it.

Another approach is the opponent-process theory. It asserts that all shifts of arousal level produce an antagonistic process that moderates the motivational ups and downs. Thus, if taking a drug leads to a feeling of euphoria, there is an opponent process that has the opposite effect. While the drug is still active, the opponent process simply dampens the motivational high. When the drug is finally withdrawn, the opponent process stands revealed—there is a withdrawal effect, and the person feels "down" and depressed.

Another attempt to answer the question of what different motives have in common comes from work on the rewarding effect of brain stimulation. This has led to the hypothesis that some regions of the brain are "pleasure centers," a view that is still a matter of considerable debate.

Organizational Notes

This chapter focuses on certain motives that are primarily biological—hunger, thirst, avoidance of violent threat, and so on. Learned motives such as the need for achievement or the desire for prestige, which are probably based on our socialization history, are discussed in Chapters 12 and 16. But the present chapter does not deal with all of the biological motives. Sex is no less rooted in our biology than is thirst or hunger, but it is not discussed here. The reason is that while sex is a biological motive, it is also a social one. As a result, it is more profitably considered in the context of other social-reaction patterns. Its essence involves not just the action of one organism (as do hunger and thirst) but rather the *inter*action of two organisms. Its biological roots will be discussed in Chapter 10, together with those of a number of other social motives that are probably also based on built-in tendencies (at least in animals), such as certain facets of aggression, parental and filial reactions, and so on.

A final point. In some accounts, learned motives are regarded as synonymous with social motives. But they shouldn't be. Not all social motives are primarily learned (e.g., sex), nor are all learned motives primarily social (e.g., the desire to amass possessions). In effect, then, motives can be classified as shown in the table below, which highlights the reasons why they are discussed in different contexts:

	Primarily biological (built-in)	*Primarily learned*
Primarily involving the individual	e.g., hunger (see Chapter 3)	e.g., the desire to acquire possessions, need for achievement (see Chapters 12, 16)
Primarily social	e.g., sex (see Chapter 10)	e.g., the need for prestige, for reassurance (see Chapters 12, 16)

Discussion Topics

1. *Machines that mimic directed behavior.* A discussion of various machines that use negative feedback principles may help to underline the point made in the chapter—the relationship between directed action and negative feedback. The direction of the machine may come from outside. An example is provided by military rockets that home in on their targets by orienting to heat. (See Gallistel, C. R. 1980. *The organization of action.* Hillsdale, N.J.: Erlbaum.) The direction may also come from the inside. An example is *M. Speculatrix*, an "organism" constructed out of nuts and bolts. This organism scurries about on the floor, pursuing light to charge its solar battery. Should its energy stores fall

below a specified level, a switch is thrown in *Specularix*'s inside which makes it (him, her?) plug itself into the wall to recharge its battery (a machine version of homeostasis).

Taking all this into account, one might ask students in what sense these devices—especially *M. Speculatrix*—may or may not be considered organisms and in what sense they should be considered machines. (See Grey, W. 1953. *The living brain*. New York: Norton.)

2. *Peripheral vs. central control of hunger and thirst.* An old account of hunger, thirst, and other basic, biological motives is that they are produced by certain annoying peripheral sensations. Thus hunger was said to be caused by the rumblings of an empty stomach and thirst by dryness of the mouth and throat. This account is false.

Regarding thirst, people given the drug pilocarpine salivate profusely, bathing their mouths and throats in fluid. Nevertheless, they report that they get thirsty if deprived of water. Conversely, people born with ineffectual salivary glands drink no more water than normal people (although they do gargle much more frequently). Significantly, these people distinguish being thirsty from having a dry throat and mouth.

As regards hunger, people who have had gastrectomies, an operation in which the stomach is surgically removed, report getting hunger pangs. When sugar solutions are fed into their veins or through their intestines, they report that they feel sated.

In sum, thirst is not dependent on whether the mouth and throat are dry, nor is hunger determined appreciably by whether or not the stomach is full. Instead, these motives are triggered by neural systems that monitor less peripheral cues (e.g., the glucose—glycogen conversion in the liver and the utilization of nutrients in the blood).

3. *Obesity.* The causes of overweight are of considerable current interest. The text discusses some of the factors that might lead to obesity. Until fairly recently, many investigators inclined toward the externality hypothesis, the view that obese persons were disproportionately sensitive to external factors that govern feeding such as palatability. In a food-rich society such as ours, such external factors might tilt the balance toward overeating, especially given the impetus of the advertising industry. The externality hypothesis, however, has been brought into question by recent studies which suggest that some of the earlier results that seemed to favor it were produced by a "diet-busting effect" found in restrained eaters. At least some cases of so-called overweight may simply be due to different weight set-points.

For further discussions of obesity, see:

Fitzgerald, F. T. 1981. The problem of obesity. *Annual Review of Medicine* 32: 221–31. A discussion which concludes that the health hazards of overweight may have been exaggerated.

Rodin, J. 1981. Current status of the external-internal hypothesis for obesity. *American Psychologist* 36: 361–72. A reconsideration of the externality hypothesis by one of the major figures who first proposed it.

Stricker, E. M. 1978. Hyperphagia. *New England Journal of Medicine* 298: 1010–13. An influential attack on the interpretation of hyperphagia along the lines of the hypothalamic dual-center theory of hunger.

Stunkard, A. J., ed. 1980. *Obesity.* Philadelphia: Saunders. An excellent collection of papers on the topic.

4. *Opponent-process account of motivation.* A powerful example of an opponent process in motivation comes from the behavior of a drug addict. For example, chronic users of amphetamines report that administration of this drug makes them feel powerful and alert and uninterested in sleep or food. When they stop taking the drug, these feelings reverse in sign: They now feel exhausted, very sleepy, and very hungry.

Another example is love. Often, love begins with ecstasy; it then settles into contentment (though hopefully not boredom). When the lover leaves (or dies), the opponent process shows itself as grief, depression, and so on.

Still another example is the amateur parachutist. At first, there is terror at the jump. But this turns into relief and intense pleasure upon successful landing. (See Solomon, R. L. 1977. An opponent-process theory of acquired motivation: IV. The affective dynamics of addiction. In Maser, J. D., and Seligman, M. E. P., eds. *Psychopathology: Experimental models*, pp. 66–103. San Francisco: Freeman. See also Solomon, R. L. 1980. The opponent process theory of acquired motivation: The costs of pleasure and the benefits of pain. *American Psychologist* 35: 691–712.)

Demonstrations

1. *A demonstration of the relative unimportance (or, at least, the variability) of peripheral cues.* Ask students (by show of hands, etc.) how they know they are hungry. How many say they feel dizzy? Or feel a headache? Feel stomach pains? Hear stomach noises? Feel weak? (No doubt there are other possibilities.) The students will give all kinds of answers, indicating that it is by no means clear that they know what cues they are using and that different people use (or think they use) different cues. (Suggested by P. Rozin.)

2. *A classroom test of sex differences in perceptions of desirable body shape.* The text suggests that some of the factors that underlie popular concerns about body weight are a matter of cultural ideal rather than simply a matter of health. In our society, there is a cultural premium on being slender. Women seem to be more concerned about this than men—they diet more, are more likely to regard

themselves as overweight, and so on. Is this because they feel that the ideal they aspire to is more attractive to men? Interestingly enough, there is some evidence that this is not the whole story, for they seem to want to be more slender than men want them to be. (See Fallon, W. E., and Rozin, P. 1985. Sex differences in perceptions of desirable body shape. *Journal of Abnormal Psychology* 94: 102-105.)

Here is a demonstration to test whether this generalization holds for your class. Below are nine figure drawings of women, ranging from 1 (thinnest) to 9 (heaviest). (Taken from Stunkard, A., Sorensen, T., and Schulsinger, F. 1980. Use of the Danish Adoption Register for the study of obesity and thinness. In Kety, S., ed., *The genetics of neurological and psychiatric disorders*, pp. 115-20. New York: Raven Press.) Put these figures on a transparency and show them on an overhead projector. (Another way is to photograph them and present them on one or more slides.)

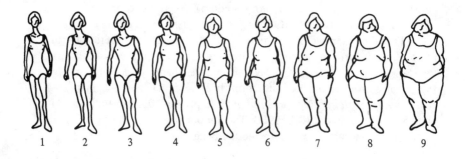

The female students should be asked to indicate the number of the figure (from 1 to 9) that most closely approximates what they would like to look like. The men should be asked to indicate the number of the figure that approximates the female figure they find most attractive.

After the ratings are made, a separate show of hands for men and women ("How many voted for 1, for 2, for 3, etc.?") should indicate whether there is or isn't a sex difference in the female body weight ideal as judged by men and women.

If the results found by prior studies are any guide, the women will vote for a thinner figure than will the men. Such a result might lead to an interesting class discussion because it's by no means obvious why this should be so. One interesting possibility is that the preference has a basis in social class. There is some evidence that men and—especially—women in the upper socioeconomic bracket are thinner than those in the middle class. Perhaps the middle-class college women want to be as much like upper-class women as possible. A simpler possibility is the effect of the advertising and fashion industries, which have promoted slenderness as a special female ideal.

3. *The sympathetic emergency reaction.* The autonomic underpinnings of fear can be demonstrated by having students measure their heart rate under various conditions. Begin by telling the students where to feel for the heartbeat, and ask them to count as you indicate the beginning and end of a one-minute period. Do this initially without special instructions, in order to get a base rate. Then ask the students to think of something that frightens them. To make this vivid, ask them to conjure up a mental image of this frightening something. Now ask them to count the number of heartbeats per minute while they experienced the frightening image. On the average, their heartbeat will go up. Simply ask for a show of hands of all for whom the rate went up, for whom it went down, for whom it remained the same. This will demonstrate that even the mere thought of a frightening situation will provoke the sympathetic emergency reaction—a point that is worth coming back to in the discussion of certain behavior therapies, such as systematic desensitization.

4. *A demonstration that we don't remember all the dreams we have.* As we know, each of us goes through several REM periods per night (about four to five). But do we remember the dreams? Ask students how many remember a dream they had the night just before the class. How many remember a dream the night before, and the night before that? The tally will show (*a*) considerable forgetting and (*b*) variability. Some people seem to be better able to remember their dreams than others. The reasons are still under debate. (Some psychologists suggest that those who use imagery well can remember their dreams better, but the evidence is very meager so far.)

For other demonstrations in this manual that concern dreams, see Chapter 1 (Demonstration 1) and Chapter 12 (Demonstration 1).

Selected Readings

GENERAL WORKS

Dement, W. C. 1974. *Some must watch while some must sleep.* San Francisco: Freeman.

Gray, J. 1971. *Psychology of fear and stress.* New York: McGraw-Hill.

Luce, G. G., and Segal, J. 1969. *Sleep and dreams.* London: Panther Books. Published by Heinemann, London, in 1967, under the title *Sleep.*

CLASSICS

Cannon, W. B. 1929. *Bodily changes in pain, hunger, fear and rage,* rev. ed. New York: Appleton-Century.

Cannon, W. B. 1932 and 1960 (rev. and enl.). *The wisdom of the body.* New York: Norton.

REFERENCE WORKS

Carlson, N. R. 1981. *Physiology of behavior*, 2nd ed. Newton, Mass.: Allyn and Bacon. (Already mentioned in Chapter 2.) See especially Chapters 12-15.

Gallistel, C. R. 1980. *The organization of action*. Hillsdale, N.J.: Erlbaum. (Already mentioned in Chapter 2.) Excellent chapters on servomechanisms and motive states.

Mook, D. 1986. *Motivation: The organization of action*. New York: Norton. A first-rate undergraduate text that is broad, integrative, and very well written.

Teitelbaum, P. 1967. *Physiological psychology*. Englewood Cliffs, N.J.: Prentice-Hall. (Already described in Chapter 2.) Of particular interest here because its author is the major exponent of the dual-center theory of hunger.

CHAPTER 4

Learning

Overview

The previous chapters have focused on the built-in aspects of human and animal behavior. But there is no doubt that we can't possibly account for all behavior in terms of innate prewiring, for much of it is clearly modifiable through experience. A number of investigators, whose modern descendants are sometimes called behavior theorists, believed that the organism's prewired repertory of behaviors is supplemented by continual rewirings—new connections in the nervous system that are formed by experience. This general assumption motivated the approach to learning taken by Pavlov in the study of classical conditioning, and was later developed and reformulated by Thorndike and then Skinner in the study of instrumental conditioning. Despite the differences in the theoretical views of Pavlov, Thorndike, and Skinner, these pioneers share some important characteristics. (1) They believed that all learned activities are ultimately composed of simpler ones, just as complex chemical compounds are made up of simpler atoms. (2) They believed that learning is governed by certain general laws that apply to all situations and all species including humans. (3) Given this belief in the generality of the laws of learning, they studied learning as it occurred in relatively simple situations, using a few animals such as dogs, rats, and pigeons.

While the chapter emphasizes findings that come from the animal laboratory, it also illustrates the relevance of these for human behavior. Of particular interest are attempts to explain certain behavioral disorders (for example, phobias and depression) or to lay the foundation for therapeutic changes through psychotherapy (for example, flooding and systematic desensitization) or behavioral medicine (as in work with biofeedback).

While traditional behavior theory can account for a wide range of phenomena and can boast of some important applications, its generality has been criticized on two main accounts. To begin with, it seems to *over*estimate the flexibility of many kinds of learning in various species. Studies on belongingness show that the way in which animals associate events is not as arbitrary as it was originally assumed to be. There seem to be certain species-specific, biological constraints

which determine what kind of association is most readily acquired. This holds
for both classical conditioning (some CS-UCS associations are more easily
formed than others, as shown in studies of learned taste aversions) and instrumental conditioning (some responses are more easily reinforced by certain
reinforcers than by others, as shown by work on species-specific defense
reactions).

A second criticism of behavior theory is that it *under*estimates what animals—
especially the primates—can learn. A number of investigators have argued that
animals can acquire cognitions, representing a change in what they *know* rather
than in what they *do*. In certain cases, these cognitions indicate an ability to
respond to quite abstract conceptual relationships, as shown by work on insightful learning and on the acquisition of higher-order concepts such as "same-
different" in chimpanzees.

Summary of the Main Topics

HABITUATION

Habituation is a decreased tendency to respond to stimuli that have become
familiar. It is perhaps the simplest form of learning known, and it occurs at
virtually all levels of the animal kingdom. It serves an important adaptive function by limiting the range of stimuli that provoke escape reactions from an
organism. One is better able to focus on what is new if there is a way to ignore
that which has already become familiar.

CLASSICAL CONDITIONING

In contrast to habituation, in which the organism only learns to recognize an
event as familiar, other forms of learning require the animal to form an association. Ivan P. Pavlov was one of the first to study such associations experimentally. His studies introduced the four major components of the classical conditioning procedure: the unconditioned stimulus (UCS), the unconditioned response (UCR), the conditioned stimulus (CS), and the conditioned response
(CR). The UCS elicits the UCR automatically and without prior learning (e.g.,
food powder in the mouth produces salivation). In contrast, the relation between the CS and the CR is clearly learned (e.g., the click of a metronome produces salivation, but only after many pairings of metronome and food powder).

A CR can be eliminated by presenting the CS alone, omitting the UCS. This
leads to extinction. Extinction can be removed by reconditioning or spontaneous recovery, which suggests that the CR was masked rather than completely
abolished during extinction training.

If an animal is presented with a stimulus that is not identical to the CS, there
will be stimulus generalization: the animal will tend to give a CR to this new

stimulus. The more the new stimulus differs from the original CS, the weaker will be the generalized CR. A related procedure is stimulus discrimination in which animals are trained to respond to one stimulus which is paired with USC (CS+) and not to respond to another which is never accompanied by the UCS (CS-).

Classical conditioning is found in a wide variety of animal species and with a wide range of UCSs and UCRs that transcend the simple cases of food powder and salivation used in Pavlov's laboratory. The CR is often similar but not identical to the UCR. The CR, for example, may be weaker and more "preparatory" than the full-blown UCR. In some cases, such as certain drug reactions, it is the very opposite of the UCR. The compensatory-reaction hypothesis proposes that this kind of a CR may represent a tendency to counteract the effects of an anticipated UCR. This hypothesis may explain phenomena of drug tolerance and addiction.

Pavlov believed that the primary factor which leads to an association between CS and UCS is contiguity in time. More recent work suggests that the story is more complicated than that. One suggestion comes from studies of the temporal relations of CS and UCS, which show that the strength of the CR will be maximal if there is forward pairing (CS before UCS) and the time interval is relatively small—indications that the CS serves a signaling function. When there is simultaneous pairing (CS simultaneous with UCS), the CS provides no new information, so CR is weak. If there is backward pairing (CS after UCS), the CS predicts the nonoccurrence of the UCS. If the UCS is an aversive stimulus (e.g., electric shock), the CS may act as a safety signal.

If what is learned in classical conditioning is that one stimulus (the CS) serves as the signal for another (the UCS), how does the animal extract this relationship from a context in which there are often many other irrelevant stimuli? One answer is that the most effective signal is one that is not only present when the UCS is about to occur, but is also one that is absent when the UCS will not occur. According to this analysis, what matters is the contingency between the stimuli (that the UCS is contingent—or dependent—upon the CS) rather than the mere contiguity. But contingency alone is not sufficient, for the animal has to attend to the relevant stimuli, as shown by the phenomena of overshadowing and blocking.

INSTRUMENTAL CONDITIONING

Instrumental conditioning differs from classical conditioning in several respects. First, in classical conditioning, reinforcement (UCS) is presented regardless of what the animal does, while in instrumental conditioning reinforcement is contingent upon the instrumental response—presented only if the animal performs that response. Second, while the response is essentially forced in classical conditioning, in instrumental conditioning it must be selected from among a number of alternatives. Put another way, two quite different relationships have to be learned in classical and instrumental conditioning respectively. In classical conditioning, the animal must learn a relation between two stimuli, the CS and the UCS. In instrumental conditioning, it must learn the relation between a response and a stimulus, the instrumental response and the reinforcement.

The classic experiment is Thorndike's study of hungry cats who learned to perform an arbitrary response to get out of a puzzle box and obtain food. The course of the cat's behavior can be described as an increase in the strength of the correct response together with a corresponding decrease in the strength of the various incorrect responses. This led Thorndike to formulate the law of effect, which states that behavior is governed by its consequences. Responses that are (immediately) followed by reinforcement will be strengthened; responses that are not followed by such reinforcement will be weakened.

The study of instrumental conditioning has been considerably elaborated and refined by B. F. Skinner's so-called operant approach. Behavior is studied in the highly simplified situation provided by the operant chamber. If the desired instrumental response is fairly low in the animal's behavior repertory it can be shaped by reinforcing successive approximations of the behavior.

As Skinner sees it, stimuli in instrumental conditioning (or, to use his terms, operant conditioning) do not elicit a response (as they do in classical conditioning). Instead, they serve a discriminative function by signaling a particular relationship between the response and reinforcement (e.g., a light, S+, indicates that bar pressing will produce food reward; the absence of light, S-, indicates that bar pressing will not produce any food reward).

There are various distinctions between reinforcers. One concerns the difference between positive reinforcers which animals will strive to attain, and negative reinforcers which they will try to escape and avoid. Another distinction is between primary reinforcers (e.g., food, water, access to a sexually responsive mate) and conditioned or secondary reinforcers whose capacity to reinforce a response is based on prior pairing with an already established (usually, a primary) reinforcer. As a general rule, the effectiveness of a reinforcer declines as the delay between the response and the presentation of the reinforcer is increased. However, humans can overcome this by using symbolic means to relate past, present, and future.

An important contribution of the operant approach is its emphasis on the fact that, in general, responses are rarely reinforced every time they occur. In the laboratory, such partial-reinforcement conditions are created by means of various reinforcement schedules (e.g., fixed-ratio and variable-ratio). Responses acquired under partial-reinforcement conditions are much more resistant to extinction than those acquired under continuous reinforcement.

Also important in instrumental conditioning are negative reinforcers (aversive stimuli). In punishment training, the animal learns to suppress a response that leads to an aversive stimulus. In escape and avoidance learning, the animal learns to produce a response to get rid of an aversive stimulus, or to avoid it altogether. Phobias are an example of avoidance learning in human life. One explanation for the persistence of phobias is that they don't extinguish because the person never stays in the feared situation long enough to discover that the expected negative reinforcer will not occur.

In a previous section, the text considered the association formed in classical conditioning, that between CS and UCS, and concluded that this association was based on contingency rather than contiguity. Much the same seems to be true for the association between the instrumental response and the reinforcer formed in instrumental conditioning. Here the relevant contingency is estimated by comparing the probability of reinforcement when the response is performed with the probability of reinforcement when it is not performed. There is evidence that animals and humans do in fact discover and respond to such response-outcome contingencies. Thus infants seem to prefer conditions in which they have control over a desirable outcome, and numerous studies attest to the devastating effects of learned helplessness in animals and humans.

BEHAVIOR THEORY AND HUMAN DISORDERS

While classical and instrumental conditioning procedures have been used primarily with animals, their relevance to human behavior has been demonstrated in such areas as behavior therapy and behavioral medicine. Two techniques of behavior therapy are based on principles of classical conditioning: systematic desensitization and flooding. Various operant techniques have also been employed to modify maladaptive behavior patterns in disturbed persons. Desired behaviors are strengthened by reinforcing them, as in token economies. Unwanted behaviors are weakened by extinction, or in some cases by the application of a satiation principle: the person is presented with such a surfeit of the reinforcer that he gets sick of it.

Learning about the contingencies between one's own actions and subsequent events in the world may have profound effects on bodily functioning. Thus some practitioners of behavioral medicine, a new field concerned with medical conditions brought on or aggravated by psychological factors, have tried to apply conditioning techniques, often coupled with biofeedback, to effect therapeutic change. A promising new development is the study of the biological effects of learned helplessness, which may involve the impairment of the body's immune system.

SOME LIMITATIONS OF BEHAVIOR THEORY

A number of critics have challenged behavior theory's insistence that a few basic principles are sufficient to characterize and explain all learned behavior in all organisms.

Some critics take issue with behavior theory's claim that the associations learned in classical and instrumental conditioning are essentially arbitrary. They argue that there are species-specific biological constraints that allow some animals to learn certain associations more readily than they learn others because the relevant items (CS and UCS in classical conditioning, response and reinforcement in instrumental conditioning) have some built-in "belongingness."

Studies of belongingness show that the laws of learning are not identical for all animals but depend on the species and the items to be associated. But while behavior theory may have overestimated the flexibility of rats and pigeons, it seems to have underestimated that of other species, including monkeys, apes, and humans. An issue raised by critics of behavior theory is whether human reasoning and understanding can be explained by principles of behavior theory. Edward Tolman, for example, argued that an animal acquires knowledge, rather than a tendency toward some behavior, and that overt behavior is only an index of the knowledge gained. This type of view allows for latent learning and learning without performance.

In a classic series of experiments, Wolfgang Köhler showed that chimpanzees can create solutions to problems. In these tasks, learning seems to be best described as gaining insight into the relevant relationships leading to problem solution, rather than the acquisition of a set of associations. The work of Harlow on "higher-order concepts" and rule formation in monkeys and the work of Premack on symbol manipulation in chimpanzees provide further examples of learning that is hard to characterize in terms of behavior theory.

The chapter ends with a statement of an important characteristic of human intelligence: it can be accessed and applied to different situations. Thus a pigeon may be brilliant in its homing capability, but its genius is severely limited to navigating. Unlike humans (and, to some extent, chimpanzees), who are "generalists," the pigeon cannot apply its particular genius to other tasks. It is an intellectual "specialist."

Discussion Topics

1. *Methodology and classical conditioning.* There are some interesting methodological issues in the study of classical conditioning that may introduce the student to one of the joys of the scientific enterprise: there is fun in discovery, and there is fun in discovering how to make a discovery. Examples include such questions as: How can you determine whether a flatworm can be conditioned (e.g., controls for pseudoconditioning)? Can a human fetus be conditioned (can we be sure we've conditioned the fetus rather than its mother)? (See Spelt, D. K. 1948. The conditioning of the human fetus *in utero*. *Journal of Experimental Psychology* 38:338-46.)

2. *Applications of classical conditioning.* There are some fascinating areas of application of classical conditioning—human phobias, various realms of sexual behavior (e.g., fetishism), and of course behavior therapy. While some of this material is considered in the text, it can be very much expanded. One possibility

is a comparison of desensitization and flooding. Both try to extinguish learned fears, but one does so by gradually sneaking up on the fear-evoking stimulus, while the other immediately confronts it head on. Which method is preferable and when? (See Stampfl, T. G., and Levis, D. J. 1967. Essentials of implosive therapy: A learning-theory-based psychodynamic behavior therapy. *Journal of Abnormal Psychology* 72:496-503.)

3. *On the negative effects of positive reinforcement.* Teachers often wonder why learning—an experience one would imagine to be naturally reinforcing— must be maintained artificially by giving grades. Perhaps the problem is giving grades in the first place.

To explain this suspicion, consider a rat in a running wheel. In this situation, a rat will very often run seemingly for the fun of it. However, if you alter its cir- cumstances for several days by requiring it to run in order to get food, the ani- mal now will not run as much as before if returned to the situation where run- ning does not produce food. (See Skinner, B. F., and Morse, W. H. 1958. Fixed- interval reinforcement of running in a wheel. *Journal of the Experimental Anal- ysis of Behavior* 1:371-79.) In other words, paying running with food trans- formed running from fun into work. This result might lead one to expect that Jack Nicklaus might well turn down the privilege of playing a round of golf for fun over the weekend.

Similar effects have been observed with young children. Preschoolers draw pictures quite spontaneously. But after a period during which they were re- warded for such drawings with gold stars (a conditioned reinforcer), they stopped drawing when no more gold stars were forthcoming. According to some investigators, this result reflects the operation of cognitive dissonance, a process dealt with in a later chapter (see Chapter 11). But it's quite possible that the underlying mechanism is similar to that observed in the wheel-running rats. (For a description of the gold-star study, see Lepper, M. R., Greene, D., and Nisbett, R. E. 1973. Undermining children's intrinsic interest with extrinsic rewards: A test of the overjustification hypothesis. *Journal of Personality and Social Psy- chology* 28: 129-37.)

4. *Commitment and self-control in the pigeon.* Many of us who are over- weight have encountered the following problem. Each night as we go to sleep we promise ourselves that tomorrow we will begin to diet in earnest. The trouble is that when we wake up hungry the next morning, we find that we have lost our self-control.

One solution to this problem is to commit ourselves to the diet in *advance*. Many diet clinics work in just this way. We sign a contract to abide by certain dietary rules while in the clinic, and as long as we remain, we are not tempted by fattening foods, because none are present. A more extreme version of com- mitment to insure self-control can be seen in the cases of people who have their mouths wired shut so that they cannot eat.

Interestingly, it is possible to demonstrate commitment to insure self-control in pigeons. Just like our dieters, pigeons will choose a small, immediate reward over a delayed, large reward even though the delayed reward provides more total reinforcement over time. In other words, pigeons tend to be impulsive rather than exercise self-control. However, if you give the pigeons a key to peck which denies them the choice between these two rewards, they will often peck it, committing themselves thereby to receiving the large, delayed reward. It appears that, in some ways, pigeons are like people. (See Rachlin, H., and Green, L. 1972. Commitment, choice, and self-control. *Journal of the Experimental Analysis of Behavior* 17:15–22.)

5. *Behavior theory, avoidance learning, and psychopathology.* There is a so-called defense mechanism, sometimes found in certain disturbed persons, known as "reaction formation" (see Chapters 12 and 19). This is an exaggerated response that seems to cover up its opposite, which the person tries not to acknowledge. For example, a child may really feel great hostility to, say, his father. But he cannot face the fact that he feels that way; for if so, he would be racked with guilt and anxiety. As a result, he has to push this unwanted feeling out of his mind. He tries, but it returns, together with the associated guilt and anxiety. He finally hits on a solution, but, according to many clinical psychologists, without knowing that he has. He becomes extremely worshipful and affectionate toward his father, strenuously denies that he could possibly harbor any resentment, and so on. In short, he has developed a reaction formation against his own hostility. This reaction protects him against his own anxiety. By performing acts of affection, he protects himself against the possibility that he might perform an act of hostility. The two acts are opposites, in the same way in which raising one's arm is the opposite to lowering it—one cannot perform the one while performing the other. As a result, the dangerous act is blocked from execution, and the anxiety this forbidden act (attacking father) might give rise to is forestalled. Much the same holds for unfriendly thoughts about one's father. These are similarly interfered with by competing thoughts of friendliness and affection.

Note that this analysis is quite compatible with a behavior theory analysis of avoidance. The patient's problems would be described as follows. To begin with, there is a classically conditioned association with fear. Its stimulus is hostility toward the father, in thought or deed. This was presumably paired with some punishment. Perhaps the child started to kick at his father, or to shout, "I hate you," or whatever. The result might have been physical punishment, or, for that matter, a scolding, loss of love, or the like. The result is as follows:

$$CS \qquad\qquad\qquad\qquad CR$$

thought or act of   ⟶   fear
hostility

Given this conditioned response, the child feels fear (anxiety and guilt or closely related experiences) whenever he acts or thinks in a hostile manner in regard to his father. These hostile responses are the CS to which fear is conditioned. The trick is to get rid of this CS. But how? He can't physically run away from this CS, because it is inside of him, produced by his own thoughts and acts. All he can do is to block them. He eventually discovers that this is most easily done when he performs a response that is antagonistic to the one that is to be blocked. And that of course is the opposite response—acts and thoughts of friendliness and affection. Such competing responses necessarily block the fear-evoking ones. But as a result they reduce anxiety by removing the stimulus which produces it. This anxiety reduction is reinforcing, and it reinforces the instrumental response—the reaction formation. Thus:

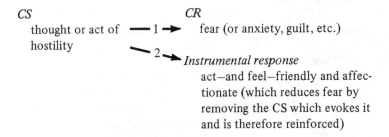

CS

thought or act of hostility

CR

fear (or anxiety, guilt, etc.)

Instrumental response
act—and feel—friendly and affectionate (which reduces fear by removing the CS which evokes it and is therefore reinforced)

The first arrow is the classically conditioned response; the second, the instrumentally conditioned one.

For some case examples of reaction formation, see Chapters 12 and 19. This defense mechanism is particularly striking in cases of so-called obsession-compulsion in which the patient has strange, frightening thoughts which he tries to shut out of his consciousness but can't (the obsessional thought—e.g., of cutting someone's throat) and in which he has developed odd bits of behavior which he feels compelled to perform on pain of great anxiety (the compulsive acts—e.g., locking all the knives in the house in an inaccessible drawer).

6. *Belongingness and phobias.* Seligman has noted an interesting aspect of phobias: only certain kinds of objects are likely to be feared. For example, people with phobias may fear snakes or elevators, but they never fear the grass or the air. Conventional learning theory has a hard time with this phenomenon. When a loud noise scared little Albert while he was playing with a rabbit, why didn't he develop a fear of the rug the rabbit was on rather than of the rabbit itself? The answer may be akin to what we studied in the taste-aversion experiment by Garcia and Koelling (see text). In the same fashion that the rat is more likely to associate nausea with tastes than with flashing lights, little Albert is more likely to associate the fear-evoking noise with the rabbit than the rug. (See Seligman, M. E. P. 1971. Phobias and preparedness. *Behavior Therapy* 2:307–20.)

7. *The continued vitality of behavior theory.* The text questions the adequacy of behavior theory on various grounds. And indeed, some of the attacks on the general approach are very telling, for the theory does not seem capable of han-

dling them at all. But even so, many behavior theorists refused to throw in their theoretical towels and continue (to be sure, with some modifications) their general enterprise. Why is this? A number of reasons may be suggested.

One has to do with the fact that behavior theory is more explicit than the cognitive approach—at least as they both apply to animals. And one may argue that it is better to have a theory that makes explicit assertions that are wrong than a theory whose assertions are so vague that it is not clear how they can be tested. The explicit theory can be disproved, and if disproved, can be modified so that it can be tested once again. A related fact is that the behavior-theory approach suggests experiments—questions one can pose to nature and can answer one way or another.

A very different answer has to do with American society. Behavior theory—especially Skinner's version of it—has been enormously influential in American psychology. In part this may be because it fits in with some underlying assumptions of American society. One is the prevailing environmentalism—the belief that learning is all-important and that innate factors matter little, which fits in with the American faith in education, the infinite possibilities of self-improvement, and so on. It presumably grows out of the view (e.g., the Declaration of Independence) that all persons are created equal, a view often denied in practice (e.g., slavery, racism, sexism) but still widely believed. If true, this suggests that differences between people reflect differences in the environment in which they were brought up—that is, the way they were taught. (It is ironic that a view which held that all men—that is, all humans—are equal may be the origin of a theory that holds that, in some vital psychological aspects, all vertebrate animals are alike.)

A second factor that might account for the ready acceptance of behavior theory by American society may be the American emphasis on action over thought. The admired hero tends to be the person who "does things"—the pioneer who clears the wilderness or the captain of industry who builds railroads and factories—rather than the "impractical egghead" who just sits and thinks. This fits in with the behavior theorist's emphasis on responding as opposed to cognition.

A third factor may be the American emphasis on payoff. Factory workers are paid in dollars, rats in food pellets. The similarity may be compelling enough in a society such as ours to make it willing to give Thorndike and Skinner a ready ear. (For further discussion of this, see Schwartz, B., Lacey, H., and Schuldenfrei, R. 1978. Operant psychology as factory psychology. *Behaviorism* 6:229-54.) These points are extremely speculative, but they may well make for an interesting class discussion.

8. *What is really meant by insight.* A very interesting little book is Wertheimer's *Productive Thinking* (New York: Harper, 1945), which presents a Gestalt psychological analysis of various problems posed to children and adults. One is Wertheimer's discussion of how high-school students learned a theorem in geom-

etry, specifically the one about the area of a parallelogram. The question is, did they learn it by rote or by insight and understanding? For details, see Wertheimer. Some of the examples show how children tried to prove the theorem (area = base × altitude) when confronted by oddly shaped parallelograms, and sometimes by figures that weren't parallelograms at all. This should be of considerable interest, especially to students considering careers in teaching.

Demonstrations

1. *Shaping.* It is easy and fun to demonstrate the operant process of "shaping a response by successive approximations" in a class.

Have one student leave the room. While he is absent, the rest of the class decides on the response they want him to perform. Let us say that it is "pick up a piece of chalk." The subject is then invited back into the classroom and is told to imagine that he is hungry and that a given signal (say, a tap on the table) means he received a bite of food. His job is to get as much "food" as possible. You wait for him to move in the direction of the blackboard. When he does, you tap the table. You then proceed to make the criterion for table tapping progressively more specific: initially he receives "food" just for walking toward the blackboard, then for standing in front of a piece of chalk, then for touching the chalk, and finally for lifting the chalk.

2. *Conditioning without awareness.* According to some authors, instrumental conditioning in humans sometimes occurs without the subject's awareness of just what response is being reinforced (e.g., Greenspoon. 1955. The reinforcing effect of two spoken sounds on the frequency of two responses. *American Journal of Psychology* 68:409–26; Philbrick, E. B., and Postman, L. 1955. A further analysis of "learning without awareness." *American Journal of Psychology* 68:417–24). Other authors disagree (e.g., Paul, G. L., Eriksen, C. W., and Humphreys, L. G. 1962. Use of temperature stress with cool air reinforcement for human operant conditioning. *Journal of Experimental Psychology* 64:329–35). Whatever the ultimate verdict on this issue, it makes an interesting classroom demonstration, for it brings home some aspects of the operant procedures rather clearly.

A subject is asked to play the role of a job applicant who has to tell you about himself for, say, ten minutes. It is not important that he tells the truth; all that matters is that he impresses you sufficiently so that you offer him the job. After the subject has been given these instructions, he or she is asked to leave the classroom for a moment.

You then tell the class that during your conversation with the subject, the class is to record the number of personal pronouns used in the volunteer's statements during the two five-minute periods of your ten-minute conversation. During the first five minutes, you respond to the volunteer only when absolutely necessary, and then in as perfunctory a fashion as possible. During the next five minutes, however, your behavior changes: you nod, smile, and say "Um-hm" after each personal pronoun the volunteer uses. Be sure the class knows how you plan to apply these contingencies before the experiment begins, so that they will know which five-minute period you are in.

After the experiment ends, ask the subject whether he was aware of the contingency being used. If your results are similar to Greenspoon's, the subject will be unaware of the contingency. Then ask the class which five-minute period had more personal pronouns. If the contingency was effective, more personal pronouns should have been used in the second five-minute period. In variants of this same experiment, one might try to reinforce some other verbal-response class, for example, plural s's or past tense ed's, or whatever.

3. *The role of irrelevant dimensions in discrimination.* The text points out that learning to discriminate between two stimuli involves attentional selection— the organism has to decide which stimulus dimensions are relevant and which irrelevant. Here is a demonstration of attentional selection. Present the class with the following pairs of stimuli, one pair at a time. Their job is to decide which stimulus is "correct"—the one on the right or the one on the left. Immediately after making the choice (which they write down), they are given the correct answer. They then proceed to the next pair. (The correct item in each pair is indicated by a plus sign next to it.)

MOTHER +	SISTER
SON	FATHER +
NIECE +	UNCLE
HOUSE +	CANOE
SHIP	LADDER +
CAT	TIGER +
LION +	GIRAFFE
RAIN	FIRE +
	and so on

The principle is very simple, but very few subjects will catch on to it. The correct word is one that begins with a letter whose capital form has no curves in it (that is, A, E, F, H, I, K, etc., but not B, C, D, G, etc.). But the trouble is that few if any subjects will hit upon this notion. They will be concerned with irrelevant dimensions of meaning. After hearing (or seeing, if you can put the pairs on slides) MOTHER + SISTER -, SON - FATHER +, they may assume the correct equals "older"; they will then form some new hypothesis when they hear NIECE + UNCLE -, and so on. Eventually, they may give up the meaning hypothesis and recognize that certain letters are always correct. But will they come to understand the principle? To test this, make up pairs that use only *some* of the letters in the alphabet. Keep a few to test whether the subjects have really caught on to the principle or have merely learned that A, E, etc., are correct, while B, C, etc., are incorrect. The way to test this is to later give the subjects pairs of words that obey the same principle but that begin with letters that have not been used before in the first position. Given the examples presented, a new pair might be:

DAGGER   ZEBRA   +

To show that the problem's difficulty has to do with irrelevant dimensions, perform one variation. Before the experiment starts, ask half of the class (say, everyone whose birthdate is an even number) to close their eyes, while the others look at one or two pairs (this assumes visual presentation). Specifically, the pairs use nonsense *forms* such as:

)   vs.   /   (the second being correct)
(vs.   –   (the second again being correct)
          and so on

The subjects who had the prior experience which taught them to pay attention to shape (and especially to curved vs. straight lines) in one situation will surely do better in the next experiment.

4. *A demonstration of belongingness.* The earliest demonstration of a belongingness effect goes back to Thorndike. In a variant of his study, read the following sentences to a class. Make sure that the time between the underlined words is always the same, whether they are within the same sentence or across adjacent sentences. The subjects are told that they will be tested for their memory of the material that was read to them. The pairs are the following:

> *John* rides a *car.*
> *Frank* rides a *horse.*
> *Henry* rides a *bicycle.*
> *Peter* rides a *train.*
> *Clark* rides a *trolley.*
> *Robert* rides a *pony.*
> *Jules* rides a *rocket.*

The subjects are then asked to answer the following questions:

1. Which word followed: Frank rides a _____? (Answer = horse)
2. Which word followed: rides a trolley _____? (Answer = Robert)
3. Which word followed: Henry rides a _____? (Answer = bicycle)
4. Which word followed: rides a train _____? (Answer = Clark)

The results will probably show that the number of correct responses is considerably greater for questions 1 and 3, which test for within-sentence associations, than for questions 2 and 4, which test for across-sentence associations. The items within a sentence are understood as belonging together, more so than are items across sentences, even though the time elapsed between, say, *Frank* and *horse* is the same as that between *trolley* and *Robert*. In this case the belongingness is based on the (presumably learned) structure of language. But the basic principle is the same as the built-in belongingness that occurs in animals who are prepared to associate, say, tastes and digestive illness more than they associate tones and illness.

5. *Insightful problem solving.* To demonstrate this, jump ahead to Chapter 8 (on thinking), which discusses this and related issues as they apply to human problem solving. Some of the problems used there can be adapted for a classroom demonstration to give a sense of what it may have felt like to be one of Köhler's chimpanzees. An example not used in the text is Katona's matchstick problems. (See Katona. 1940. *Organizing and memorizing.* New York: Columbia University Press, discussed in Woodworth and Schlosberg. 1954. *Experimental Psychology*, rev. ed. New York: Henry Holt, p. 828.) The matchstick problems can be presented on slides or cardboard, or drawn on a blackboard before the class enters. The subject's job is to take each drawing (made up of separate lines, or "matchsticks") and move *three sticks* to change the number of squares. The instructions are as follows: "Here are five equal squares. Make four similar squares out of the five by changing the position of three of the sides." On the left are the drawings that are to be changed; on the right are the correct solutions.

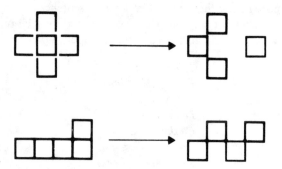

Note that there is an underlying principle. The task requires that the number of squares become smaller even though the number of sides must stay the same. In order to accomplish this, one must see that in the original drawing some of the sides have two functions: they serve as sides not to one but to two squares. Remove one or more of these and make them "one-sided," and the problem is solved. To test whether the students understood the principle, shift to new drawings in which the task is to change from four to three, and so on. (See Katona or Woodworth and Schlosberg for examples.)

Selected Readings

GENERAL WORKS

Fancher, R. E. 1979. *Pioneers of psychology.* New York: Norton. (Already mentioned in Chapter 2.) See especially Chapter 8 and the first part of Chapter 9 for a well-written historical introduction to pioneers like Pavlov, Watson, and Skinner.

Premack, D., and Premack, A. J. 1983. *The mind of an ape.* New York: Norton. This book gives a fine idea of the comparative complexity of chimpanzee cognition.

Skinner, B. F. 1971. *Beyond freedom and dignity.* New York: Knopf. The Skinnerian world view applied to the world at large.

Wertheimer, M. 1945. *Productive thinking.* New York: Harper & Row. Charming, well written. Contains the views of Gestalt psychology's founder on insight and human problem solving in a popular, lecturing style.

CLASSICS

Köhler, W. 1925. *The mentality of apes.* New York: Harcourt Brace and World. The early classic that's still worth reading.

Pavlov, I. 1927. *Conditioned reflexes.* Oxford: Oxford University Press.

Premack, D. 1976. *Intelligence in ape and man.* Hillsdale, N.J.: Erlbaum. A rather technical account of a series of brilliant experiments on symbol manipulations in chimpanzees.

Skinner, B. F. 1938. *The behavior of organisms.* New York: Appleton-Century-Crofts.

Thorndike, E. L. 1898. Animal intelligence: An experimental study of the associative processes in animals. Psychological Monographs 2 (whole no. 8).

Tolman, E. C. 1932. *Purposive behavior in animals and men.* New York: Century. The major account of the experiments that led Tolman to insist that animals acquire cognitions of various kinds.

With the possible exception of Köhler's and Thorndike's books, the preceding are not for the casual reader. They represent landmarks in the history of the field and require serious study.

REFERENCE WORKS

Dickinson, A. 1980. *Contemporary animal learning theory.* Cambridge, England: Cambridge University Press. An excellent paperback text that considers animal learning from a cognitive, rather than a behavioral theoretical point of view. Well written but rather technical.

Fantino, E., and Logan, C. 1979. *The experimental analysis of behavior: A biological perspective.* San Francisco: Freeman. A short review of the major experimental phenomena of animal learning, with an emphasis on operant processes. The last chapters of the book discuss ethology and learning in invertebrates.

Hilgard, E. R., and Bower, G. H. 1975. *Theories of learning.* Englewood Cliffs, N.J.: Printice-Hall. This work compares and contrasts the major theories of human and animal learning. It deals with theoretical approaches discussed in this chapter, as well as with theories of human learning, memory, and thinking discussed later on (e.g., in Chapters 7 and 8). A relatively advanced text, useful for reference.

Schwartz, B. 1984. *Psychology of learning and behavior*, 2nd ed. New York: Norton. Perhaps the best undergraduate text on the topic. Focuses on the major theoretical issues in behavior theory and shows how recent discoveries have altered the field. Very readable.

Schwartz, B., ed. 1984. *Psychology of learning: Readings in behavior theory.* New York: Norton. A paperback volume that is a collection of some influential experimental papers in the field of animal learning.

Seligman, M. E. P., and Hager, J. L. 1972. *Biological boundaries of learning.* New York: Meredith. A selection of readings on the effects of biological predisposition on learning.

CHAPTER 5

Sensory Processes

Overview

This chapter opens with a discussion of the origins of human knowledge, contrasting the opposing views of empiricists and nativists and describing how the nature-nurture controversy that grew out of their debate runs through much of the entire field. It shows how the empiricists' claim that all knowledge comes from the senses leads immediately to the question of what information these senses can provide and what the mechanisms are by which they provide it.

The chapter describes the main approaches to the study of sensory processes, including psychophysics and psychophysiology. After a brief tour of the different senses, it takes up one of them in detail—vision. The discussion is organized around some characteristics not only of vision but of the senses generally— reworking of the proximal stimulus, transduction, sensory interaction, and coding. In line with this organization, the section on vision begins with the proximal stimulus and its transformation by various accessory structures of the eye, turns to the visual receptors that transduce the stimulus, considers various phenomena of visual interaction such as brightness contrast that depend upon neural mechanisms beyond the receptor level, and finally takes up the sensory qualities of color and the way they are coded by the nervous system.

Summary of the Main Topics

THE ORIGINS OF KNOWLEDGE

This section takes up the empiricists' and the nativists' accounts of the origins of human knowledge. The empiricists' belief that all knowledge comes through the senses leads to an examination of what these senses can provide us with and to the distinction between the distal stimulus (e.g., a tree out there) and the proximal stimulus that this distal stimulus gives rise to (e.g., the retinal image cast by that tree). This in turn leads to one of the central problems of the entire field: how can the perceiver find out about the distal stimulus when all he is given is the proximal stimulus? The question arises because we perceive many qualities of a distal object—for example, its distance from us and its constant size and shape—which do not seem to be given in the proximal stimulus (e.g., the retinal image of a five-foot tree ten feet away is just as tall as one cast by a fifty-foot tree a hundred feet away).

To get around such difficulties, empiricists appealed to learning by association, which they held to be the mechanism that provided the various aspects of our perceptual experience not given in the proximal stimulus. Nativists disagreed, asserting that sensory input is organized according to innately given perceptual categories that are built into the nervous machinery.

PSYCHOPHYSICS

Psychophysics is the branch of sensory psychology that studies the relation between various stimulus characteristics and the sensory experiences they produce. The first topic of the section is the *quality* of different sensory experiences. This varies between the different sensory modalities (e.g., sensations of sight vs. those of hearing). It also varies within a given modality (e.g., red vs. green). In trying to account for such qualitative differences, psychologists still follow the general line formulated in Johannes Müller's doctrine of specific nerve energies. This doctrine asserts that such qualitative differences are not produced by differences in the stimuli that correspond to different sense modalities (e.g., light vs. sound) but rather to differences in the neural structures that are excited by these stimuli.

Sensory experiences differ not only in quality but also in *intensity* (e.g., a soft sound vs. a loud sound). This section takes up a number of issues that concern the measurement of such sensory intensities. An important approach to this problem grows out of the measurement of the absolute threshold (the lowest intensity of some physical stimulus that produces a response) and the difference threshold (the amount by which a given stimulus must be increased or decreased to produce a just noticeable difference or j.n.d.). A fundamental psychophysical relationship is Weber's law, which states that the amount that has to be added to a stimulus to yield a j.n.d. (that is, the size of the difference threshold) is a constant fraction of that stimulus. An extension of Weber's law is Fechner's law, which tries to express a general relationship between physical stimulus intensity and the intensity of the sensory experience it gives rise to in the observer. According to Fechner's law, this sensory experience grows as the logarithm of the physical stimulus intensity.

Modern investigators have become concerned by the fact that an observer's psychophysical judgments are affected not only by his sensitivity to the stimulus but also by his expectations and beliefs that produce response biases. A way of disentangling sensory sensitivity and response bias is provided by the signal-detection approach. In a typical detection experiment, the stimulus is presented on half of the trials, and it is absent on the other half. In this procedure, there can be two kinds of errors: misses (saying a stimulus is absent when it is present) and false alarms (saying it is present when it is absent). Their relative proportion is partially determined by a payoff matrix. When this payoff matrix is varied, the effects can be graphically expressed by an ROC curve. According to signal-detection theory, distinguishing between the presence of a stimulus and its absence depends on a process in which the subject has to decide whether some internal event (the so-called sensory process) is produced by the signal or by the background noise.

AN OVERVIEW OF THE SENSES

The chapter next presents an overview of the human senses: kinesthesis and the vestibular senses, taste, the skin senses, the sense of smell, and finally, hearing. Concerning hearing, this chapter gives a brief account of how various accessory structures in the middle and inner ear transform the sound-wave stimulus into a deformation of the basilar membrane, which is then transducted by the auditory receptors. It also discusses pitch and the theories that try to explain it—place theory and frequency theory.

The overview of the senses concludes with a list of several characteristics that are not specific to any one sensory system but are found in many if not all of them. They are (1) the presence of accessory structures that help fashion a "better" proximal stimulus for the receptors to work on; (2) the transduction of the physical stimulus energy into a neural impulse by the receptors; (3) further processing of the stimulus input by neural centers beyond the receptor level which code (that is, translate) the information into the various dimensions of sensory experience; and (4) various phenomena of sensory interaction, some dependent upon events in the immediately preceding past, others dependent upon activity in adjacent parts of the sensory system. These four summary points provide an organizing framework for the detailed discussion of the sense of vision which follows.

VISION

The stimulus for vision is electromagnetic radiation in the region of the visible spectrum (about 400 to 750 nanometers). Various structures of the eye, such as the lens and iris, act as accessory devices that transform the incoming light into a proper proximal stimulus, the retinal image.

Once on the retina, the physical stimulus energies are transduced into neural impulses by the visual receptors, the rods and cones. According to the duplexity theory, these two differ in function. The rods are the receptors for night vision; they are sensitive to relatively low light intensities and lead to achromatic sensations. The cones are the receptors for day vision; they respond to much higher levels of light intensity and lead to chromatic sensations. The case for the duplexity theory is bolstered by the fact that the two receptor systems yield different spectral sensitivity curves.

This section also takes up the photochemical events in the receptors which underlie transduction.

A number of phenomena show that the components of the visual system never function in isolation, that instead they constantly interact. One kind of interaction takes place over time, as in various forms of adaptation. An interesting laboratory example is provided by the stabilized image, which keeps all parts of a given image on the same part of the retina. Under these circumstances, the image tends to fade away.

Even more important is interaction in space—the fact that the response to a visual stimulus applied to any given region depends in part on how neighboring regions are stimulated. An example is brightness contrast. A similar effect results in the accentuation of contours as shown by Mach bands. The neural mechanism that underlies brightness contrast and related interaction processes is lateral inhibition.

Visual sensory experiences vary in an important qualitative respect: they have color. Color sensations can be classified according to three dimensions: hue, brightness, and saturation. Two pairs of hues are composed of color antagonists: red-green and blue-yellow. This antagonistic relationship is shown by the fact that each member of a pair (e.g., red vs. green) tends to oppose the action of the other. One example is additive color mixture, as in simultaneously stimulating the same region of the retina with two or more stimuli. In such additive mixture, the mixture of two color antagonists (that is, red with green, and blue with yellow) leads to gray. Related results come from negative afterimages (after staring at a red light and then looking away, you see a green spot) and simultaneous color contrast (a gray patch surrounded by red seems to have a greenish tinge).

To explain the mechanisms that underlie these and similar phenomena of color vision, one first has to ask about the way in which different frequencies of light are transduced into the receptor discharge. This is done by the joint action of three different kinds of cones, each of which is maximally sensitive to a somewhat different region of the spectrum.

Another question concerns the way the receptor message is coded into sensory experience. According to the opponent-process theory, this is accomplished by three neural systems, each of which corresponds to a pair of sensory antagonists: red-green, blue-yellow, and black-white.

Discussion Topics

1. *The nature-nurture controversy.* This is one of the great issues that runs through the entire field of psychology. The students may be interested to know just how pervasive this controversy really is. It is encountered in the discussion of learning and behavior theory, where the question was whether the laws of learning hold for all animals or whether there are species-specific biological constraints upon them (Chapter 4). It is encountered again in several other chapters on cognition. One instance is the discussion of cognitive development which takes up Piaget's theory that human intellectual growth goes through a fixed

series of changes that is presumably based on built-in patterns (Chapter 14). Others are the chapters on language, which contrast the view (e.g., Skinner's) that language is entirely learned with the hypothesis (e.g., Chomsky's) that it is species-specific to humans, who are innately predisposed to organize language inputs in certain ways (Chapers 9 and 15). The nature-nurture issue crops up in still other areas. One is concerned with the biological bases of social behaviors. Are there some built-in predispositions that make various animals and ourselves capable of aggression or love or self-sacrifice? (See Chapter 10.) Other chapters in which this issue comes up in another form concern individual differences. Here the question is whether certain differences between individuals are attributable to hereditary or to environmental factors and what the relative contributions of each are. These differences may be in their intelligence-test performance (Chapter 17), personality traits (Chapter 18), or the extent to which they are susceptible to certain mental disorders (Chapter 19).

This catalog makes it clear that the nature-nurture issue is an extremely pervasive one. Some further points:

(a) A psychologist who has a nativist bias in one area need not have this bias in another. Consider a nativist approach to perception. A psychologist who has this bias tends to believe that various properties of the perceptual world are based on the biological equipment the perceiver brings to the world rather than on his experience. It may well be that this equipment is different for humans than for some other animals. But there is no assumption that this built-in basis for perception differs from person to person. Much the same holds for the view that language is a species-specific human capacity. Again the view is that some aspect of our ability to understand and produce speech comes from the way we are built. In this respect we are different from, say, ducks who are built to quack, but we are not different from each other. In regard to perception and language, the nativist bias says nothing about differences between human beings. The situation is quite different in topic areas like human intelligence. Here, the nature-nurture issue concerns the difference between human beings, the extent to which differences in intelligence-test performance (or personality or tendency toward certain mental disorders) are attributable to hereditary differences or to environmental ones. One can well maintain a nativist position on such questions as the nature of human perception and language while holding to an environmentalist view on differences in IQ.

(b) Part of the popularity of the empiricist position in American society comes from the American belief that all men are created equal and that what makes them unequal is the cumulative effect of environmental differences. It is very likely that this general philosophical outlook led to an intellectual climate which welcomed behavior theories such as Skinner's. But there is something rather ironic about all this, because the one position does not really follow from the other. For it is perfectly possible to hold that all men are created equal (an environmentalist view about individual differences among humans) without subscribing to the view that all animals are created equal, that psychologically speaking, rats, pigeons, and even humans are essentially alike (an environmental-ist view that rejects the belief in species-specific, built-in factors that govern such processes as learning, perception, and language).

2. *Different sensitivities in different creatures.* The stimulus energies to which different animals are sensitive are different, sometimes enormously so, for different species have evolved different sensory mechanisms to fit their special needs. An example is the fine interplay between the sensory apparatus of bats and that of the moths upon which they prey. Bats locate these moths by emit-ting ultrasonic sounds which bounce off small objects in midair and produce an echo which the bat can hear. This is of obvious adaptive value to the bat. But evolution works for the prey no less than for the predator. It turns out that the moths upon whom the bats feed have also evolved a sensitivity to ultrasonic sounds. When they hear the bat's cries—especially when those cries are short and loud, as the bat comes in for the kill—they reflexively take evasive action. They drop in midair, take a power dive, and veer off to one side or another—evasive maneuvers reminiscent of naval vessels trying to outrun a larger foe. Such facts highlight the adaptive value of the sensory systems which equip their posses-sors—ourselves no less than moths and bats—to go about their business and survive. (For details on the moth-bat battles, see Roeder, K. D. 1965. Moths and ultra-sound. *Scientific American* 212:94–102.)

3. *Image resolution in the visual system.* Anyone looking at the original pho-tographs of Mars taken by the Mariner space probe might have felt discouraged about our ever getting a clear picture of the Martian surface. The problem was that everything looked gray, with no features of the landscape distinguishable from others. This discouragement was premature, however, because each pic-ture was altered subsequently by a computer to remove the "noise" from the picture. After computer filtering, each picture clearly showed the Martian land-scape. Enhancement techniques were thus used to create a clear picture from one that was not.

Something akin to this process goes on in the visual system. The visual image reaching the retina is not perfectly refracted by the lens; it is diffused by the aqueous and vitreous humors that maintain the shape of the eye; and it passes through a yellowish substance over the fovea (the macula lutea) and strikes the rods and cones, both of which are pointed toward the brain (a direction obvi-ously ill-suited for seeing), not toward the lens of the eye.

All of these factors tend to degrade the quality of the image reaching the brain. Nevertheless, humans see very well—for example, they see clear contours even though the image is fuzzy. The reason is that we have our own image-enhance-ment system which improves the quality of our vision. One mechanism, dis-cussed in this chapter, is lateral inhibition, which enhances contours (see p. 164). A second mechanism, discussed in the next chapter (see pp. 197–99) is provided by feature detectors in the brain, which are sensitive to organized stimulus patterns such as edges or straight lines. All these mechanisms tend to perfect the imperfect image on the retinal surface.

4. *The effect of complete homogeneity.* The text has argued that the visual system is geared to notice change, whether over time or over space. What happens when there is no change of either kind?

This question has been attacked experimentally by exposing the retina to a continuous, homogeneous stimulus (a procedure that is quite analogous to what is done by means of the stabilized image). Such a homogeneous stimulus is often called a *Ganzfeld* (in German, "whole field"). One way of achieving a *Ganzfeld* is to cover the eye with half of a translucent ping-pong ball which admits only diffuse light. Thus outfitted, the subject (who now looks somewhat like Little Orphan Annie) is exposed to light of some particular intensity and wavelength, which now will provide the identical stimulus to all parts of his retina. For a short while the subject reports, say, a bright red mist, but this quickly fades and ultimately disappears, leaving virtually no sensation of definite color or brightness, a nondescript experience that one subject reported as "a visual nothing." Interestingly enough, this experience changes instantly if we provide some inhomogeneity of stimulation, for example, by holding a finger against part of the ping-pong ball. Now the subject immediately sees a blackish (actually a black-green) area surrounded by the original red field. (See Hochberg, J. E., Triebel, W., and Seaman, G. 1951. Color adaptation under conditions of homogeneous stimulation (*Ganzfeld*). *Journal of Experimental Psychology* 41:153–59.)

The *Ganzfeld* phenomenon is probably due to the fact that in this situation all of the antagonistic processes of the visual system cancel each other out. All areas inhibit each other equally, and adaptation effects do the rest. This is yet another demonstration of the fact that the visual system notices differences and is much less concerned with absolute intensities. W. S. Gilbert was satirizing class distinctions in Victorian England, but one of his lyrics applies equally well to the role of distinctions in the nervous system: "When everyone is somebodee, then no one's anybody."

5. *Relational perception—a pervasive effect.* The facts of sensory adaptation and of spatial interaction (as in brightness contrast) show that the visual system is meant to note change—in time or space or both. When there is no change, nothing is noted. The extreme case of this is the *Ganzfeld*, where all visual experience seems to disappear. But such effects are not confined to vision or even to sensory processes in general. They run through many aspects of psychological experience.

Needless to say, such phenomena are found in the other senses. There is sensory adaptation in all of them—smell is a good case in point. And there are contrast effects of certain kinds in the other senses too: thus a medium weight appears heavier if it is lifted after a light weight, and it will appear lighter if it is lifted after a heavy weight. Similar effects have to do with the judgment of the psychological value of certain outcomes such as rewards and punishments. These are related to expectation. Rats that have been running an alley at the end of which they find ten pellets of food will stop running (and act very frustrated) if their reward is suddenly switched to one pellet; in contrast, rats that had been running to one pellet all along have no such frustration effects. Similarly for school grades. A "B" is a success or a failure—depending on what the student expected to get. Related effects pertain to emotional feelings. This point is explicitly made in Solomon's opponent-process theory, which is deliberately modeled on some phenomena observed in the sensory realm. Intense passion gradually turns into contentment as it is muted by the opponent process; when the stimulus for the positive experience (say, the lover) departs, the opponent process reveals itself more directly as grief and depression (see Chapter 3, pp. 81-82).

Demonstrations

1. *Auditory "beats."* The text points out that all sounds can be represented in terms of the frequency and amplitude of their constituent sine waves. The way in which the different sine waves interact can be illustrated by taking a guitar and adjusting one of its strings so that it makes a sound only slightly higher or lower than that made by another string. Now pluck both strings simultaneously. The intensity of the sound should wax and wane, its period equaling the difference between the two sounds' frequencies. For example, if the frequency of the sound wave from one string is 1,000 Hz and the other is 1,006, the listener should hear six beats per second as the sound envelope produced by the addition of the separate waves waxes and wanes.

2. *Brightness contrast.* To demonstrate brightness contrast, take a gray piece of cardboard (C) and put it in plain view of the class. Now take a masking screen (M) made up of two halves—one white, the other black. In each half, there are two small square-shaped holes. If the mask is now placed over the gray cardboard, the viewer will see two small gray squares—one surrounded by black, the other by white. Ask for a show of hands to indicate which of the two squares looks brighter. (If the illumination on the entire setup is even, the gray on black will appear brighter to most of the students.) Now perform a simple control. Reverse the mask, so that the half that was formerly on the right (say, the black side) is now on the left and vice versa. Again ask which square is brighter. The judgment will now change, for again the one on the black ground will appear brighter.

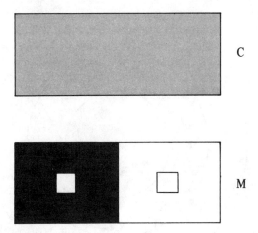

3. *A demonstration of Mach bands.* Mach bands are one of the traditional ways of demonstrating the way the visual system "sharpens" the input, creating contours where physically there are none. The classical—and easy—demonstration uses a color wheel. If you have a color wheel, prepare a disk as shown in Diagram I below.

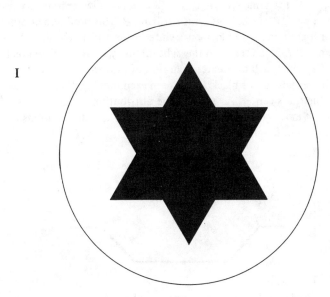

II

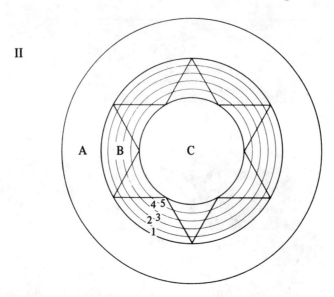

The disk in Diagram I shows a black star on a white background. What happens when this disk is rapidly rotated? To understand the resulting light distribution, consider Diagram II, which shows two bands, *A* and *B*, surrounding a central circle *C*, all corresponding to regions of the rotating disk. In band *A*, there will be a relatively high light intensity which is even throughout, for the entire band *A* is white. By the same reasoning, *C* will produce a lower intensity level, for the entire circle *C* is black. Now consider band *B*. This produces intermediate intensities, for it contains both black and white regions. If we consider *B* to consist of minibands *B-1*, *B-2*, etc., then the light intensity on *B-1* will be greater than that of *B-2*, which will be greater than that of *B-3*, and so on. The reason is simply that the proportion of black to white in each miniband increases as one gets closer to the star's center. As a result, the distribution of light intensities goes down as one moves from miniband *B-1* inward. These distributions are graphically plotted in Diagram III.

III

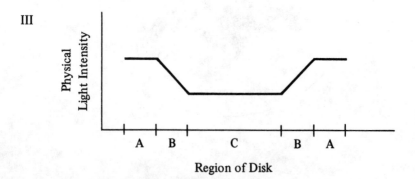

The important point is that, physically speaking, the decrease in light intensities from *B-1* to the center of the star is perfectly gradual. But this is not the
way it looks. For what the observer sees is different. He sees a central dark circle (corresponding to *C*), surrounded by a gray ring (*B*), which in turn is surrounded by a white one (*A*). But that's not all. He also sees bands that accen-
tuate the transitions. He will see a brighter band at the transition from *A* to *B*,
and a darker band at the transition from *B* to *C* (as shown schematically in Diagram IV). These are Mach bands—contours produced by the visual system
(pp. 162-63).

IV

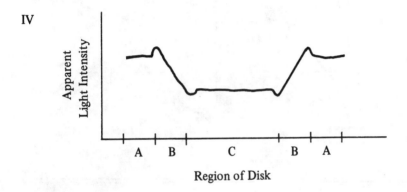

Region of Disk

Needless to say, the demonstration can also be performed by having a white
star on a black background, with appropriate (but color-reversed) results.

4. *Simultaneous color contrast.* Color contrast is readily (and often rather
prettily) obtained by colored lights and shadows. To perform the demonstration, you need a gray or white background, a desk lamp, a stick or rod that can
throw a shadow (the ring stands that chemists use work fine), and four colored
light bulbs—red, green, blue, and yellow. The demonstration should be done in
dim light provided by a regular light bulb. The setup is shown on the next page
using red light.

Note that the arrangement of the lamp and rod means that there is reddish
illumination on the screen. But there is also something else: the shadow cast
by the rod. What light falls on the region outlined by the shadow? Only that
thrown by the general room illumination, which is presumably white. As a
result, the shadow should look gray. But it doesn't. It is surrounded by red,
and it therefore takes on the tinge of the red's antagonist: green. There is
another effect in addition to this color-contrast phenomenon. The shadow
looks darker than it should if all that mattered were the physical light intensity reflected by it. For example, it looks darker than does a region of the
screen that gets the same room illumination but is outside of the light cone

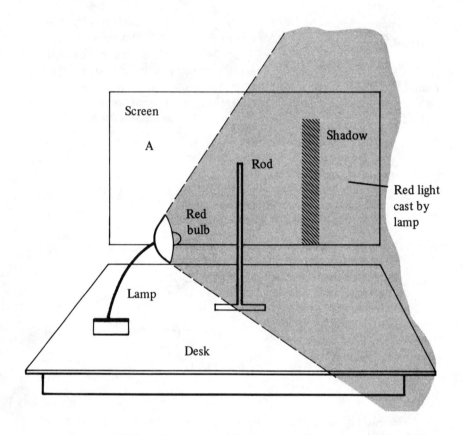

thrown by the red lamp (for example, point A on the diagram). This is another demonstration of the phenomenon of brightness contrast.

Similar effects will be obtained by substituting blue, yellow, or green bulbs. The shadow will tend to look yellow if the bulb is blue; blue if the bulb is yellow; and red if the bulb is green.

5. *Additive color mixture.* The same setup of the rod and desk light can be used to show (in a rough and ready form) additive mixture. One now uses two desk lamps—say, red and blue—to illuminate the same general region of the screen. (The easiest way is to place them at opposite sides of the desk.) There will be little doubt that the region in which the two light cones thrown by the two lamps overlap looks more purplish (and, incidentally, brighter) than the other two. To show color antagonism, use red and green. The region of overlap will probably not be gray. That would be too much to hope for, since the intensities of the colors are not adjusted and since the colors won't be the unique colors (e.g., the red will probably be too yellow). But there will be some ten-

dency in that direction, for the overlap region will surely look less saturated, more grayish (and, again, lighter). Most effective will be blue and yellow. The students (who simply can't forget the happy childhood days when they mixed blue and yellow crayons subtractively to get green) will expect green; in fact, the region of overlap will look desaturated, approaching gray.

6. *Negative afterimages.* Some rather impressive demonstrations are actually in the text. (The flower on p. 170 could be photographed and shown as a slide. After, say, sixty seconds of fixation, and then looking at a white background, the effect is very strong. One sees the flower in its true colors.) A fast way of getting the effect is again by the use of the colored lamps. Now a few seconds (ten at most) should do. Ask the students to look, say, at the red lamp, then at a white screen. They'll see a dark, greenish splotch which—naturally—moves with their eyes, being "painted" on the retina. If they don't fixate the red light but move their eyes around a bit, they may see greenish streaks.

7. *The interaction of smell and taste.* For those who like to mix science and humor, here is a demonstration of the fact that much of what we regard as taste depends upon smell. Assuming you have a small class (or section), you can ask one student to serve as subject. Begin with a control in which he or she tastes various liquid foods (e.g., juices) while blindfolded and is asked to identify them. Identification will be nearly perfect. Now keep the blindfold but get rid of the sense of smell. This can be done by having a student assistant hold the subject's nose while he or she is trying to taste the stimuli. Or, if you prefer technological devices, clamp the nose with a clothespin. All this will lead to some mess as liquids get slopped over the desk (let alone the poor subject's face), a fair amount of merriment over the total situation, and the clear-cut result that the subject will not be able to identify quite a few of the liquids by taste alone.

Selected Readings

GENERAL WORKS
Békésy, G. von. 1957. The ear. *Scientific American* 197:66–78. Clear discussion of some basics of the auditory process written by one of psychology's Nobel laureates.

Wald, G. 1950. Eye and camera. *Scientific American* 183:32–41. Beautiful presentation of some basic facts about the eye and the receptor processes, written by a major figure in the field. Excellent illustrations.

CLASSICS
Boring, E. G. 1950. *History of experimental psychology.* New York: Appleton-Century-Crofts. Sections on Locke, Berkeley, Hume, Kant. The authoritative history of experimental psychology.

Crombie, A. C. 1964. Early concepts of the sense and the mind. *Scientific American* 210:108-16. Readable account of some early workers in the field of sensory process; includes good illustrations.

Fancher, R. E. 1979. *Pioneers of psychology.* New York: Norton. (Already mentioned in Chapter 2.) Chapter 3. A readable introduction to the greatest figure in the study of sensory processes, Hermann Helmholtz.

REFERENCE WORKS
Brown, E. L., and Deffenbacher, K. 1979. *Perception and the senses.* New York: Oxford University Press.

Coren, S., Porac, C., and Ward, L. M. 1984. *Sensation and perception*, 2nd ed. New York: Academic Press. Both this, and Brown and Deffenbacher (see above) are good undergraduate texts for material covered in Chapters 5 and 6 of this text.

Kling, J. W., and Riggs, L. A., eds. 1971. *Woodworth and Schlosberg's experimental psychology*, 3rd ed. New York: Holt, Rinehart and Winston. More advanced treatments of sensory processes.

CHAPTER 6

Perception

Overview

Whereas the preceding chapter was concerned with the crude raw materials of our sensory experience, the present one asks how this sensory input is organized and interpreted to let us apprehend the objects and events in the external world around us: how we come to perceive, not just a bright red, but an apple—a tangible object of constant shape and size, that has depth and is stationary. But while this is a valid description of the distal object, it does not correspond to the proximal stimulus, which is two-dimensional, changes in both size and form with changes in the observer's distance and angle of regard, and moves as the observer moves his eyes. This poses a problem, perhaps the central problem in the entire field of perception: how can we perceive the constant properties of the distal stimulus, given the inevitable variations in the proximal stimulus? Much of this chapter revolves around this question and around the nature-nurture controversy that has formed the background of all attempts to answer it.

Summary of the Main Topics

THE PROBLEM OF PERCEPTION

This section takes up the essential problem of perception. The perceiver wants to know about an unchanging distal object, but all he is given is the proximal stimulus which lacks many of the properties of the distal object and changes continually as the observer moves about. Two approaches to the question have been framed by the empiricists and the nativists, the first based on learning, the second on innately given reactions to certain stimulus invariants. These two approaches form the poles of the nature-nurture controversy, which helps to provide an organizational framework for much of the material discussed in this chapter.

PERCEPTUAL ORGANIZATION

Our perceptual experience is organized and structured. Many aspects of this organization can be described as they help the perceiver answer three questions about something he observes in the external world: What is it? Where is it? What is it doing?

In humans, the determination of *what* something is, is largely based upon its form. A number of perceptual processes serve as a prelude to the perception of form. One is the segregation of a figure from its background; another is the grouping of its components according to such factors as proximity, similarity, and good continuation. Reversible figure-ground effects, grouping, and certain related phenomena such as subjective contours, all testify to the fact that what we see cannot be solely accounted for in terms of the proximal stimulus.

A similar point applies to the processes that come into play when the form of the figure is perceived (pattern recognition). While we still don't know just how pattern recognition is attained, it's clear that it depends on the recognition of some relation between the component parts rather than on the parts in isolation. This point was stressed by the Gestalt psychologists, who buttressed their view by repeated demonstrations of the phenomenon of form transposition.

The chapter turns next to the perceiver's attempts to determine *where* something is by discussing the perception of depth. It begins by considering the binocular cues for depth—retinal disparity and convergence—and then takes up the monocular cues—linear perspective, relative size, and interposition. It finally turns to motion parallax as yet another vital source of information about the layout of objects in the environment.

The next topic is the perception of movement. Here, as so often throughout this chapter, we see that what is perceived is not a mere copy of what the proximal stimulus gives us. Movement can be perceived when in fact there is none. One example is stroboscopic movement in which there is no motion at all on the retinal image. A related example is induced movement. Here all that moves is a framework, but what is seen is the (induced) motion of an enclosed figure that in fact is stationary. A final point concerns the role of eye movements. When we move our eyes over a stationary scene, we see the various objects in the scene at rest, even though the images projected by these objects necessarily move across our retinas—a demonstration that the nervous system compensates for the retinal displacements produced by eye movements.

PERCEPTUAL SELECTION: ATTENTION

Our perceptual systems have a limited capacity. At any one time they are assailed by a myriad of stimuli, however they cannot respond to all of them but must select among them. This perceptual selection can be accomplished in either of two ways. One is based on physical orienting movements, such as moving the eyes. The other is based on central processes (that is, attention), by means of which information from the sensory channels is selected and registered so that it can be processed further. An example is selective listening.

INNATE FACTORS IN PERCEPTUAL ORGANIZATION

This section considers some of the built-in factors that underlie perceptual organization. It begins by considering the evidence for such an innate basis, including studies of human infants and the young of other species. It then turns to the search for the underlying physiological mechanisms. This leads to a discussion of feature detectors in the retina and brain, whose existence is inferred from single-cell recordings and whose adaptation may explain certain perceptual aftereffects, such as the waterfall illusion.

LEARNED FACTORS IN PERCEPTUAL ORGANIZATION

This section considers the ways in which perception can be modified by the experience and/or the expectations of an observer. These are discussed under three major headings: (1) perceptual adaptation—a recalibration process exemplified by the adjustment to various optical distortions; (2) perceptual differentiation—a process whereby certain distinctive features in the stimulus are singled out and attended to; and (3) perceptual problem solving—a constructive process based on the interplay between the features of which the pattern is composed (bottom-up processes) and higher-level knowledge and expectations (top-down processes). Several phenomena are considered to illustrate this latter process, including context effects, ambiguous figures, phonemic restoration, fragmented figures, some apparent motion effects, and impossible figures.

THE PERCEPTION OF REALITY

The chapter now asks how the various aspects of perceptual organization contribute to the larger goal described at the beginning: perceiving the real world outside. To accomplish this goal, the perceiver must apprehend certain unchanging characteristics of the distal object despite various contextual factors—illumination, the observer's distance and orientation—that lead to enormous variations in the proximal stimulus. But the perceiver manages to do so nonetheless, as shown by the perceptual constancies. Some of these are probably based on built-in factors. An example is lightness constancy, in which the perceiver responds to the object's reflectance and somehow discounts the level of illumination that falls upon it—a phenomenon that seems to be based on the same innate mechanisms (e.g., lateral inhibition) that underlie brightness contrast. Other constancies may well be based on learning in very early life, such as size and shape constancy, in which the perceiver responds to the actual size and shape of an object regardless of its distance and its orientation.

The same perceptual strategies that allow us to construct a constant, realistic perceptual world from a fluctuating and ambiguous proximal array, can occasionally lead to misperceptions—the so-called perceptual illusions. The moon illusion, the Müller-Lyer illusion, and the Ponzo illusion are cases in point.

THE REPRESENTATION OF REALITY IN ART

Phenomena such as object permanence demonstrate the shadowy boundary between perception and conception, in which it is not clear where seeing ends and knowing begins. The same theme is struck in this section, on visual art, which shows that representation is both of what is seen and what is known. During different historical periods, artists had different representational aims, as exemplified by a comparison of Renaissance painters, Impressionists, and certain modern artists.

Discussion Topics

1. *The nature-nurture issue and its ramifications.*   This topic may be even better suited for discussion at this point than at the end of Chapter 5. (For details, see Chapter 5, Discussion Topic 1.)

2. *Illusion and reality.*   There is an odd paradox about the psychology of perception. It tries to find out how people perceive the world as it really is, but it goes about doing so by studying various effects that produce illusory perceptions. An example is brightness contrast, in which a gray on black looks brighter than the same gray on white, even though in reality they are both the same. Or take various depth cues as displayed in two-dimensional figures which look as if they were three-dimensional, though of course they aren't. Or take the waterfall effect, in which the observer looks at a stationary line after looking at a series of stripes moving downward. He now sees the line as floating upward even though it is really stationary. In all these cases, perceptual processes produce illusion, and yet perception normally leads to seeing what is really there. How can we resolve this paradox?

The answer is that in such demonstrations one deliberately isolates a factor that normally lets us see reality as it truly is, without presenting the normal context in which that factor operates. Take brightness contrast. In real life this accentuates the difference between an object and its background, so we see it as it really is, a separate thing that exists in its own right. Brightness contrast also helps us see the object's true lightness, for the real world, the same illumination hits both figure and ground so that brightness contrast can compensate for the increase in illumination, thus producing lightness constancy. But these aids to seeing what is really there occur in the real world. In the laboratory, the experimenter wants to isolate the individual factors that produce perceptual effects. He uses gray patches on white and black rather than real objects that are separate from their backgrounds. And he suspends other rules of the world. He may choose not to illuminate figure and ground equally so that a factor which normally preserves reality (brightness contrast) operates to yield an illusion. Similar arguments apply to, say, perspective drawings. These are drawn on a two-dimensional surface. As a result, the perspective depth cues that are valid under normal conditions—in the real, three-dimensional world—produce an illusory appearance of depth.

This situation is not really all that different from the one that holds in other sciences. Physicists drop objects in a vaccum in order to isolate certain factors that govern the behavior of falling bodies. They do this, even though there are normally no vacuums on earth. To understand reality, one must sometimes isolate some of its aspects at the expense of others. As a result, one may well exaggerate one or another facet. In the study of perception, this exaggeration may produce an illusion.

A related point concerns some cases (such as the Müller-Lyer illusion) in which the illusion may simply be a perceptual overcompensation. In most cases, compensating for distance leads to size constancy—thus preserving reality. But occasionally this perceptual strategy backfires and leads to illusory effects. (For discussion of this last point see pp. 210-11 of the text, and Gregory, R. L. 1968. Visual illusions. *Scientific American* 219:66-78.)

Demonstrations

1. *The effect of perceived distance upon perceived size.* The text often refers to size constancy and related effects, which show that the organism responds to the distal stimulus (the true size of the object) rather than to the proximal stimulus alone (that is, the size of the retinal image). (See pp. 180-82, 208-10, among others.) To do this, the perceiver must somehow compensate for the distance at which the object is seen. He presumably does so by responding to various depth cues, noting the distance, and then adjusting his perception of the object's size accordingly.

Proof that the observer perceives size in terms of perceived distance is easy to find. Let the subject first form an afterimage, using the setup described in Chapter 5, Demonstration 6. After he inspects the colored lamp, let the subject look at a blank piece of white paper held out at arm's length. He will see, say, a green spot on that paper. Let him next look at the screen (or white wall, etc.) in front of the classroom. He will now see a green spot on that wall. (If he fails to see an afterimage, ask him to blink. This often brings a fading image back for a while.) The key question is, how large does this image (that is, the green spot) appear? Does it look smaller, equal, or larger when it is seen on the white paper, or on the white wall? The subject will answer that the image seems much larger when it is on the screen or wall. The reason is simple: the wall is much farther away. Note that the retinal size of the image is identical in both cases. After all, the afterimage, is, so to speak, "painted" on the retina—it is an area where certain receptors have become overexcited and that area is the same whether the subject looks at a nearby plane or one much farther away. The result demonstrates that the perception of size does not depend on retinal size alone. It also depends upon the apparent distance. (This relation between the apparent size of an afterimage and the apparent distance of the surface on which it is seen is called Emmert's Law.)

2. *Induced motion.*   Induced motion is a simple illustration of the general effects of a framework upon that which it encloses. A simple way to demonstrate it is to use a screen (or white wall) and first attach a small piece of black tape somewhere in the middle. Now use a projector and project a grid upon the screen. This may be done (if you have the right projector) by using a piece of chicken wire or something similar. This gridwork is then moved back and forth by hand. This projects a moving framework against a stationary figure (that is, the piece of tape). Even so, the piece of tape will seem to move (in the opposite direction of the movement of the grid)—an effect of induced motion.

Another way of producing the same result is by means of an overhead projector that uses transparencies. Now the grid is inked on the transparency, which is then moved back and forth over the stationary figure.

3. *The aftereffect of motion.*   Motion aftereffects are often ascribed to the adaptation of special feature detectors sensitive to directional movement (that is, movement in one direction rather than another). To illustrate this phenomenon prepare a spiral figure like the one shown below.

Paste it on cardboard and then attach it to a rotating wheel (say, a color wheel) that rotates rather slowly (somewhere between fifteen and thirty revolutions per minute should work). Ask the subjects to look at this for about one minute (thirty seconds may be enough). Now stop the wheel and hold it completely still. After a short interval, the subjects will see a rotation in the opposite direction from that they observed a moment before.

4. *Perceptual construction.*   Hochberg's study on the perceptual schemas built up by momentary glimpses (see text, p. 193) lends itself to a nice classroom demonstration. The easiest way is with an overhead projector that works with transparencies. First draw a cross (say, a red cross) much like Hochberg's on a transparency. Then get a piece of black cardboard and make a circular hole in it whose diameter is roughly the width of any one arm of the cross (as in the diagram on p. 193). Place this over the transparency that bears the red cross. Initially cover even the small hole, so that the students see nothing. Next open the hole and slowly move it around, following the edges of the cross as shown in the figure on page 193. Go all around the cross and then around again. The subjects will start to perceive the figure. It's not just that they know that the figure is there. They will say that it seems as if they really saw it—a demonstration of a perceptual schema by expectation.

In the event you have no overhead projector, you can create the same effect by using two large pieces of cardboard. One holds the red cross and is attached to some holder (perhaps an easel) that holds it upright. The other should be a large black cardboard that has the circular hole. This is now slid around the cross in much the same manner that is used for the transparency.

5. *The effect of context (and expectation) on visual perception.*   The role of context on some aspects of form perception is neatly illustrated in the figure below.

B A K E R

B 64 59

Note that the identical figure is perceived as a B when in the context of letters, but may be seen as a 13 when in the context of two-digit numbers. (From Bruner, J. S., and Minturn, A. L. 1955. Perceptual identification and perceptual organization. *Journal of General Psychology* 53:21-28.)

6. *The role of context (and expectation) on auditory perception.*   The way in which expectations and knowledge can bias auditory perception can be illustrated in the following way. Tape record someone saying the nonsense syllable "tress" repeatedly, at the rate of about three times per second, for a period of about one minute. Attempt to keep each repetition of the syllable as uniform as possible, so that the entire string has few intonational contours and is monotonous. Play this to the students without informing them of the content of the tape. Simply ask them to listen carefully, and then to write down exactly what they hear. A collection of students' responses will reveal distortions that illustrate the constructive nature of auditory perception. In addition to the actual syllable "tress," students are likely to report having heard words such as "rest,"

"stress," "dress," "distress," "dressed," etc. This effect was first noted by Gregory and Warren, and was considered analogous to visual reversible figures. (See Gregory, R. L., and Warren, R. M. 1958. An auditory analogue of the visual reversible figure. *American Journal of Psychology* 71:612-13.)

   7. *Seeing vs. knowing—a demonstration of the Gelb effect.*   The Gelb effect (named after a German psychophysiologist who worked in the 1930s) is a striking demonstration of two points described in the chapter (see pp. 207 ff.). One is that the very mechanisms that normally let us see the world as it really is will sometimes produce illusions. The second is that seeing is not always the same as knowing, for we sometimes cannot help but say that something *looks* in a certain way, even though we *know* perfectly well that it actually is not that way at all.

   To set up the Gelb effect, take a piece of *black* construction paper (8½ by 11 inches is a convenient size) and suspend it from the ceiling of an otherwise darkened room with black thread, so that it is at some distance from any walls that are in back of it. (The top of an open door frame may do as well.) Now set up a slide projector so that the beam of light from the projector falls on the *entire* piece of black paper (see Diagram I). Ideally, the beam should illuminate just the paper and none of the background behind it. To create a beam of light of the appropriate shape and size, one will probably have to adjust the aperture of the projector. This can be done quite easily by using a blank glass slide (easily obtained from any camera shop) and creating the appropriate shape by covering its edges with opaque masking tape. The more precisely the beam is shaped and aimed (to cover the paper alone and none of the background behind it), the more dramatic the result will be, but some effect will be obtained even if the conditions are not altogether perfect.

   When observed under these conditions, the black piece of construction paper (let's call it *A*) will look white (or perhaps, a lightish grey).

   Now comes the next step. Keep everything as it was, but hold a second, *white* piece of paper (let's call this one *B*) so that part of it is in front of *A*, the original, black piece of construction paper (see Diagram II). After a brief moment, the perceived color of paper *A* will change: originally seen as white, it will now appear in its true color and will look black.

   Now for the third step. Simply take the white piece of paper *B* away, so that everything goes back to the way it was. What do the observers say now? They will all say that now the (objectively black) piece of construction paper *A* looks white again. They may add that they know that it really *is* black, but that knowledge does not change the fact that it now looks white. These steps can be repeated again and again, and the result will always be the same. When a corner of the white piece of paper *B* is in front of the black paper *A*, they will see *A* as black. When it is removed, *A* will look white again, and so on.

   What explains these effects? As we saw in the chapter (pp. 207 ff.) lightness constancy—that is, seeing the color of the paper as it really is, regardless of the illumination—is a side effect of brightness contrast. Under normal circumstances, the illumination falls equally on both the figure and its background. If so, then both figure and background will reflect more light. As a result, there will be lateral inhibition from the background which will nullify the effect of increasing the amount of light reflected by the figure. Under these circumstances, there will be lightness constancy—a black object will look black even if the illumination that falls upon it is increased.

But note that the viewing conditions in this demonstration are *not* normal. For here, the illumination does not fall on paper A's immediate background. (It has no immediate background, because it is hung away from any walls directly behind it.) Here, the illumination falls on A and only A, and as a result there is no lightness constancy, for there is no brightness contrast (that is, lateral inhibition) that can offset the increased amount of light reflected from A. But con-

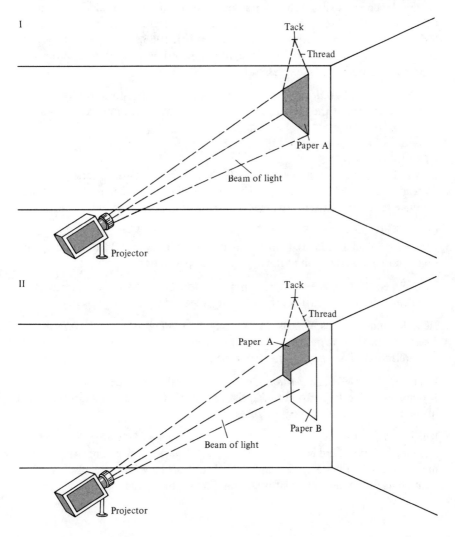

trast is immediately introduced when the white paper *B* is placed adjacent to *A*. Because paper *B* is white, more light is reflected from it than from *A*. As a result, there is contrast and inhibition, and paper *A* looks as it ought to look— black. (For further details, see Coren, S., Porac, C., and Ward, L. M. 1984. *Sensation and perception*, 2nd ed. New York: Academic Press.)

Selected Readings

CLASSICS
Gibson, J. J. 1950. *The perception of the visual world.* New York: Houghton Mifflin. Lucid and excellently illustrated statement of the Gibsonian position. Gibson subsequently altered his views in some significant respects and expressed his newer theories in later books (e.g., Gibson, J. J. 1966. *The senses considered as perceptual systems.* New York: Houghton Mifflin). But the essence of the approach is probably best expressed in his 1950 treatment.

Köhler, W. 1947. *Gestalt psychology.* New York: Liveright. A beautifully written statement of the Gestalt positions on perception, learning, and memory by one of its founders.

REFERENCE WORKS
Brown, E. L., and Deffenbacher, K. 1979. New York: Oxford University Press. (Already mentioned in Chapter 5.) The emphasis in this—rather advanced—undergraduate text is on the sensory aspects of perception.

Coren, S., Porac, C., and Ward, L. M. 1984. *Sensation and perception*, 2nd ed. New York: Academic Press. (Already mentioned in Chapter 5.) Good undergraduate text, whose emphasis is on cognitive aspects of perception.

Held, R., ed. 1976. *Recent progress in perception.* San Francisco: Freeman. An excellent collection of articles from *Scientific American.*

Held, R., and Richards, W., eds. 1972. *Perception: Mechanisms and models: Readings from Scientific American.* San Francisco: Freeman. Another excellent collection of *Scientific American* articles.

Hochberg, J. E. 1978. *Perception*, 2nd ed. Prentice-Hall foundations of modern psychology series. Englewood Cliffs, N.J.: Prentice-Hall. The best short treatment of the field by one of the major figures in it.

Kling, J. W., and Riggs, L. A., eds. 1971. *Woodworth and Schlosberg's experimental psychology*, 3rd ed. New York: Holt, Rinehart and Winston. (Already mentioned in Chapter 5.) See chapters by J. E. Hochberg for more advanced treatments of the perception of brightness, depth, form, and motion.

CHAPTER 7

Memory

Overview

Whereas the preceding two chapters (on sensory processes and on perception) discussed how knowledge is acquired, the present chapter asks how this knowledge is stored in memory and later retrieved.

The chapter makes several major points. One is that there seem to be several memory systems. Most of the discussion concerns distinctions based on the duration over which memories are held and the form in which they are stored (e.g., sensory registers, short-term memory, long-term memory). Other distinctions involve the memory modality (e.g., verbal vs. visual) or the degree to which the memory concerns particular events as opposed to timeless information (episodic vs. generic).

Another theme is the role of organization. This is contrasted with the effects of rote connections as postulated by associationists and is likened to the importance of organizing factors in perception. Organization is discussed in two contexts: as a way of getting material into long-term memory (by recoding it into larger chunks) and as a means of facilitating its later retrieval.

A third point is that remembering is by and large an active process. Acquisition often requires an active effort to organize the material (e.g., rehearsal, mnemonics through imagery), while recall may demand an active search process and is not infrequently supplemented by reconstruction.

A last topic concerns forgetting—the opposite side of the coin of remembering. This can arise from a variety of sources, including faulty acquisition, disruption during storage (e.g., decay, certain forms of interference), and difficulties at the point of retrieval (e.g., interfering memories acquired before or after original learning, inadequate retrieval cues).

Summary of the Main Topics

ACQUISITION, STORAGE, AND RETRIEVAL

The act of remembering means success in three phases of the memorial process: acquisition (learning what has to be remembered), retention (storage of what has been learned), and retrieval (recognition or recall of what has been learned).

THE SENSORY REGISTERS

Many modern investigators believe that material placed in memory passes through several successive memory systems. Some are thought to hold materials for relatively brief periods; others store them for much longer intervals. The initial stage seems to involve several sensory registers which have a very large capacity, and which hold inputs in a relatively unprocessed form but only for a few seconds (the echo of the auditory register) or for fractions of a second (the icon of the visual register).

SHORT-TERM MEMORY

The text then turns to short-term memory, which stores materials for a minute or so. A major difference between short-term memory and long-term memory concerns their capacities. For long-term memory this is enormous; for short-term memory it consists of only seven or so items.

Most items that enter short-term memory are quickly forgotten, perhaps by decay or through displacement by later items. But some are transferred into the long-term memory store. Given this transfer, recall may reflect retrieval from either short-term memory or long-term memory. The text discusses studies of free recall (primacy and recency effects), which suggest a way of finding out which items come from where.

This section ends with a look at experimental studies of retrieval from short-term memory, which use reaction-time measures to test whether the search for an item in short-term memory involves parallel or serial search. The results support the latter.

THE ACQUISITION OF LONG-TERM MEMORIES

Much of the earlier work on what we now call long-term memory grew out of the associationist tradition. This tradition led to techniques to study rote connections between arbitrary and presumably meaningless items as exemplified by Ebbinghaus's lists of nonsense syllables. Later studies of paired-associate learning allowed an analysis of positive and negative transfer of training when one task is learned after another.

This section takes up an alternative view (consistent with the tradition of Gestalt psychology). It holds that the key to understanding of human memory is organization rather than association. One line of evidence is the fact that memorial capacity can be dramatically increased by recoding (organizing) materials into larger chunks, thus overcoming the bottleneck of short-term memory with its limited capacity. This organization may be visual (as in imagery) or verbal. If the second, it may be by use of grammatical units, by semantic categories (e.g., recall clustering), or by thematic content. Such organizations are often imposed by an active effort, as shown by the usual superiority of intentional to incidental learning.

RETRIEVAL FROM LONG-TERM MEMORY

Recall depends not just on acquisition (and of course storage) but also on retrieval. This depends in part on trace accessibility, which in turn depends on the presence of appropriate retrieval cues. Most effective retrieval cues seem to follow the principle of encoding specificity—that is, memory is better to the extent that the cue context available at the time of retrieval approximates that during original encoding. Retrieval, like acquisition, depends on organization and is often a very active process, as suggested by the search strategies subjects report in thinking-aloud tasks and by the tip-of-the-tongue phenomenon.

Memory retrieval also frequently involves reconstruction from partial knowledge. Tasks asking subjects to reproduce stories from an unfamiliar culture and serial reproduction tasks demonstrate reconstruction. Recent studies of hypnotized subjects also indicate that subjects actively (and often incorrectly) reconstruct memories to please the hypnotist. These findings argue against the popular notion of memory as a kind of tape recorder from which we can potentially read a complete record of our experiences.

STRATEGIES FOR REMEMBERING

Learners frequently try to remember something by rehearsing it. One form of rehearsal is maintenance rehearsal, which simply holds material in short-term memory, with no long-term benefits. A second rehearsal technique is elaborative rehearsal, which does have long-term effects. With elaborative rehearsal, material is organized so that it is stored more efficiently and connected with other material already in long-term memory, thereby increasing the number of potential retrieval paths.

Mnemonics are special strategies for improving memory. Many are quite effective because they provide a way to organize material into larger units. The method of loci and the peg method are time-proven techniques that rely on the use of imagery.

FORGETTING FROM LONG-TERM MEMORY

A final topic in the discussion of long-term memory is forgetting. The text asks why failures to remember increase as the time between learning and recall test increases. It considers three possible factors: decay, interference by retroactive inhibition (in which new learning hampers the recall of the old) or by proactive inhibition (in which previously learned materials hamper the recall of newly learned items), and changes in retrieval cues that increase as time goes by. Each of these factors seems to account for some of the phenomena of forgetting; no one of them seems able to explain them all.

VARIETIES OF LONG-TERM MEMORY

This section takes up some distinctions within long-term memory. It first looks at episodic memory versus generic memory.

A second distinction concerns the way in which the materials are stored in memory. There are reasons to suppose that some long-term memory systems are essentially visual. An extreme and very rare case is eidetic imagery.

DISORDERED MEMORY

Still another approach to the study of memory is the study of disorders of memory caused by injury to the brain. Anterograde amnesia is a condition in which the patient's ability to enter new material into long-term memory is compromised. In the case of retrograde amnesia, the patient is unable to remember events from some period prior to the onset of the condition (usually caused by a head injury). One hypothesis accounting for the loss of memory for events just prior to an injury is that the consolidation of memory traces during this period was impaired, leaving the memories vulnerable to loss.

Traditionally, amnesia phenomena were interpreted as fitting the distinction between short-term and long-term memory quite neatly. More recently, however, it has been demonstrated that patients suffering from anterograde amnesia are able to acquire some new skills, such as learning a maze. The patients have no memory of repeated experiences with the maze, yet their performance improves. This finding has led to a number of proposed explanations, including the postulation of different memory processes for procedural and declarative knowledge, and of impairments to the patient's conscious access to memories.

Discussion Topics

1. *The enormous importance of retrieval cues.* Much of what is often called forgetting is simply the result of inadequate retrieval cues at the time of recall. If these are provided, the "forgotten" memories come back—often in a rush. This fact is probably relevant to many phenomena of real life, some of which have been discussed in the text. (a) The difficulty of remembering childhood events, given the fact that the retrieval cues in adulthood are so very different from the conditions under which the memories were laid down. (See text, p. 249; also see Schachtel, E. 1949. On memory and childhood amnesia. In Mullany, P., ed. *A study of interpersonal relations.* New York: Hermitage, pp. 3–49.) But even so, such memories can be brought back by various triggers: the discovery of an old toy stuffed away in an attic box, going through old family albums, meeting a childhood acquaintance, and so on. It may be worthwhile asking the students for the age of their very first memory. (A show of hands is simple enough: How many can recall anything before their first birthday? Before their second? And so on.) It is sometimes said that there is a sex differ-

ence here—that women can remember back earlier than men. If so, one might speculate that this reflects earlier language development, since girls tend to speak at an earlier age than boys. (b) The fact that psychoanalysis, or similar psychotherapies, may bring back such childhood memories (see Chapters 12 and 19) fits in with this point. On the psychoanalytic couch the patient is encouraged to think about his childhood. One thought leads to another, especially in a context in which the patient may feel somewhat dependent and regards the therapist as a kind of parent figure—all conditions that tend to reinstate the appropriate retrieval cues. It may be that such cues (rather than the removal of various repressions, as Freud supposed) are the main cause of the restoration of childhood memories that is often said to occur during psychoanalysis. A similar explanation may apply to enhanced recall under hypnosis. (c) It is worth reflecting upon what happens when we meet an old acquaintance whom we haven't seen for many years. One result is the mutual triggering of memories. Another phenomenon that happens occasionally is the strange feeling that the other person hasn't changed at all, a feeling that again tends to be mutual. This feeling may partially reflect reality; perhaps people do have some constant personality characteristics that remain over much of the life span (see Chapter 18 for a discussion). But part of the reason has to do with retrieval cues. Joe sees Jim, whom he hasn't met for two decades. He recognizes him, and this triggers various memories—of his own feelings toward Jim, his own ways of dealing with him, and so on. As a result, he behaves as he did twenty years ago, even though he may have changed substantially. And Jim necessarily responds to Joe's behavior, which evokes the old reaction patterns in him. The two clap each other's shoulders, act boisterously as they used to do, and then part—each convinced the other is just as he used to be, when in fact he may well be quite different.

2. *Remembering and the courtroom.* The legal system often depends on witness testimony. But even with the best of intentions, this testimony may be flawed, for it is dependent on human memory with all its problems. What should prospective lawyers and judges learn about memory to help them understand how to evaluate witness testimony? What can be done about instructing those who question witnesses to provide better conditions for unbiased recall? Some of these matters are discussed in the text (see pp. 240-42). (For studies relating such matters to eyewitness testimony, consult Loftus, E. F., and Palmer, J. S., 1974. Reconstruction of automobile destruction: An example of the interaction between language and memory. *Journal of Verbal Learning and Verbal Behavior* 13:585-89. Loftus, E. F., and Zanni, G. 1975. Eyewitness testimony: The influence of the wording of a question. *Bulletin of the Psychonomic Society* 5:86-88. Bourne, L. E., Dominowski, R. L., and Loftus, E. F. 1979. *Cognitive processes.* Englewood Cliffs, N.J.: Prentice-Hall, pp. 95-101.)

3. *The physical basis of memory.* The text provides relatively little discussion of hypotheses about the physiological bases of memory. To be sure, neurological and physiological evidence is discussed in some detail where it pertains to

the functional organization of the memory system, as exemplified by the discussion of anterograde and retrograde amnesia. But questions about the physical basis of memory (e.g., changes in the structure of the neurons caused by neural activity) are not dealt with, in part, because so little is known as yet. (A good introduction to this subject is the discussion in Rosenzweig, M. R., and Leiman, A. L. 1982. *Physiological psychology.* Lexington, Mass.: Heath, Chapter 15.)

Demonstrations

1. *The limited capacity of short-term memory.*   The limited capacity of short-term memory is easily demonstrated in a study of digit span. In this and the following demonstrations, the students need scratch paper and pencil. They are told that they will hear a series of unrelated digits. They are to listen to them and write them down in the same order in which they heard them as soon as the experimenter says "go." Immediately after this they again listen when the experimenter says "ready" and reads the next list of digits, write down what they recall when he says "go," and so on. Here is a suggested series:

Span of 4:   Ready?   6 1 9 4   Go.

Span of 5:   Ready?   3 7 8 5 2   Go.

Span of 6:   Ready?   9 6 5 2 8 3   Go.

Span of 7:   Ready?   4 2 6 9 8 5 1   Go.

Span of 8:   Ready?   8 1 6 3 7 2 4 9   Go.

Span of 9:   Ready?   6 2 5 7 3 4 9 8 1   Go.

Span of 10:   Ready?   9 3 8 2 4 7 1 5 3 6   Go.

Span of 11:   Ready?   5 8 1 4 7 9 3 2 6 1 7   Go.

After the last series has been read and responded to, read the correct answers to the class (or perhaps have them ready on a hitherto hidden blackboard). Each student can now score himself at each span level, indicating he was correct if all digits were in the correct order, incorrect for anything else. A simple show of hands will indicate how many students were correct at each span level, and will indicate that the mean is at about six or seven (the exact number varies, depending in part on the rate at which the items are read). The results document the capacity limit of short-term memory. The groans of the subjects, particularly as they listen to the span of eight and up, testify to the fact that they are quite conscious of items slipping out of memory even as they try to hold on to them.

2. *Chunking in short-term memory.*   The following is presented as a study of letter span, where subjects hear an unrelated series of letters and have to recall

them immediately afterward. The letters are read at about the same rate as the digits were, preceded by the experimenter's warning "ready" and followed by the command to write down the recall "go." The series is as follows:

F

B

I

C

I

A

I

B

M

T

W

A

This is a series of twelve letters, and many—though not all—of the students will have considerable difficulty with it. Now write the correct response on the blackboard. First in a simple horizontal line (there will be a few "ahs"):

F B I C I A I B M T W A

Then with appropriate spaces:

F B I   C I A   I B M   T W A

Now the point will be completely obvious. The letters form four well-known abbreviations which by now are words in our vocabulary. As a result, there are four chunks rather than twelve.

3. *The primacy and recency effects of short-term memory.* In the recall of information from short-term memory, there is a tendency for items at the beginning and end of a list to be remembered more readily than items in the middle (see text, p. 227). To show that this is so, the students are read a list of unrelated nouns, at a rate of about one per second. As before, the list is preceded by the warning "ready" and followed by the command "go." The students are told that their job is to recall as many of the words as they can, regardless of the order in which they were presented. The items are as follows:

Candle

Maple

Subway

Poison

Tiger

Ceiling

Lawyer

Ocean

Paper

Garbage

Thunder

Sofa

Mountain

Dollar

Wagon

Doorbell

After the last word is read, the experimenter says "go" and allows one minute for the subjects to write down as many of the words as they can recall. He next reads the items in the same order as they were presented and asks subjects to score themselves as follows: number of correct words recalled in the first quarter of the list (items 1-4), in the second quarter (items 5-8), the third (items 9-12), and the last (13-16). A show of hands should make it fairly apparent that more items are recalled from the first and last quarter than from the two middle ones—that is, there will be a primacy-recency effect.

4. *Imagery as a mnemonic aid.*   The text describes the role of imagery in forming paired-associate connections (pp. 245-46). This is readily illustrated in the classroom. Begin by dividing the class into two groups. Group I consists of all students whose birthday falls on an even day of the month; group II, of all students whose birthday falls on an odd day. Both groups will hear a list of paired associates. They are told that they should try to associate the members of each pair, and that they will later be asked to supply the second member of each pair when presented with the first. But they are also told that they should use different methods of forming the association depending upon the group to which they are assigned. Group I is to use a standard method of verbal rehearsal. Immediately after hearing the two members of each pair, they must repeat the

items silently to themselves (that is, "A–B, A–B, A–B") until the next pair is read by the experimenter. Group II uses a different method. In this group, the subjects are asked to form a mental image that connects the two items mentioned in one mental picture, seen in "the mind's eye." The experimenter repeats the instructions: "Now remember, the subjects in group I silently say the pair over and over again; the subjects in group II form an image." He or she then reads the pairs, making sure to leave a six-second pause between each pair. (This is important, for it seems to take some time—say, five seconds—to find an image.) The pairs are as follows:

Locomotive	—	Dishtowel
Jacket	—	Asparagus
Mask	—	Sailboat
Oyster	—	Telephone
Pencil	—	Elephant
Curtain	—	Liver
Blackboard	—	Suitcase
Rock	—	Bottle
Alligator	—	Thermometer
Piano	—	Banana
Carpet	—	Rainbow
Sugar	—	Headlight

Six seconds after the last pair has been read, the experimenter says, "I will now test you for your memory of the pairs. Please take a blank piece of paper and put down the numbers 1 to 12 on twelve lines. Have you done so? Are you ready? I will now read you the first items of each pair (though not in the order in which you heard them). Your job is to write the second member of each pair on the appropriate line. I will give you five seconds for each item. Are you ready?" (This long speech is useful, for it lengthens the retention interval, which probably adds to the difference between the verbal rehearsal and the imagery group.) He or she now reads the first members of the pairs (the correct responses are in parentheses):

1. Pencil	(Elephant)
2. Mask	(Sailboat)
3. Piano	(Banana)

4.	Locomotive	(Dishtowel)
5.	Carpet	(Rainbow)
6.	Oyster	(Telephone)
7.	Alligator	(Thermometer)
8.	Jacket	(Asparagus)
9.	Curtain	(Liver)
10.	Rock	(Bottle)
11.	Sugar	(Headlight)
12.	Blackboard	(Suitcase)

After the test, the instructor reads the correct responses (or perhaps shows them on a previously hidden blackboard). The students are next asked to score themselves and to add the total number of correct responses. A show of hands will quickly indicate the results. (E.g., How many members of group I got more than six—or seven, or eight—correct? How many members of group II did? How many members in each group got every single item?) The superiority of the imagery group will be very impressive.

Selected Readings

GENERAL WORKS
Loftus, E. F. 1979. *Eyewitness testimony.* Cambridge, Mass.: Harvard University Press. A discussion of the use of eyewitness testimony in courtroom procedures, which should be of considerable interest to would-be lawyers and the public at large.

Luria, A. R. 1968. *The mind of a mnemonist.* New York: Basic Books. A fascinating account of a man who could not help remembering much more than he wanted to and became a vaudeville entertainer as a way of living with his unwelcome gift.

Neisser, U. 1982. *Memory observed: Remembering in natural contexts.* San Francisco: Freeman. An interesting selection of works on memory as it occurs in natural contexts rather than in laboratory settings.

CLASSICS
Bartlett, F. C. 1932. *Remembering: A study in experimental and social psychology.* Cambridge, England: Cambridge University Press. The classic statement of the role of construction in remembering.

Ebbinghaus, H. 1964. *Memory: A contribution to experimental psychology.*
New York: Dover Publications. (Originally published in 1885.) One of the very first
experimental studies of human learning, memory, and forgetting, which affected
virtually all subsequent research in the area.

Neisser, U. 1967. *Cognitive psychology.* Englewood Cliffs, N.J.: Prentice Hall.
Already a classic, this book established cognitive psychology as a subject matter
in its own right. Its emphasis is on the earlier stages of the information-processing sequence, such as perceptual organization, attentional selection, and various
aspects of the sensory registers and short-term memory. Beautifully written.

REFERENCE WORKS
Baddeley, A. D. 1976. *The psychology of memory.* New York: Basic Books. An
undergraduate text on memory, written—and very well written at that—from a
constructionist point of view. More advanced than Klatzky's text (below).

Howard, D. V. 1983. *Cognitive psychology.* New York: Macmillan. Well-organized, very clear undergraduate text that considers memory as well as thinking
and language.

Klatzky, R. L. 1980. *Human memory: Structures and processes*, 2nd ed. San
Francisco: Freeman. A good undergraduate text on the subject.

Norman, D. A. 1976. *Memory and attention*, 2nd ed. New York: Wiley. The
best short introduction in the area. An excellent, extremely well-written book
that presents the material from a modern information-processing perspective but
still places it in a broad (and often historical) perspective.

CHAPTER 8

Thinking

Overview

This chapter continues the discussion of cognition by asking how knowledge is transformed and manipulated by the process of thinking. There are two main themes that provide the framework for the discussion. The first concerns the nature of the representations that underly thinking and problem solving—are they images with picturelike qualities, or are they of a more abstract propositional nature? Evidence is presented to suggest that there is some truth to both of these possibilities. The second theme concerns the nature of the processes that are involved in problem solving: reasoning and decision making.

Problem solving appears to be a directed and hierarchically organized activity whose structure is in some ways akin to that of various skills. Mastery of such skills, as of various forms of problem solving, depends upon the formation of appropriate chunks that permit automatization. The general approach to problem solving is mirrored in the study of artificial intelligence, wherein various aspects of human thinking are simulated by computer programs. The chapter also takes a look at failures in problem solving caused by mental set. It discusses the sudden restructuring that may occur when sets are broken and the relation between such restructuring and creative thinking and humor.

Finally, the chapter considers evidence concerning the nature of the thinking process involved in deductive and inductive reasoning, and decision making under uncertainty. It appears that people are not always as rational and logical as one might like to believe. A number of biases and commonly applied heuristics often lead people to draw erroneous conclusions when reasoning about syllogisms, to use inappropriate means of testing hypotheses, and to make various errors when estimating the relevant probabilities for the decision at hand.

Summary of the Main Topics

THE ELEMENTS OF THOUGHT

The chapter begins with a discussion of an old question: What are the elements of which thought is composed? One view (a descendant of an early version of behavior theory; see Chapter 4) holds that thought is equivalent to implicit motor action, especially as this occurs in the form of small movements of the throat and larynx. This position is shown to be false given the fact that people can solve problems while engaged in irrelevant vocalizations (e.g., saying "la-la-la") and that they can think even when totally paralyzed by the drug curare. Another possibility is that thought is entirely made up of mental images. This view, however, cannot tell the whole story as evidenced by studies that support imageless thought. More modern theorists prefer to describe the components of thought at a more central and abstract level. An example of such a central component is a concept, a class descriptor that subsumes a number of individual instances (e.g., "dwelling" subsumes "house," "tent," "igloo"). Another is a proposition, which is a way in which concepts can be combined with each other (e.g., "dogs generally bite mailmen").

PROBLEM SOLVING

The next section turns to the manner in which thinking proceeds. Its emphasis is on directed thinking as it occurs during problem solving. This is described as an internal process which is structured and organized, a mental sequence whose parts do not stand in isolation but fit into an overall plan whose end (the goal) determines the preceding steps.

The organization of such mental plans is generally hierarchical, in which the overall goal includes subgoals, sub-subgoals, and so on. The efficiency with which such activities can be executed depends in part on the degree to which its constituents have become chunked and automatized. A process of increasing chunking of subcomponents seems to characterize many directed activities, including various skills such as sending Morse code and typing, playing chess, and solving diverse problems. In all of these, mastery seems to depend on having acquired the relevant chunks.

Once behavior is automated, it may persist even when one wants to stop it. An example is the Stroop effect; when subjects have to call out the color of the ink in which a word is printed, they are seriously slowed down if the word is a color adjective that is not the same as the color of the ink.

Many of these notions of how problem solving proceeds have been incorporated in attempts to simulate certain aspects of human thinking by computers. Such efforts are based on the belief that both humans and computers can be regarded as information-processing systems. Attempts to create computer programs that can solve problems fall into two main classes. One uses algorithms; another is based on heuristics. One limitation of most existing attempts to simulate human intelligence by computers is that they can cope only with problems that are well defined; they are inadequate when it comes to problems that are ill defined.

Problem solving is not always successful. Its failures are sometimes caused by a strong, interfering mental set, which may be produced by prior mechanization of particular (now inappropriate) solution techniques and heightened by intense motivation. When misleading sets are overcome, there is sometimes a radical restructuring of the way in which the problem is seen. Such restructurings seem to be at the basis of creative thinking, where it tends to occur after a period of incubation that helps to disrupt competing sets. A related restructuring effect may be responsible for some aspects of humor, which, like creative thinking, also involves a dramatic shift from one cognitive organization to another.

SPATIAL THINKING

One way of solving spatial problems is by using mental images. While there are some studies which support the view that spatial thinking involves mental maps that have picturelike properties, other studies suggest that some spatial knowledge is represented in terms of propositions. Whatever the nature of our mental maps, studies of a congenitally blind child's navigational abilities confirm that spatial knowledge is not necessarily visual.

REASONING AND DECISION MAKING

The question of whether people reason according to the formal laws of logic provides the framework for this section. The discussion is organized around the evidence from three domains: deductive reasoning, inductive reasoning, and decision making under uncertainty.

Deductive reasoning—the ability to deduce a particular consequence from a general rule—has been studied through the use of syllogism tasks. Contrary to expectations of early philosophers who believed syllogistic reasoning was a fundamental aspect of human rationality, people tend to make systematic errors in evaluating syllogisms. These errors appear to be caused by several factors including: (1) a tendency to accept conclusions consistent with the context established by the premises of the syllogism (the atmosphere effect), (2) a tendency to apply inappropriate logical transformations, or (3) difficulty in separating empirical from logical knowledge.

Just as there are obstacles to deductive reasoning, so there appear to be obstacles to the reverse process of inductive reasoning—generating a rule from a set of particulars. People have a strong tendency that impairs the inductive process; they seek evidence that will confirm, as opposed to falsify, a hypothesis (the confirmation bias).

People often have to make decisions based on estimates of probabilities. Recent studies suggest that they sometimes make certain mistakes in performing such tasks. One reason is that they tend to overestimate the likelihood of events because they base their estimates on the ease with which an instance of the event comes to mind (the availability heuristic). Another is that they sometimes assume that the joint occurrence of two independent events is more likely than the occurrence of just one event or the other (the conjunction fallacy).

These various lines of evidence suggest that human reasoning is often guided by faulty and irrational processes. But if so, how can we explain the obvious achievements of the human intellect in mathematics, philosophy, and science? One factor may be the collective nature of these disciplines; science, mathematics, and philosophy are based on the efforts of many persons who check each other's errors and thus provide a protection against the reasoning flaws of any one individual. Another possibility is that the errors of thinking we have discussed are analogous to perceptual illusions; they may represent distortions of thought patterns that by and large function correctly and rationally, and may therefore provide insight into the general processes of thinking.

A BACKWARD LOOK AT MEMORY, PERCEPTION AND THINKING

The chapter closes by reminding the reader that the boundaries between memory, perception, and thinking are by no means clear or exact. Perception, for example, frequently depends on memory (e.g., context effects), and it may also involve processes akin to those involved in problem solving (e.g., unconscious inference). These three domains are all aspects of the general process of cognition.

Discussion Topics

1. *Understanding and insight.*   Many aspects of problem solving in humans are related to the issues the text brought up in the discussion of Köhler's study of insightful behavior in chimpanzees (see Chapter 4, pp. 127–29). To achieve insight is to acquire a mental organization of the problem that really gets at the heart of the issue, solving not just the one task but others that have a similar structure. An excellent example of the kind of thinking that leads to such broad, insightful classes—that creates broad, useful chunks—can be found in a book by Max Wertheimer, the founder of Gestalt psychology, entitled *Productive Thinking* (see selected readings, Chapter 4). One of his topics concerns the way in which some high school students learned to prove that the area of a parallelogram is equal to its base times its altitude. The students learned how to prove this by extending the base of a parallelogram (ABCD below) and drawing two altitudes (that is, BE and CF in the figure shown below).

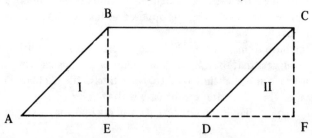

The teacher readily shows the students how to prove the theorem. They already know that the area of a rectangle is the product of its two sides, and the teacher shows them that the area of the parallelogram is equal to that of rectangle BEFC. (The trick is to show that the two triangles labeled I and II in the diagram are identical.) All this is straightforward enough, but Wertheimer asked whether the students have really understood the essential point. He did so by drawing some parallelograms of his own on the blackboard (see below). Can the students handle this new parallelogram?

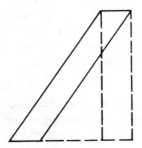

Many cannot. To be sure, quite a few use the old familiar trick of drawing altitudes as shown in the diagram, but not too many know how to proceed from there. The teacher may side with them, arguing, "You certainly gave them a queer figure. Naturally they are unable to deal with it." (Wertheimer 1945, p. 17).

Wertheimer argued that the trouble is that at least some students did not understand the essence of the proof. They learned to show that two triangles are congruent, but they didn't get the basic idea—that a rectangle can be regarded as a parallelogram one of whose pieces (triangle I) has been cut off and then moved over to the other side (where it becomes triangle II). Students who see this won't have any problems with oddly tilted parallelograms. For that matter, they can even cope with strange figures such as the one below.

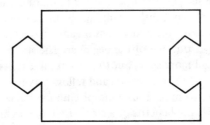

When asked to find the area of that figure, they simply say it is the area of the rectangle that forms the main frame. They recognize that this figure is just another version of the parallelogram proof. One of the sides has an odd-shaped protrusion that bulges out; the other has a protrusion that comes in. The two areas are the same, so they cancel.

Wertheimer argued that students who have understood this point have really achieved insight. Their solutions are productive, not blind. Much of the rest of the book contrasts such productive thinking (in students, as well as in great scientists) with blind, rote attempts. This makes for an interesting discussion—both in its own right, and in relation to educational issues. How can we educate children (and adults) so that their solution efforts will be productive rather than blind?

For additional readings on this topic, you may want to look at Johnson-Laird, P. N., and Watson, P. C., eds. 1977. *Thinking: Readings in cognitive science.* Cambridge, England: Cambridge U. Press, pp. 1–34 (see selected readings) and some of the papers in a selection edited by J. M. Mandler and G. Mandler, especially pp. 234–98 (Mandler, J. M., and Mandler, G., eds. 1964. *Thinking: From association to Gestalt.* New York: Wiley).

2. *Mental calculators.* The text describes the hierarchical structure that characterizes skills in various experts. An interesting example is provided by persons who have unusual abilities at performing mental calculation. One such lightning calculator could express fractions such as 4/47 in decimals. He would be silent for about four seconds, then give the answer at a uniform rate of three digits every four seconds. "Point 0851063829787234042551914, that's about as far as I can carry it . . ." (See Hunter, p. 35, in Johnson-Laird 1977). Upon inquiry, it became clear that this amazing feat depends on a large repertoire of calculative strategies which allow him to transform the task into a—for him—easier sequence. (For details, see Hunter, I. M. L. Mental calculation. In Johnson-Laird, P. N., and Wason, P. C., eds. 1977. *Thinking: Readings in cognitive science.* Cambridge, England: Cambridge U. Press).

Such unusual abilities may provide a springboard for the discussion of competence in other skills. Chances are that while few students (or, for that matter, instructors) have attained a level of mastery in any skill that has reached the heights of the mental calculator described by Hunter, most of them have surely attained some competence in a skill that others do not have. Some may be bridge players who can see patterns in the distribution of cards; others may be chess players; still others may excel at some sport. In all these cases, the competent practitioner, let alone the expert, has organized the relevant components in a quite different way from that of the beginner. The star basketball player may well be stronger and more agile, but that is not all it takes; he sees overall patterns in the position of the opponents and fellow players, has coordinated his movements so that they form organized motor chunks—he, no less than the chess player, exemplifies the benefits of a structured, hierarchical organization.

3. *The confirmation bias and hypothesis testing.* The text describes a classic experiment that shows how the confirmation bias can lead to errors in hypothesis testing—the so-called four-card problem in which subjects repeatedly fail to

select the appropriate information that is required to test a hypothesis (see text, pp. 288, 290). (From Wason, P. C. 1968. Reasoning about a rule. *Quarterly Journal of Experimental Psychology* 20:273-81.)

Why are subjects so consistently remiss in looking for *dis*confirmation of the hypothesis to be tested? One possibility is that the confirmation bias exhibited in this problem may partially reflect the operation of the availability heuristic we've encountered previously. The hypothesis the subjects had to test was that "If a card has a vowel on one side, it has an even number on the other side." Nothing was explicitly said about consonants and odd numbers. As a result, these concepts may not have been so readily available when the subjects tried to find ways of testing the hypothesis, and therefore, they didn't come to mind. This suggestion finds some support in the fact that the confirmation bias in tasks of this kind is more readily overcome when the problem is stated in more concrete terms.

An example comes from a study that used a task with the same formal properties of the four-card problem. But now the problem did not involve cards that had letters on one side and numbers on the other. Instead, the components of the problem were much more concrete and related to real life; they were envelopes that were either sealed or unsealed on one side, and that either did or did not have postage stamps on the other. Now the hypothesis was "If a letter is sealed then there is a stamp on the other side." Analogous to the four-card problem, the subjects were presented with four envelopes and their task was to turn over those envelopes that are required to test the hypothesis—no more and no less (see diagram below). In this situation, the subjects behaved much more rationally. Most of them turned over the sealed envelope *and also* the envelope with no stamp. (See Johnson-Laird, P. N., Legrenzi, P., and Legrenzi, M. 1972. Reasoning and a sense of reality. *British Journal of Psychology* 63:395-400.)

 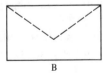 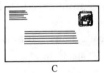 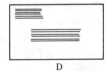

A   B   C   D

It appears that when problems are concretely stated, success is much more likely than when they are posed in an abstract form. We saw examples of this general principle when we took up syllogisms (p. 286). Many subjects have trouble with abstractly phrased syllogisms. For example, they won't recognize that the syllogism

                        Some A are C.
                        Some B are C.
          Therefore: Some A are B.

is invalid. If the same syllogism is put in concrete terms, such as

                        Some dogs bite mailmen.
                        Some vampires bite mailmen.
          Therefore: Some dogs are vampires.

its invalid nature is much more readily appreciated.

The fact that subjects may perform quite well at a certain task when that task is formulated in concrete terms but fail at the same task when it is stated more abstractly is a rather general phenomenon in thinking and problem solving. We will return to it when we take up the novice-expert distinction in the chapter on cognitive development in children (see Chapter 14).

Demonstrations

1. *Insightful problem solving.* This manual describes a demonstration of insightful problem solving for use in connection with Chapter 4, but it could well be used in connection with the present chapter (see Chapter 4, Demonstration 5).

2. *Mental set based on sound.* The experimenter explains that he wants to demonstrate some interesting facts about the way we understand our language. He begins as follows:

"In English, many words are pronounced somewhat differently from the way they are spelled. An example is O–L–K (he writes it on the blackboard), which in a number of cases is pronounced OAK without sounding the L at all. For example . . .

"Can you give me a synonym for *people* or *family* that fits this pattern?" (He encourages the class to speak up, and most of the students will surely respond, "*Folk.*")

"Now, can you give me the name of the American president at the time of the Mexican War?" (The class will now respond, "*Polk.*")

"Now, can you give me a word that means *egg white*?" (At this point quite a number of students will shout, "Yolk." The experimenter says nothing, and a few of the yolk-sayers will start to laugh as they get the point. A few will not get it, and look puzzled. They may still persist even when the experimenter asks, "Did everyone catch on to the mental set?")

The yolk-sayers were clearly victims of a mental set. They were used to responding with *-olk* words, ignoring what all of them certainly know: that *yolk* is hardly a synonym for *egg white*.

3. *A demonstration of the Stroop effect.* The Stroop effect is an excellent example of automatization. Reading is a hugely overlearned skill. We know it so well that we can't help employing it even when we don't particularly want to. This phenomenon is well known to anyone who drives on a highway. You may not want to read the billboards as you pass by them, but you can't help yourself. The Stroop effect makes use of the same principle. The subject is shown words printed in different colors of ink and is asked to name the color. This is easy enough, unless the words are color adjectives which do not fit the color of the ink. It turns out that it is rather difficult to say *green* when you encounter the word *brown* printed in green ink. Having learned to read, you can't help thinking of *brown* and this necessarily interferes with the response *green*.

The present demonstration will use numerals rather than colors, a procedure that seems to produce the same effect. (See Reisberg, D., Baron, J., and Kemler, D. G. 1980. Overcoming Stroop interference: Effects of practice on distractor potency. *Journal of Experimental Psychology: Human Perception and Performance* 6:140-50.) The idea is to show subjects a line of numerals such as

$$6 \quad 6 \quad 6$$

and to ask them to say how many numbers there are in the line (that is, "three" rather than "six"). Here too there will be an interference—though perhaps to a lesser degree—between the automatized reading response and the response the task asks for.

The subjects are first divided into two groups, I and II, to the right or left of some midline. All subjects are told that they will receive a sheet that contains four columns of typewritten characters, some numerals, other characters like # and $. The characters will be in lines, and the subjects are told that their job is to whisper the number of characters in each line, as quickly as they can. To make sure they understand, the experimenter should give some examples on the blackboard. For example:

$$\$ \quad \$ \quad \$$$
$$7 \quad 7$$
$$4 \quad 4 \quad 4$$
$$\& \quad \& \quad \& \quad \&$$

which should be read, "Three, two, three, four."

After the preliminaries are over, the stimulus sheets are handed out, face down. (A model for this sheet is provided below.) The subjects are told that the sheet contains four columns, labeled A, B, C, and D. The subjects in group I are asked to read off—or rather, to whisper—the number of characters in columns reading down one column and then the other, A and B, as quickly and accurately as they can. The subjects in group II are asked to do the same for columns C and D. The experimenter tells them to flip the sheet over as soon as he gives the signal. He also tells them to raise their hand immediately upon completing the two columns they are assigned. Two assistants have the job of watching the hands shoot up. One notes when three-fourths of the subjects in group I are finished; the other does the same for group II.

Stimulus Sheet for Use with Stroop-Effect Demonstration

			Columns				
A		B		C		D	
3 3		2 2 2		$ $		& & &	
2 2 2		3 3		& & &		$ $	
4 4		3 3 3 3		# #		$ $ $ $	
3 3 3 3		4 4		$ $ $ $		# #	
2 2 2		2 2 2 2		& & &		& & & &	
2 2 2		4 4 4		& & &		# # #	
3 3		3 3 3 3		$ $		$ $ $ $	
4 4 4		4 4		# #		# #	
2 2 2 2		2 2 2		& & & &		& & &	
4 4		3 3 3 3		# #		$ $ $ $	
2 2 2 2		4 4		& & & &		# #	
3 3 3 3		4 4 4		$ $ $ $		# # #	
4 4 4		3 3 3 3		# # #		$ $ $ $	
4 4		2 2 2 2		# #		& & & &	
3 3 3 3		4 4		$ $ $ $		# #	
2 2 2		2 2 2 2		& & &		& & & &	
4 4		4 4		# #		# #	
3 3 3 3		3 3		$ $ $ $		$ $	
4 4 4		2 2 2		# # #		& & &	
2 2 2 2		3 3 3 3		& & & &		$ $ $ $	
4 4		2 2 2		# #		& & &	
3 3 3 3		4 4		$ $ $ $		# #	
3 3		2 2 2		$ $		& & &	
2 2 2		3 3		& & &		$ $	

4. *A demonstration of the availability heuristic.*   The following demonstration indicates how availability rests on two reasonable suppositions. One is that

the more frequently something is encountered, the more readily it will be re-called. The second is that the more readily an item is recalled, the more *available* that item will be for the purposes of making various estimates. (The study is adapted from one reported by Tversky, A., and Kahneman, D. 1982. Avail-ability: A heuristic for judging frequency and probability. In Kahneman, D., Slovic, P., and Tversky, A., eds. 1982. *Judgment under uncertainty: Heuristics and biases.* New York: Cambridge University Press, pp. 163–78.)

The students are read a list of thirty-seven names. Nineteen of these names belong to women; eighteen belong to men. Most of the men are rather well known; most of the women are less well known. The order in which these names are presented is random. The students hear the names read aloud and are asked to listen carefully because they will be tested later for various aspects of the list.

Whether the list presented here is appropriate for the particular students in a class has to be judged by the instructor. The main point is to make the shorter list consist of persons who on the whole are better known (and thus more readi-ly available) than the longer one. But this may have to be adjusted depending on the particular group. Thus, for a class made up of many feminists, the women on the list may be more available than the men, and so on. So, if any of the names seem inappropriate given the background and interests of the students in a particular class, simply replace them with names that seem about as well known (that is, available) as the other names on the list of the same sex.

This list is as follows (the names should be read, at the rate of about one every two seconds):

Robert Redford
Mick Jagger
Helen Reddy
Martin Luther King
Lana Turner
Elizabeth Blackwell
Elvis Presley
Carly Simon
Emily Brontë
Margot Kidder
Emily Dickinson
Ronald Reagan
Amelia Earhart
John McEnroe
Sandra Day O'Connor
Abigail Van Buren
Frank Sinatra
Tracy Austin
Henry Kissinger
Muhammad Ali
Benjamin Franklin

Katharine Hepburn
John Travolta
Karen Magnusson
Robert F. Kennedy
Rita Coolidge
Arnold Schwarzenegger
Millicent Fenwick
Wilt Chamberlain
Annette Funicello
Margaret Atwood
Richard Burton
Jack Nicholson
Margaret Thatcher
Richard Nixon
Teri Garr
John Wayne

After the list is read, ask the students to perform the following tasks:

(a) Take out a pen or pencil and some scrap paper. (This request should be made now rather than before the demonstration started. The idea is to let some time elapse between list presentation and test, for any forgetting that occurs will probably enhance the bias effects.)

(b) Now say to the students: "You just heard a list of persons. Please judge whether the list contained more men than women." Give them five seconds to make their judgment.

(c) After this, ask them to write down as many names as they can remember from the entire list.

By a show of hands, count up the students who felt that there were more men's than women's names on the list. This tally will probably show that the majority of students judged that there were more men rather than women (though in fact, of course, the reverse was true).

To convince the students that there were indeed fewer men than women, you may want to show them the original list on a slide or an overhead transparency, separated by men and women as shown below:

Robert Redford
Mick Jagger

                              Helen Reddy

Martin Luther King

                              Lana Turner
                              Elizabeth Blackwell

Elvis Presley

                              Carly Simon
                              Emily Brontë

Margot Kidder
Emily Dickinson

Ronald Regan

Amelia Earhart

John McEnroe

Sandra Day O'Connor
Abigail Van Buren

Frank Sinatra

Tracy Austin

Henry Kissinger
Muhammad Ali
Benjamin Franklin

Katharine Hepburn

John Travolta

Karen Magnusson

Robert F. Kennedy

Rita Coolidge

Arnold Schwarzenegger

Millicent Fenwick

Wilt Chamberlain

Annette Funicello
Margaret Atwood

Richard Burton
Jack Nicholson

Margaret Thatcher

Richard Nixon

Teri Garr

John Wayne

The final step in the demonstration is to look at the memory results. Simply ask the students to indicate whether they recalled (1) more men's names than women's, (2) more women's names than men's, or (3) the same number of men's as women's names. A show of hands will probably indicate that a majority remembered more men's names than women's. (In the original study, fifty-seven of eighty-six subjects recalled more well-known names than less well-known names.)

5. A demonstration of the conjunction fallacy.   In estimating the likelihood of events, people sometimes erroneously judge the *joint* occurrence of two events to be more probable than either of the two events taken alone. The text discusses this bias as yet another manifestation of the availability heuristic and provides some examples of (fallacious) reasoning based on this conjunction fallacy (see Chapter 8, pp. 290-91).

Below is a classroom experiment that should demonstrate the conjunction fallacy. (The examples are taken from a study reported by Tversky, A., and Kahneman, D. 1982. Judgments of and by representativeness. In Kahneman, D., Slovic, P., and Tversky, A., eds., *Judgment under uncertainty: Heuristics and biases.* New York: Cambridge University Press, pp. 84–100.)

The instructions are as follows:

"I am going to ask you to evaluate the likelihood of various events that may occur in the future. In each case, I will describe a certain situation and will then indicate four possible outcomes."

(If at all possible, present each of these situations in writing, perhaps on the blackboard, or by way of a transparency and an overhead projector.)

"Consider each of the four outcomes carefully and then decide which outcome is the most likely, which is the next most likely, and so on down to the least likely. Call the most likely outcome "1," the next most likely "2," and so on down to "4," which is the least likely.

The problems are as follows:

(1) Suppose John McEnroe makes it to the finals at Wimbledon next year. Which of the following outcomes is the most likely ("1"), the next most likely ("2"), the next most likely after that ("3"), and the least likely ("4")?

(a) McEnroe will win the match.
(b) McEnroe will lose the match.
(c) McEnroe will win the first set but lose the match.
(d) McEnroe will lose the first set but win the match.

(2) Again, rank order the following events (with "1" most likely and "4" least likely):

(a) President Reagan will argue against federal support for any services related to abortion.
(b) President Reagan will cut federal support to state governments.
(c) President Reagan will increase the defense budget by less than 10 percent.
(d) President Reagan will argue against federal support for any services related to abortion and will cut federal support to state governments.

A show of hands will indicate whether the students fell victim to the conjunction fallacy. In Problem 1, outcomes *c* and *d* are conjunctions that are less probable than outcomes *a* and *b* because they make a prediction about *both* winning the match (or losing it) and winning (or losing) the first set. In Problem 2, the conjunction is outcome *d*, for it predicts that the President will perform both of two actions (e.g., outcomes *a and b*) rather than making a prediction about either one alone.

6. *A demonstration of the representativeness bias.*   The text discusses the

availability heuristic and the conjunction fallacy as factors that produce biases that lead people to errors in estimating probabilities. Another bias is the so-called *representativeness bias*, which reflects a tendency to judge the likelihood of an event by assessing the degree to which that event seems particularly representative of what people regard as a likely occurrence. Suppose a subject is told that a certain (perfectly honest) coin will be tossed eight times in a row. He is now asked which of two possible outcomes, *A* or *B*, is the most likely:

A. First toss: Heads
   Second toss: Heads
   Third toss: Heads
   Fourth toss: Heads
   Fifth toss: Heads
   Sixth toss: Heads
   Seventh toss: Heads
   Eighth toss: Heads

B. First toss: Heads
   Second toss: Tails
   Third toss: Tails
   Fourth toss: Heads
   Fifth toss: Tails
   Sixth toss: Heads
   Seventh toss: Heads
   Eighth toss: Tails

Most subjects will say that *A* is more likely than *B*. But they're wrong. For in fact, both are *equally* likely. If there are eight coin tosses, there are 256 (that is 2^8) possible sequences of heads and tails. Each of these sequences is just as likely as any other one. The reason why most people believe that the sequence H H H H H H H H is more likely than the sequence H T T H T H H T is that the second one seems so similar to many other sequences (e.g., H T H T T H T H) whereas the sequence of eight heads in a row is unmistakable. As a result, the second sequence *seems* to be more random, more "representative" of what we regard as a chance process.

A similar bias probably accounts for the so-called "gambler's fallacy." After a long run of reds on the roulette wheel, most people falsely believe that on the next trial black is more likely to occur. But in fact, of course, it is no more—and no less—likely to occur than it was before. On any one turn of the wheel, the ball is just as likely to hit on red as on black, and this is so no matter what happened on the spin before (assuming the wheel is honest). For the ball, each trial is a separate event, and the probabilities remain identical.

To demonstrate the representativeness bias, tell the students that a coin has been tossed ten times in a row and ask them to judge which of the sequences *A* through *C* shown below is most probable, which next most, and so on down to least probable.

```
Toss: 1  2  3  4  5  6  7  8  9  10
   A: H  T  H  T  H  T  H  T  H  T
   B: H  H  H  H  H  H  H  H  H  H
   C: T  H  T  T  H  T  H  H  T  H
```

A show of hands will probably indicate that the students will be quite consistent in regarding *B* as least likely, *C* as most likely. But as the prior discussion shows, they are all *equally* likely. (See Kaheneman, D., and Tversky, A. 1974. Judgments under uncertainty: Heuristics and biases. *Science* 185:1124–31 for a general discussion of this and related effects.)

Selected Readings

GENERAL WORKS

Adams, J. L. 1980. *Conceptual blockbusting: A guide to better ideas*, 2nd ed. New York: Norton. A well-written paperback that provides an abundance of games, puzzles, and conundrums that might provide an excellent source of additional class demonstrations of thinking and problem solving.

Dreyfus, H. L. 1979. *What computers can't do*, rev. ed. New York: Harper & Row. An important critique of the claims for artificial intelligence.

Ghiselin, G., ed. 1952. *The creative process.* New York: Mentor Books. An interesting collection of autobiographical materials by various artists and scientists, writing about the way they went about creating what they did.

CLASSICS

Wertheimer, M. 1945. *Productive thinking.* New York: Harper. (Already mentioned in Chapter 4.) A delightful book by the founder of Gestalt psychology, which discusses blind and "productive" problem solving in children and famous scientists.

REFERENCE WORKS

Howard, D. V. 1983. *Cognitive psychology.* New York: Macmillan. Well-organized, very clear undergraduate text that considers memory as well as thinking and language.

Johnson-Laird, P. N., and Wason, P. C., eds. 1977. *Thinking: Readings in cognitive science.* Cambridge, England: Cambridge University Press. A first-rate collection of excellent papers in the field, including work on problem solving, reasoning, comprehension, and imagery. The papers vary in difficulty, but some of them—such as Luchins and Luchins, and Hunter—should be accessible to the beginning student.

Kahneman, D., Slovic, P., and Tversky, A., eds. 1982. *Judgment under uncertainty: Heuristics and biases.* A fine collection of papers on judgmental biases in thinking and decision making, including some of the classic papers in the field.

Nisbett, R., and Ross, L. 1980. *Human inference: Strategies and shortcomings of social judgment.* Englewood Cliffs, N.J.: Prentice Hall. A discussion of the implications of the various biases in thinking uncovered by Tversky, Kahneman, and others, for judgment in the social realm.

CHAPTER 9

Language

Overview

In this chapter we begin by immediately relating the topic of language to earlier chapters.* We do this by reminding the student of Descartes's speculations about human action and behavior, as discussed in Chapters 2 and 3. Descartes was the father of mechanistic psychology, whose descendants such as Pavlov and Sherrington gave us the theory of reflexes—man as machine. However, we state here that Descartes drew the line at language, for here was "the mark of thought hidden and wrapped up in the body" that defied mechanistic description. Following Descartes, as well as most linguists and psycholinguists today, we show that language is not describable in terms of the notions of reflex, association, or stimulus-response bond that do so much work elsewhere in psychology. Rather, an organizational view is required to explain the human capacities and behaviors with language.

Summary of the Main Topics

MAJOR PROPERTIES OF HUMAN LANGUAGE

The chapter begins with a discussion of two important properties of language: it is creative and structured. The creative aspect of language allows us to utter and understand a limitless number of sentences we have never heard before. This creativeness is produced by organizing principles of sound, meaning, and grammar, which permit ever-new sentences to be spoken and understood. Every language is organized as a hierarchy of structures, going from sentence down to words, with phonemes at the bottom level, and different organizing principles come into play at each level of the hierarchy.

*This chapter was prepared by Lila R. Gleitman.

THE STRUCTURE OF LANGUAGE

The chapter first discusses phonemes, which are the sound elements of a language. Each language restricts itself to using only some of these speech sounds. Structural principles determine various restrictions as far as the combinations of sounds that are allowed in a language.

The chapter continues by considering the structural principles that hold at the level of morphemes (the smallest units of language meaning) and words. Two major approaches to the nature of word meanings are discussed. One is the definition theory, which tries to describe meaning as a combination of features (e.g., grandmother is a female parent of a parent). The other is the prototype theory, which tries to describe meaning by resemblance to a typical instance (e.g., grandmother is a gray-haired, smiling lady who gives cookies to children). The section concludes by considering an important distinction between morphemes. The great majority of morphemes belong to the open class (examples are *green, hit, horse*) and are primarily relevant to word (that is lexical) meaning. A smaller but no less important group belongs to the closed class (examples are *the, in, -ed, -er*) and are primarily relevant to grammatical (that is, syntactic) organization.

The chapter next turns to the organization of words and phrases into sentences. The meanings of sentences cannot be read off their outward form (that is, their surface structure). Sentences with quite different surface structures can mean the same thing (have the same underlying structure, as in *John hit Bill* and *Bill was hit by John*), and sentences with the same surface structure can mean different things (have different underlying structures, as in *Flying planes can be dangerous*). A number of experimental studies have shown that listeners are much more likely to attend to and remember the underlying structure than its surface manifestation.

THE ORGANIZATION AND USE OF LANGUAGE

The chapter continues by a discussion of the mechanisms by which listeners comprehend the sentences they hear. It appears that they do so by utilizing various strategies (such as left-to-right analyzing procedures, with an initial assumption that the doer comes first, the done-to comes second). To understand complex sentences that contain several propositions (some of which may be deformed in the surface structure), the listener employs still further sentence analyzing strategies that include the utilization of various closed-class cue words, such as *and* and *who*.

Further discussion concerns the way in which the speaker produces sentences. Clues for how this is accomplished come from an analysis of speech errors which suggest that the process begins with the construction of a syntactic framework built out of closed-class items, after which open-class morphemes are chosen and inserted. Studies of aphasia yield similar conclusions.

LANGUAGE AS A HUMAN CAPACITY

The chapter concludes with a discussion of attempts to teach language to chimpanzees, using either a modified version of sign language or an artificial visual system. In the authors' view, the results show that chimpanzees can acquire a respectable vocabulary and some beginnings of propositional thoughts, but that there is no evidence as yet that they can learn syntactic principles. To this extent, the results are in line with the view that language is a uniquely human endeavor.

Organizational Notes

Language and thought. Unlike many other texts, this one introduces language (Chapter 9) and thought (Chapter 8) in separate discussions. This is because the two topics are in fact partly distinct. Some thought, even by human beings, is nonlinguistic (for instance, much spatial reasoning), and certainly much speech is thoughtless! Another reason for introducing these two topics separately is that inquiry about them by psychologists has traditionally followed quite separate lines. Nonetheless, and as Descartes saw clearly, there are some obvious links between thinking and speaking. We try to suggest these links to the student particularly in the discussion of "chimpanzee language" in this chapter. The most interesting finding here, from Premack, is that the chimpanzee is a clever creature, indeed, despite his linguistic deficiencies. That is, psychologists merely penalize the chimpanzee by forcing him to express his thoughts in language. When we allow him to think "nonlinguistically," we see his intelligence. This is one demonstration that, although language and thought are related, they are not the same. Language is a human vehicle for thought. But if a creature lacks this vehicle, he may still have other means for thinking.

Discussion Topics

1. *Slips of the tongue.* Slips of the tongue are very often amusing linguistic phenomena, but as the text points out (p. 326), they have recently been investigated systematically, both as revealing of normal linguistic processing and of speech pathologies. A recent volume edited by Victoria Fromkin (1980. *Errors in linguistic performance: Slips of the tongue, ear, pen, and hand.* New York: Academic Press) presents many interesting psychological perspectives on speech errors, beginning with an article (by John Potter) on the unfortunate Dr. Spooner who gave his name to such errors ("spoonerisms"). M. Garrett's article in this volume (Chapter 18) shows how speech errors can give information about how thought is processed into speech. As one example, the phrases

"... a kice ream cone ..." (target = an ice cream cone)

"... an anguage lacquisition course ..." (target = a language acquisition course)

suggest that the sentence is not planned out, word by word, from left to right. Notice that we use *an* when the following word begins with a vowel, and *a* when the following word begins with a consonant. To believe that the phrase "a kice ream cone" was constructed literally from left to right (mentally) we would have to imagine a sequence in which the language-processing mechanism reasoned as follows: "I'm going to make a speech error on the next word I say, such that it will start with a consonant, when usually it starts with a vowel; therefore, to ac- commodate this speech error to come, I'd better begin with *a* rather than *an.* According to Garrett, it makes more sense to say that the nouns and adjectives are specified at a stage of processing earlier than the specification of the article (*a* or *an*). This latter is specified as a function of these other, prior specifications. In short, the order of events in speech (the article before the adjective and noun) is different from the order of events in planning that speech (adjective and noun prior to the article). In general, this volume contains many appealing and in- teresting interpretations of the common slip-of-the-tongue phenomena, which make very informative and engaging lecture topics.

2. *Reading.*   One major issue here is whether learning to read is like learning to talk, and whether fluent reading is like fluent comprehending. For example, does reading a sentence or word require, as a component process, converting that word into some phonologic form, or could reading be "immediate," a direct translation from print to meaning? (A general review of the psychological issues appears in Rozin, P., and Gleitman, L. R. 1977. The structure and acquisition of reading. In Reber, A., and Scarborough, D., eds., *Toward a psychology of read- ing.* Hillsdale, N.J.: Erlbaum. A recent interesting discussion is in M. S. Seiden- berg. 1985. The time course of phonological code activation in two writing systems. *Cognition* 19:1-30. A simpler discussion is in Gibson, E. J., and Levin, H. 1975. *The psychology of reading.* Cambridge, Mass: MIT Press.)

3. *Chimpanzee language.*   In the discussion of this topic, we took the view that chimpanzees and other primates, even under specific tutelage, do not seem capable of acquiring anything like a human language. Our view is controversial, of course, because others (Gardner and Gardner) assess the same evidence quite differently. Many of the animal researchers (particularly, Premack and Terrace) take the same view of the enterprise that we have. Whatever the final truth of the matter, it has evidently been very attractive to suppose that the higher pri- mates are much like humans in linguistic regards, only covered with velour. This accords with the recurrent hope and fantasy that, like Dr. Doolittle, we can aspire to communicate with the beasts. It accords as well with certain positions within psychology itself. For example, if learning is by a single mechanism (asso- ciation), then chimpanzee cognition *could* differ from human cognition *only* quantitatively, not qualitatively. Clearly, we have favored an opposing view, but the instructor might wish to take the other position, in which case the following readings would provide useful background: Gardner, B. T., and Gardner, R. A. 1971. Two-way communication with an infant chimpanzee. In Schrier, A. M.,

and Stollnitz, F., eds., *Behavior of nonhuman primates*, vol. 4, pp. 117–84. New York: Academic Press; Gardner, R. A., and Gardner, B. T. 1969. Teaching sign language to a chimpanzee. *Science* 165:664–72; Gardner, R. A., and Gardner, B. T. 1978. Comparative psychology and language acquisition. *Annals of the New York Academy of Science* 309:37–76. For a position close to the one we sketched in the chapter, see Seidenberg, M. S., and Petitto, L. A. 1979. Signing behavior in apes: A critical review. *Cognition* 7:177–215.

4. *Language in retarded and autistic children.* For an interesting collection of articles on this topic, see Morehead, D. M., and Morehead, A. E. 1976. *Normal and deficient child language.* Baltimore: University Park Press.

Demonstration

Why we say hafta. Below is a detailed lecture-demonstration which is designed to show the student that language is governed by principles (which linguists often call "rules") and that such principles determine his own speech, no matter how informal and "unruly" he may think it is. To drive these points home, we will look at a speech form that is usually regarded as sloppy and informal and show that its use is actually remarkably systematic and governed by principles.

Start out by asking the class what they think of *hafta*. They will undoubtedly agree that

(1) hafta

is an informal or sloppy way to say

(2) have to

and, in particular, that

(3) I hafta sleep

is the informal way to say

(4) I have to sleep.

Now ask the class to notice that the same pronunciation as in (4) occurs, with the exception of changing an "*l*" to an "*h*" in:

(5) I have two sheep.

(This works best if you are writing each sentence on the blackboard, after you pronouce it.) Now ask the class to notice that you would never say,

(6) I hafta sheep

as an informal way to say (5). At this point, the class will be laughing. For it

becomes intuitively obvious that the English speaker is very careful about when
to be careless! He will substitute *hafta* for *have to*, never for *have two*. The point
is finally driven home by showing that, in the careful form, the following two
sentences can be pronounced identically:

(7) I have to fish.
(8) I have two fish.

Now tell the class you're going to substitute *hafta*, and then take a vote on
whether you meant (7) or (8):

(9) I hafta fish.

All the students will know that (9) means (7), never (8). If you're extremely
lucky, there'll be a foreign student in the class, who'll be completely bewildered
—for this subtle fact about English is rarely learnable by nonnative speakers. This
makes your point all the more forcefully. It is a piece of knowledge of language,
not a piece of sloppiness.

The next step here is to tell the class what kind of fact this really is, about the
structure of English. Ask the class to tell you some words in which the sounds
f and *t* occur right next to each other. (Note that we are speaking of sounds,
that is, oral speech, and not alphabetic writings. The sound *f* precedes *t* in spoken *laughed*, but there is no *f* in written *laughed*.). They'll think of many; e.g.,
after, laughed, nifty, and *lift* are words in which the sound *f* immediately precedes the sound *t*. Now ask them to think of words in which *v* precedes *t*. If they
can think of any at all (and they probably can't), it will be only in words that
are really two words combined together by compounding (e.g., *dovetail*). In
short, *ft* is a common sequence within English words, *vt* almost nonexistent.
However, *v* can precede *t*, and often does, *between* words, e.g.,

(10) I drive trucks.

So it isn't the case that it's just "hard to pronounce" a *v* and then a *t*. Rather, a
rule (that is, principle) of English prohibits this. The rule can now be stated
much more generally:

In English, two voiced consonants can occur in sequence
within a word, and two unvoiced consonants can occur
in sequence within a word, but the sequence voiced/
unvoiced or unvoiced/voiced doesn't occur.

The voiced consonants are those accompanied by vocal-chord vibration (*b, g, d,
v, z,* etc.) and the unvoiced consonants are those for which vocal-chord vibration
is less, and temporally delayed (*p, k, t, f, s,* etc.). The student can feel the vibration for the voiced consonants by placing his finger on his Adam's apple. It is
useful to ask the students to realize, as examples, that *p* and *b, s* and *z, d* and *t,*
etc., are sounds identical except for this voicing distinction.

The next step here is to show that this voicing distinction plays a major role in English structure. Ask the class to notice that, in forming a plural, sometimes *s* is added, but sometimes *z*. One says "books" but "bugz" (although we spell these both as *s*, we pronounce the plural differently in the two cases). Ask the class to notice that *z* is just the voiced variant of *s*. Now, ask the class whether they know when they add *s*, and when they add *z* to make the plural. Do they think they would know which one to add for a new word that they had never heard? Jean Berko Gleason (1958) showed that even very young English speakers do know, for new words. She showed children the following picture and said, "This is a wug."

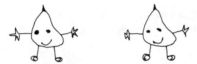

She then showed the following picture and said, "Now there are two of them; now there are two _____."

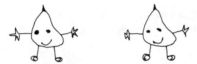

Even four-year-old children were able to answer, "wugz." For some other children, Berko said instead, "This is a wuk" and "Now there are two of them; now there are two _____." The children responded, "wuks." In short, though the children could not state the rule, they behaved as though there were a rule for when to say *s*, when *z*, even for brand new words. This is just a case of the rule we stated earlier: if the word ends with a voiced consonant (e.g., *g*), then the voiced variant (*z*) must follow; if the word ends with an unvoiced consonant (e.g., *k*) then the unvoiced variant (*s*) must follow, to make the plural. This is just because a voiced and an unvoiced consonant cannot occur next to each other in an English word.

At this point in the discussion, you are ready to return to the explanation of substituting *hafta* for *have to* but not for *have two*. Ask the class what *have* means in *have two*, and they will answer, "Own," or something of the sort. Ask them what *two* means, and they'll answer, "More than one," etc. Now ask them what the *have* means in *have to* and what the *to* means in *have to*, and they will have great difficulty answering. The correct answer is that neither has any separate meaning; rather, the sequence *have to* acts like a single word meaning. Namely, the meaning "must." Now, English speakers seem to suppose that since *have to* behaves like a single word, then, phonological rules that apply *within the word* (no voiced and voiceless consonants in sequence) apply to it. Since *have two* behaves like two words, the rule does not apply to it, so *v* remains *v*, rather than becoming unvoiced (i.e., rather than becoming *f*) to accommodate the rule.

The moral of the story here is that even the most homely and informal usages of language by ordinary speakers, that seem disorderly or even sloppy, turn out on close analysis to be highly structured: manifestations of an awesomely complex rule system that almost no speakers can state but that all, even four-year-olds, honor so as to speak and understand their language. (See Gleason, J. B. 1958. The child's learning of English morphology. *Word* 14:150–77.)

Selected Readings

ON LANGUAGE AND LINGUISTICS

Akmajian, A., Demers R., and Harnish, R. 1984. *Linguistics: An introduction to language and communication*, 2nd ed. Cambridge, Mass.: MIT Press. A good and comprehensive undergraduate text on linguistics.

Chomsky, N. 1968. *Language and mind.* New York: Harcourt Brace Jovanovich. A classic introduction to some of the basic concepts by the most influential modern linguist. Rather technical.

Fromkin, V., and Rodman, R. 1983. *An introduction to language*, 3rd ed. New York: Holt, Rinehart and Winston. Readable undergraduate text. Probably the easiest place to start.

ON PSYCHOLINGUISTICS

Armstrong, S. L., Gleitman, L. R., and Gleitman, H. 1983. On what some concepts might not be. *Cognition* 13:263–308. In the authors' view, a rather readable introduction to some important problems faced by theories of word meaning.

Fodor, J., Bever, T., and Garrett, M. 1974. *An introduction to psycholinguistics and generative grammar.* New York: McGraw-Hill. An excellent though rather technical text that in many ways laid the foundations of modern psycholinguistics.

Foss, D. J., and Hakes, D. T. 1974. *Psycholinguistics: An introduction to the psychology of language.* Englewood Cliffs, N.J.: Prentice Hall. A good and readable undergraduate text.

Howard, D. V. 1983. *Cognitive psychology.* New York: Macmillan. Already mentioned in Chapters 7 and 8 of this manual, this is a well-organized, very clear undergraduate text that considers the entire field of cognitive psychology and has several chapters on language that could serve as a first introduction to the field of psycholinguistics.

CHAPTER 10

The Biological Basis
of Social Behavior

Overview

This chapter is the first in a series of chapters that deal with social behavior. It begins with an old question, "What is the basic social nature of man?" and considers the possibility that we are essentially asocial and rapacious, a view which assumes that all the social motives that bind humans together are imposed by culture and acquired through learning.

A large section of the chapter describes various lines of evidence that suggest this view is false. For the study of animals, and to some extent of humans, indicates that there are various built-in predispositions toward social behavior which are rooted in the organism's genetic past. Examples concern reactions related to aggression, to sexual bonding, and to parental and filial behavior. Such social patterns seem to be based on a set of largely built-in communicative displays by which various animals "express" their readiness to behave one way or another.

A crucial point in all this is that natural selection is not simply a dog-eat-dog struggle in which the spoils go to the most ruthless. It rather favors those who are the most *fit*—those most likely to survive and leave offspring. As the chapter points out, this fitness is often enhanced by social and cooperative patterns of behavior. A case in point is parental behavior. Even more impressive is so-called altruism in various animals, as exemplified by alarm calls. Behaviors such as these may decrease an individual's own chances of survival but may still increase the survival probability of some genes that he shares with others of his group.

An important question considered throughout is the extent to which such findings can be generalized to humans. The chapter concludes that some of the mechanisms that underlie human social behavior—for example, in aggression, or in human altruism—are quite different from those seen in various animals in being greatly dependent upon learning and culture. But even so, there seems little doubt that some aspects of our social nature are simply part of our biological makeup. An example is emotional expression, some of which is clearly based on innately given mechanisms, as illustrated by the smile.

Summary of the Main Topics

THE SOCIAL NATURE OF HUMANS AND ANIMALS

What is the basic social nature of man? Thomas Hobbes answered that man is governed exclusively by self-interest. Man's animal nature can be tamed only by his entering a social contract, without which there will be perpetual anarchy and warfare. Man's humanity is not natural; rather, it is culturally enforced.

At first blush, Darwinian theory seems consistent with Hobbes's war of each against all: only a few can get to reproduce, and these are the fittest. But this does not mean that certain predispositions toward social behavior and coopera-tion are necessarily incompatible with biological fitness. In fact, they may well be adaptive and selected for, in both humans and animals. If so, there may be a natural predisposition to be social.

This general view has been affirmed by ethologists. This section describes the evidence that many aspects of social behavior are genetically coded in many ani-mals. It looks particularly at animals' various stereotyped, species-specific be-haviors, many of which are displays that serve as built-in communicative signals.

THE BIOLOGICAL SOURCES OF AGGRESSION

Among psychobiologists, the term aggression is generally reserved for conflict between members of the same species. This seems to have important biological roots and usually involves a struggle over some scarce resource (e.g., food, mate). To secure such resources, many animals (usually the males of the species) stake out and defend a territory. This section takes up territoriality as well as domi-nance hierarchies, ritualized combats, and various threat displays.

Some ethologists have pointed to certain parallels between animal and human aggression. But on closer examination, the differences seem more impressive. The best guess is that the underlying mechanisms are for the most part different, in that human aggression is much more dependent upon learning and culture.

THE BIOLOGICAL BASES OF LOVE: THE MALE-FEMALE BOND

The chapter next turns to love or pair-bonding. After a brief tour through the biology of the sexual reproduction process, it presents a survey of some species-specific sexual-behavior patterns in various animals (e.g., courtship rituals). In most species, the choice of the mate is up to the female, which is not too sur-prising, considering that she generally shoulders the major biological cost of reproduction.

Since sexual reproduction requires two participants, their participation has to be synchronized. In part, this is accomplished by several sex hormones. Here, the text describes the activity of these hormones (testosterone, estrogen, and progesterone) and the estrus cycle.

Despite many biological similarities, human sexuality differs from that of an-imals in being much less automatic and stereotyped. This great dependence on learning is found even in our primate relatives; chimpanzees have to learn what to rats comes naturally. Of special importance is the human female's virtual emancipation from hormonal control. She is capable of sexual behavior at any time in her cycle, a fact that may have helped to promote pair-bonding by enhancing the role of sexuality during human prehistory.

THE BIOLOGICAL BASIS OF LOVE: THE PARENT-CHILD BOND

Parental and filial behaviors are characteristic of animals that have relatively few offspring (in contrast to, say, reptiles, which lay eggs by the hundreds and then abandon them). Various parental reactions in such animals are based on natively given stimulus releasers produced by the young, such as distress calls or the human smile. This section briefly discusses the adaptive function of the infant's attachment to its mother. The mechanisms underlying this attachment are discussed in detail in Chapter 16.

SELF-SACRIFICE AND ALTRUISM

While parental self-sacrifice is readily understood in evolutionary terms, it is harder to explain what is technically called "altruism" in animals. This section looks at "altruistic" responses in which an organism endangers itself for the benefit of others of its species that are not its own offspring. One explanation (the kin-selection hypothesis) is that the danger to the individual is offset by the survival benefit to others in the flock that share some of its genes. Another biological explanation for unselfish acts is reciprocal altruism. According to this account, one animal may help another with the expectation that the favor will be returned later. In the case of reciprocal altruism, it is not necessary to postulate that the animals share genes. Sociobiology, a controversial but extremely influential movement within biology, argues that many aspects of human altruism (e.g., martyrdom) can be explained in similar biological terms.

COMMUNICATING MOTIVES

The final section of the chapter takes up the major mechanism that seems to underlie most built-in social patterns in animals—communication by displays. One question concerns their evolutionary origin. Darwin believed that displays are intention movements that have a preparatory character. But modern investigators have shown that displays are not too easily explained in this fashion, having evolved to serve a signal function and nothing else.

Built-in displays are found in humans as well as animals. (A good example in humans is emotional expression.) How does this form of communication (by display) differ from that provided by human language? Here, the text describes several differences, including the size of the vocabulary (small for display, large for language), the presence or absence of syntax (a way of arranging individual signals or words to create new "sentences" which is always present in language and never in display), and content (about one's own incipient actions in display, about just about anything in language).

Discussion Topics

1. *Social Darwinism.*   Much of this chapter is concerned with aspects of evolutionary theory which explain why a predisposition to this or another behavior pattern provides a selective advantage, increasing an individual's fitness. But the notion of "fittest" can be grossly misunderstood. And this is worth some serious discussion.

There is no doubt that Darwin's theory was and is an epochal landmark in our understanding of the forces that shaped life on earth. But in the hands of many of Darwin's contemporaries (and some of their modern descendants), the theory of natural selection was reinterpreted in terms of human society. The result was *Social Darwinism*, an extension of the biological theory to the social and political institutions of the time. In effect, this extension was little more than a means to justify the gross inequities and injustices of the age. The Social Darwinists said that in nature the struggle for existence produces what some called the *survival of the fittest.* According to Herbert Spencer, a major exponent of Social Darwinism, the same principles apply to human society. The fittest are those who prosper; the unfit, those who are poor and miserable. He therefore opposed all state aid to the poor since "the whole effort of nature is to get rid of such, to clean the world of them and make room for better." In a similar vein, other writers described millionaires as the bloom of modern civilization, the fittest of the fit, who "are a product of natural selection, acting on the whole body of men to pick out those who can meet the requirement of certain work to be done." The same line of reasoning was called upon to justify other aspects of the status quo. Some races of men were held to be less "fit" than others and were thus destined to be dominated and ultimately replaced by those of "superior" stock. This doctrine gave convenient moral sanction to racism and colonial empires. In the words of a prominent English scholar at the turn of the century, there was "cause for human satisfaction in the replacement of the aborigines throughout America and Australia by white races of far higher civilization. . . ." (Quoted in Hofstadter, 1968, pp. 41, 45; Montagu, 1952, p. 109; see below.)

The Social Darwinists obviously were not the first to proclaim that some people are inherently superior to others. They did not originate this age-old idea, but their theorizing seemed to clothe it in scientific respectability. In retrospect, it is clear that the central notions of Social Darwinism had no foundation. To begin with, they generalized from biological to social survival and assumed that the same laws hold for each. This assumption has little basis. The primary factor in human development during the last fifty thousand years or so has been *culture*: the accumulated discovery and learning of preceding generations. Genetic variation has been much less relevant. The decline of the medieval knight in armor had nothing to do with any inadequacies of biological makeup. He became extinct because of a cultural development—the invention of gunpowder. His demise had no effect on the hereditary characteristics of the human species. There was no reason why the knight's son shouldn't prosper on some future field of battle: all he had to do was trade in his father's suit for a musket.

The Social Darwinists were guilty of an even grosser error: they equated "fittest" with "best" or "highest." To Darwin himself, the fittest organism was simply the one that was best adapted to the environment of its then and there. What is fit for today is not necessarily fit for a changed tomorrow, as witness the fate of the dinosaur. Furthermore, the "best adapted" is not always the "most advanced." The tapeworm is magnificently adapted to the environment of its host's digestive tract, but few would hail it as the pinnacle of evolution. The insects outnumber us by an enormous margin; they obviously have done well at the business of survival, but does that make them better or more advanced than humans? Or, for that matter, does it make them better than whales who are currently in danger of extinction? The fact is that survival indicates only that the species is adapted to a particular environment. It implies nothing more. (For further relevant reading, see Montagu, A. 1952. *Darwin: Competition and cooperation.* New York: Schuman. Hofstadter, R. 1959. *Social Darwinism in American thought.* New York: Braziller.)

2. *Aggression as a biological facet of human nature.* This issue has been discussed in various parts of the text which cautioned about generalizing from studies of animal aggression to aggression in humans (see pp. 344-45). But even so, the topic is well worth further discussion. To set up the extremes of the argument, we note that there are, on one side, various authors who have written popularized accounts of aggression in animals that they then extend to people. (See Lorenz, K. 1966. *On aggression.* London: Methuen. See also Ardrey, R. 1961. *African genesis.* New York: Dell. Ardrey, R. 1971. *The territorial imperative.* New York: Dell.) They all agree that man is intrinsically aggressive. Ardrey's *African Genesis* probably pushes this view to its extreme by asserting that man is a naturally predatory creature derived from some killer ape whose built-in aggressive impulses are now turned against his own fellows. Various critics argue that this amounts to a "bio-theology," a refurbished version of the old idea that man is intrinsically evil, now clothed in the garb of ethological science. (An example of an opposing Man-is-naturally-good position is Montagu, A. 1952. *Darwin, competition and cooperation.* New York: Schuman. Another example, in a more popular vein is Claiborne, R. 1974. *God or beast.* New York: Norton.) Pitting these two extreme views against each other should provide a good class discussion.

Modern evolutionary theorists agree with neither extreme. They point out that both sides commit a similar error. For both seem to believe that evolutionary selection has to do with the survival of the species. But neither Darwin nor modern evolutionary theorists believe anything of the sort. Survival concerns only the individual—except that it is not the individual organism but rather the individual gene. This point is the critical one for evaluating modern ethological theories of altruism and the related arguments of sociobiologists (see the text, pp. 355–58). According to these authors, a genetic tendency to risk one's life for another will work (that is, will be selected for) only if it helps to preserve more of one's own genes than will be lost by the risk that is taken. In effect, the biological altruist is selfish. Such considerations are one reason why many psychologists feel that there is no way of explaining the real facts of human altruism without reference to learning and culture. Our built-in nature made us sociable enough to develop culture, which then did the rest. (For a discussion of modern evolutionary theory as it applies to such matters, see Dawkins, R. 1976. *The selfish gene.* New York: Oxford University Press, especially the chapter on aggression.)

3. *Possible evolutionary origins of the human smile.* The text suggests that various human emotional expressions, and especially the smile, are essentially innate. To be sure, they can be modified through learning, and they can also be faked, but even so they are initially part of our basic makeup. If so, the question is how these expressions arose in the first place. For example, what is the evolutionary history of the human smile?

As the text makes clear, questions about the evolutionary history of behaviors are much harder to answer than similar questions about the history of body structures. The trouble is that there are no fossils. Still, some hypotheses can be formed on the basis of the behavior of related species. (An example is the mating behavior of the male dancing fly described on p. 360.) In the case of the human smile, an interesting hypothesis has been suggested by Van Hoof. He proposes that smiling descends from a display found in various primates in which the animal is silent but its teeth are bared. This "grin" generally occurs as a submissive gesture. Such submissive gestures have an interesting property, because they are sometimes used in two contexts. To begin with, they serve to appease a stronger (or older) animal, signaling, in effect, "Please don't attack." But they may also serve as a form of reassurance, when directed by a stronger or older animal toward a younger one. Now the display means, "Don't worry. I won't hurt you." It has now become a gesture of what humans call friendship.

Van Hoof believes that this occurred in the evolutionary history that produced the smile. The primate grin (silent and bared teeth) was initially a submissive gesture. It gradually was also given as a friendly response. In humans, it mostly has the latter function.

Students may be interested in how the author relates all this to laughter. As Van Hoof sees it, laughter arises from a different source. There is evidently another facial expression in monkeys which occurs during periods of roughhouse play among the young. Here the mouth is open, the teeth are not bared, and the animal gives off loud, staccato noises. Van Hoof assumes that these two different displays—the one which means play, and the other which means let's be friends—come together in various ways, allowing the various combinations of smiles and laughter we see in ourselves. (For further information, as well as some excellent pictures and photographs, see the paper by Van Hoof, J. A. R. M. A comparative approach to the phylogeny of laughter and smiling. In Hinde, R. A., ed. 1972. *Non-verbal communication.* Cambridge: Cambridge University Press.)

4. *An advanced sociobiological concept—the evolutionarily stable strategy (ESS).*   Modern sociobiologists have broadened the range of social phenomena they try to explain on evolutionary grounds by advancing the concept of an evolutionarily stable strategy (ESS).

The idea is that built-in behavior patterns can be regarded as if they were strategies by which an organism maximizes the chances that its genes will survive. To be sure, the organism is not really conscious of what it is doing or trying to do, but the upshot is just the same. Consider two alternative fighting patterns (strategies) in birds that are genetically based. We will call one *hawk*, the other *dove*. A bird with the hawk gene will viciously attack any bird that impinges on its territory. A bird governed by the dove gene will spend time posturing for attack but won't ever follow through; if attacked, it will flee.

Let's now assign points to each of these strategies which define their advantage or disadvantage in genetic terms: the more points, the greater the likelihood of genetic survival. We will assume that the points for biological success are as follows:

outcome	points
win	+50
lose	0
time wasted posturing	–10
physical injury	–100

Based on these points, the average payoff to a dove in a dove-dove contest will be +15 (one wins, +50; one loses, 0; and both posture for a long time, –20). Since a dove can expect to win one-half of these contests, its expected gain is +15.

Were the bird community populated exclusively by doves, a mutant hawk gene would clearly pass like wildfire through the flock. This bird would attack all intruders and win all its battles, since every encounter would be with a pacifist. Therefore it would score +50 in every contest. But oddly enough, the upshot will not be a population composed exclusively of hawks. The reason is that as the genetic representation of hawk strategies in the flock increases, the hawkish bird increasingly runs the risk that it will encounter a similarly hawkish bird. But if it does so, the outcome is no longer so rosy. In a hawk-hawk contest, one bird wins (+50), and the other gets killed or injured (–100), for an average payoff of –25. When everyone is a hawk, aggression does not pay.

This analysis shows that given the two genes—hawk and dove—an all-dove population would not last; a hawk would be tremendously successful and would gain a large representation within the flock. But the same holds for a flock that contains all hawks with just one dove gene. This dovish characteristic would soon gain ascendancy, because the dove would score zero in every encounter with the hawk (it simply flies away), while the hawk would get an average pay-off of -25 on meeting another hawk. The result is that the final population—that is, the level at which the proportion of doves and hawks get stabilized will be 5/12 doves and 7/12 hawks. At this point, neither gene has an advantage, given the particular payoffs we have assumed.

This example illustrates a vital point. Natural selection can encourage diversity within a given gene population. In other words, individual success can often be maximized by differences that exist among members of the total group.

An interesting exercise is to ask the class to consider which of the two strategies described below is more advantageous for biological survival, given a world in which there are also hawks and doves:

a. The retaliator—acts like a dove when confronted with a dove, and like a hawk when confronted by a hawk.
b. The bully—acts like a hawk with doves, and like a dove with hawks.

Of these two strategies, the retaliator is the only ESS, because no other set of behaviors is more successful. The bully gene will be overwhelmed by the hawk gene and the retaliator gene. But the retaliator gene will not be displaced by either the hawk or dove genes, for the simple reason that around hawks and doves the retaliator acts, respectively, like a hawk and dove. (For a fuller discussion, see Dawkins, R. 1976. *The selfish gene.* New York: Oxford University Press, Chapter 5.)

Demonstration

Personal space.   This is an experiment that should be performed out of class, and reported on subsequently. It is conducted by students who operate in groups of two. One acts as observer, the other as experimenter. The procedure is modeled after a study described in the text (pp. 344–45). The pair goes to the library at a time when the library is fairly uncrowded. The experimenter finds a table at which only one or two other students are seated. In the control condition, the experimenter seats himself (herself) as he (she) would have done ordinarily. In another condition, he (she) deliberately violates another individual's personal space, by sitting directly next to him (her) even though there is a great deal of room he (she) might have kept between them. (The best bet is to choose a "victim" of the same sex; things will be complicated enough as it is without complicating them further.) The trick is to do all this without looking at the victim at all. Act toward him (her) as if he (she) were in the control condition—say, ten feet away. Go about your library business—take notes, arrange books, shuffle papers, but do so as if you were utterly unaware that you are impinging. During all this time, the second member of your pair is surreptitiously observing everything, noting the behavior of the encroached-upon person. Is there some recognition of the encroachment? Any complaint? Any attempt to turn away? To find another seat, to leave? To set up boundaries, with books or whatever? Note all this, and also observe the other person in the control condition (when there was no encroachment) to see whether anything of this sort takes place there.

The procedure for running this experiment should be discussed in a previous class or discussion section. Results should be reported on in the following class.

(For a report of a study run much like this, see Felipe, N. J., and Sommer, R. 1966. Invasions of personal space. *Social Problems* 14:206-14.)

Selected Readings

GENERAL WORKS
Dawkins, R. 1976. *The selfish gene.* New York: Oxford University Press. A lucid account of modern sociobiological fact and theory, written—and very well written at that—for the general public.

Hrdy, S. B. 1981. *The woman that never evolved.* Cambridge, Mass.: Harvard University Press. A beautifully written discussion of the evolution of the female primates. The author is a sociobiologist as well as a feminist who tries to dispel some recent myths about the evolution of sex patterns in primates.

Lorenz, K. 1966. *On aggression.* London: Methuen. Well-written, controversial description of aggression among animals by one of the founders of ethology. Rather dated in its general outlook, but worth reading anyway.

CLASSICS
Darwin, C. 1965. *The expression of the emotions in man and animals.* Chicago: University of Chicago Press. (Originally published in 1872. London: Appleton.) A great book that set the stage for much of the future work in the area.

Tinbergen, N. 1951. *The study of instinct.* New York: Oxford University Press. One of the classics of ethology and indeed of the entire field of animal behavior.

REFERENCES
Barash, D. P. 1982. *Sociobiology and behavior*, 2nd ed. New York: Very readable and balanced undergraduate text on sociobiology.

Daly, M., and Wilson, M. 1978. *Sex, evolution, and behavior.* North Scituate, Mass.: Duxbury Press. A discussion of sexual patterns in animals, with two final chapters on humans. The book emphasizes sociobiological approaches.

Gould, J. L. 1982. *Ethology: The mechanisms and evolution of behavior.* New York: Norton. Good undergraduate text on the subject.

Hinde, R. 1974. *Biological bases of human social behavior.* New York: McGraw-Hill. A fine undergraduate text that looks at the social behavior of birds and of primates and tries to abstract some factors that might be of relevance to humans.

Smith, W. J. 1977. *The behavior of communicating.* Cambridge, Mass.: Harvard University Press. The authoritative work on animal displays.

CHAPTER 11

Social Psychology

Overview

The preceding chapter explored some of the ways in which social behavior is shaped by our genetic past as this is encoded in our genetic makeup. In contrast, this chapter looks at the effects of the present situation on what we think, feel, and do in the social world.

A major theme of this chapter is that our response to any social situation depends on how we interpret it. We interpret social events in much the same ways in which we interpret other, nonsocial events, and we rely on the same cognitive processes to do so. Our interpretations are generally attempts to make sense out of whatever is seen or heard, to make it cohere with what is already known and believed. One result is a tendency to seek cognitive consistency, which may lead to various reinterpretations of prior acts and to shifts in beliefs and attitudes.

Our tendency to harmonize various events and experiences with our attitudes and beliefs is related to the way in which we perceive persons—both others and our own selves. In some ways such social perceptions are similar to the preception of inanimate objects. We have repeatedly seen how the observer manages to see through the masking surface manifestations of an ever-changing proximal stimulus to perceive the unchanging distal stimulus underneath (e.g., seeing that a tiger far off is larger than a kitten nearby; see Chapters 5 and 6). But an analogous process occurs in social perception. Here we must infer the causes of another person's behavior, which we can attribute either to the way "he really is" or to distorting surface factors in the situation. Such attribution processes also apply when we perceive our own selves, as illustrated by Schachter and Singer's theory of subjectively experienced emotions.

The chapter next deals with a set of social behaviors that seem quite unlike the various attempts to interpret the social world that were discussed before, in that they appear to be thoroughly irrational. The chapter takes up two examples —blind obedience (as in Milgram's studies) and crowd behavior (as in panics)— and discusses some attempts to explain them in cognitive terms.

129

Summary of the Main Topics

BELIEF AND SOCIAL REALITY

The text first takes up how our conception of the world and what we mean by reality is affected by confirmation from others, as shown by Asch's classic study on the effects of group pressure and by the need for social comparison.

To make sense of the world is to find consistencies in it. But it often happens that we perceive inconsistency among various aspects of our knowledge, feelings, and behavior. When such cognitive inconsistency occurs (cognitive dissonance), there is a tendency to restructure one's beliefs or behaviors so as to remove the inconsistency. This tendency may underlie many aspects of the development of beliefs and attitudes.

ATTITUDES

The text continues by discussing attitudes, that is, belief systems that are charged with emotion and are generally accompanied by a predisposition toward some kind of behavior. The section focuses mainly on attitude change and the factors that seem to bring it about. Among these factors are persuasive communications and tendencies toward cognitive consistency (as shown in justification of effort and forced compliance studies), and attempts to preserve one's self-picture. A concluding discussion concerns the fact that, by and large, attitudes seem to show more stability than change—perhaps yet another result of the tendency toward cognitive consistency, and perhaps also a result of the fact that people generally remain in the same social environment.

PERCEIVING OTHERS

The text continues its cognitive theme by elaborating on the views of theorists such as Asch and Heider who argued that the way we perceive others is in some ways similar to the way we perceive inanimate objects or events. Impressions of others can be regarded as Gestalt patterns whose elements are interpreted in terms of the whole, which may explain such phenomena as primacy effects in impression formation. The text shows how attribution theory tries to explain how we infer the causes of another person's behavior by attributing them either to situational factors or dispositional qualities ("what he's really like"). In judging others, we tend to underestimate the role of the first and to overestimate that of the second. In judging ourselves, this effect is reversed—we overrate the role of situational factors and underrate the importance of dispositional ones, an effect often called the actor-observer difference in attribution. Two facts may account for this difference: first, we know ourselves and our own history of behavior better than others do; and, second, actors and observers have different perspectives on a situation.

The last topic in this section is interpersonal attraction and the factors that seem to produce it. Some of these factors are not too surprising, including proximity, similarity, familiarity, and physical attractiveness. The text discusses some as yet unresolved questions, including what underlies physical attractiveness.

PERCEIVING ONESELF

The text next addresses the issue of self-perception: How does one know oneself? According to self-perception theory, we perceive our own selves by attribution processes similar to those which determine how we perceive others.

EMOTIONS: PERCEIVING ONE'S OWN INNER STATE

A process similar to self-attribution may also be involved in the experience of emotions. Thus Schachter and Singer's revision of the James-Lange theory of emotions argues that the emotion we feel is an interpretation of our own autonomic arousal in light of the situation to which we attribute it.

BLIND OBEDIENCE

In this section, the emphasis shifts to social behaviors that seem irrational. An example is blind obedience. This has sometimes been ascribed to factors within the person, as in studies of the authoritarian personality. But situational factors may be even more important, as shown by Milgram's obedience studies. His findings suggest that persons who were obedient to the end generally tried to make the situation comprehensible to themselves: they depersonalized it, and they tried to reinterpret it in various ways.

CROWD BEHAVIOR

An even more serious challenge to the notion that people are by and large rational comes from observations of crowd behavior. According to a view popularized by Le Bon, people become irrational and primitive when they are in a crowd; their primitive nature is presumably revealed in situations such as panics and riots. But even here, the behavior may not be as irrational as it seems. For given payoff conditions, as in the prisoner's dilemma, individuals may behave quite rationally and yet produce a collective result that is not desired by any of the participants and that is in this sense irrational. The text describes various panic situations that seem to fit this pattern, such as frantic escapes from a burning theater.

A related problem is posed by crowd violence (e.g., lynch mobs) and crowd apathy. Here too, part of the explanation probably lies in the way the individual members of the group interpret the situation. An important factor is diffusion of responsibility, which applies both to acts of commission (as in rioting mobs) and acts of omission (as in bystander apathy).

Discussion Topics

1. *The relationship between dissonance reduction and rationalization.*   People often delude themselves by giving acceptable reasons for unacceptable thoughts or actions. This is rationalization, a mechanism of defense that, according to Freud, reduces anxiety by reinterpreting a forbidden impulse in an acceptable way (e.g., a cruel beating that is "for the child's own good"; see Chapter 12, p. 421).

But the various accounts of dissonance reduction (or related means of restoring cognitive consistency) have a similar self-deluding character, as when the fact that doomsday never came is explained as a reward to the faithful. Are these two phenomena essentially the same?

The answer is not obvious. In both cases, there is clearly an attempt to make sense of something that is somehow unacceptable. But the reasons Freud offers are not the same as those suggested by consistency theorists. The psychoanalysts argue that the force behind rationalization is to blot out unacceptable impulses so as to reduce anxiety. In contrast, dissonance reduction occurs because there is an internal force to make the world seem coherent and rational. To Freud, the object of self-delusion is to avoid inner pain. To consistency theorists, the point is to avoid self-contradiction.

But this analysis is only suggestive. Further consideration may bring out some other differences or indicate that the two are ultimately the same.

2. *Collective behavior.*   The text discusses crowd behavior as one of the challenges to the belief that humans are rational animals: How can we be, when we trample each other to death in escape panics, bid valueless possessions to boom levels until they are sure to crash in acquisitive panics, and abandon ourselves to the murderous frenzy of riots or lynch mobs? This is an important issue which bears further discussion.

One possibility is to take a closer look at examples of collective behavior, to get a sense of what these crowds were really like. For an overview, see Brown, R. 1965. *Social psychology.* New York: Free Press, Macmillan. This book describes a number of such phenomena in some detail. An example is tulipomania, a speculative frenzy in which individual tulip bulbs were bid up to preposterously high prices in seventeenth-century Holland. (For more detail, see Brown's excellent bibliography.)

What do such findings tell us about human nature? One hypothesis is that humans become less than human—or at least, less rational—if they act as members of a crowd. This was the view of Le Bon, who tried to explain crowd behavior by arguing that the individual members feel protected by a sense of personal anonymity and become more suggestible to what others say and do (this last he regarded as a hypnosis-like effect). For a discussion of this approach, see Fancher, R. E. 1979. *Pioneers of psychology.* New York: Norton, pp. 197–203.

For a brief review of Le Bon in the context of his times, see Le Bon, G. 1960. *The crowd.* New York: Viking. This is well-written and lively, but it should be read with some skepticism.

An alternative view is that there are special circumstances under which individual rationality can sum to produce collective action which appears irrational. The classic example is the collective behavior produced by the payoff matrix of the prisoner's dilemma discussed in the text. Brown's chapter goes into this in considerable detail, indicating how the prisoner's dilemma matrix may underlie not just escape panics but various other forms of collective behavior as well. For further reading, see Schelling, T. C. 1978. *Micromotives and macrobehavior.* New York: Norton: This book looks at a large number of other examples in which individual decisions produce unwanted collective consequences.

Demonstrations

1. *The primacy effect in impression formation.* There is some laboratory evidence that substantiates a suspicion from real life: the first impression of a person often determines how we judge what we see him do later on (see Chapter 11, pp. 378-79). A classroom demonstration is taken from the *Study Guide* for *Psychology* (see Jonides and Rozin 1986, pp. 150-57).

Divide the class into two groups, where group I is composed of all persons whose birth date falls on an odd-numbered day, group II of all for whom it is even-numbered. Begin by reading the following instructions to both groups: "I shall show you a number of characteristics that belong to a particular person. Please watch them carefully and try to form an impression of the kind of person here described. I will later ask you to give a brief characterization of the person in just a few sentences. I will present the items one at a time, and will repeat the procedure once."

You now ask the members of group II to shut their eyes, while presenting the following list of adjectives to group I on a series of cardboards, one at a time. You present each adjective for about five seconds, until you reach the end of the list, when you repeat the entire process.

The list for group I is as follows:

> intelligent
> industrious
> impulsive
> critical
> stubborn
> envious

After the second exposure of the list, those in group I are asked to shut their eyes while those in group II are asked to open them. The list for group II is as follows:

> envious
> stubborn
> critical
> impulsive
> industrious
> intelligent

(Note that the adjectives in the list presented to group II are in the reverse order of that presented to group I.)

The members of group I are now asked to open their eyes (after the adjectives have been removed), and those in both groups are asked:

"Now please write a brief characterization of this person, using no more than a few sentences . . ."

After a few minutes of this, the experimenter says: "I will now read you a number of pairs of adjectives. For each pair, decide which of the two best fits the person we have been describing, and write that adjective on a piece of scratch paper. If in doubt, guess. Are you ready?" The experimenter now reads, allowing five seconds or so to give the subjects time to write out their responses:

> *generous* — ungenerous
> unhappy — *happy*
> irritable — *good-natured*
> *humorous* — humorless
> *sociable* — unsociable
> *popular* — unpopular
> unreliable — *reliable*
> *good-looking* — unattractive
> frivolous — *serious*
> dishonest — *honest*
> *wise* — shrewd

It is now time to look at the results. The first step is to look at the written impressions. The best bet is to read two or three aloud in each group. If the primacy effect worked, the impressions formed by group I (which began with favorable adjectives and moved to unfavorable ones) should be more favorable than those formed by group II, which saw them in the reverse order. More reliable data are provided by the check list. The experimenter first reads off the number of favorable adjectives (the ones italicized in the pairs above) and asks each subject to count the number of favorable items he chose. A show of hands should indicate whether this number is greater for group I than for group II. If so, there is support for the primacy effect—the idea that it pays to put one's best foot forward.

(For reference, see Asch, S. E. 1946. Forming impressions of personality. *Journal of Abnormal and Social Psychology* 41:258-90.)

2. *Conformity.* There is an old schoolboys' game that consists of stopping on a city street and looking up at a building across the way while a confederate watches the passersby to see how many stop and look up also. This game has become the basis of a deliberate experiment by Milgram and others to determine the effect of the size of a crowd on others. It can provide an interesting out-of-class demonstration.

The site of the study should be a city street where everyone is anonymous. (A street on campus will not work as well, for there passersby know each other and may soon catch on.) Members of the class walk around individually on this street. There is a prearranged spot to which some of them will move, but without ever indicating that they know each other. Once there, the fake crowd will look up to a building across the street (in the original study, it was up to a sixth-floor window). Four separate studies will be done, in which the size of the fake crowd is varied. Suggested numbers are 2, 6, 10, 15. Each substudy should be conducted at a different hour, to make sure that no passerby who saw the first crowd sees the second and so on.

After the crowd has been fully assembled (which may take a while so that it looks natural), two confederates, who watch the entire proceedings from appropriately placed strategic points, observe the behavior of passersby. They make a mark on a data pad to record every person who passes in either direction, and simply check whether that person looks up (or stronger yet, joins the crowd) or does not. This continues for, say, fifteen minutes. (A bit of trial and error will tell you what time interval is best for the street you pick for the study.) When the results are recorded, the score of interest is the percentage of passersby who looked up. Ideally, each crowd number ought to be run twice, to control for differences in the composition of the street population at the time the study was run (e.g., rush hour vs. afternoon crowd).

The results are reported in a later class period. They almost surely will show that the percent of uplookers increases with the crowd number. In the original study, it was 4 percent when the "crowd" number was 1; it rose to 40 percent when the crowd numbered 15. The question is why. Is it simply conformity, a dumb follow-the-leader pattern? Or is it perhaps a sensible wish to know what's going on? The greater the size of the crowd that looks up, the more likely that the crowd will be noticed. And if that many people look up, maybe there is something worth seeing. This is the kind of explanation that would be favored by a cognitively oriented social psychologist who believes that at bottom people are really rational, that they try to interpret the world so that it makes sense, and then act according to this interpretation.

(For further information, consult the original study: Milgram, S., Brickman, L., and Berkowitz, L. 1969. Note on the drawing power of crowds of different size. *Journal of Personality and Social Psychology* 13:79–82.)

Selected Readings

GENERAL WORKS

Aronson, E. 1980. *The social animal*, 3rd ed. San Francisco: Freeman. A paperback introduction to modern social psychology, stressing the role of cognitive factors; an easy and pleasant introduction to the field.

Bem, D. J. *Beliefs, attitudes, and human affairs.* 1970. Monterey, Calif.: Brooks/Cole. Excellently written paperback which may be the best introduction to the topic for the beginner.

Berscheid, E., and Walster, E. 1978. *Interpersonal attraction*, 2nd ed. Reading, Mass.: Addison-Wesley. An easy-to-read, fairly elementary paperback describing recent work in the areas of interpersonal attraction and love.

Goffman, E. 1959. *The presentation of self in everyday life.* Garden City, N.Y.: Anchor Books, Doubleday. A beautifully written description of what we do when we try to manage the impression we give to others.

Schelling, T. C. 1978. *Micromotives and macrobehavior.* New York: Norton. A well-written paperback in which a political economist looks at various group phenomena where individuals tend to be blind or indifferent to the collective consequences of their individual decisions, analogous to what happens in such crowd behaviors as panic.

Shaver, K. G. 1975. *An introduction to attribution processes.* Cambridge, Mass.: Winthrop Publishers, Inc. Good paperback introduction to the field.

CLASSICS AND REFERENCES

Asch, S. E. 1952. *Social psychology.* New York: Prentice-Hall. According to many critics, the best text on social psychology ever written. Views social psychology as a reflection of psychology as a whole, which is here regarded from a Gestalt perspective. Lucidly written, with a passionate concern for basic questions about human values.

Brown, R. 1965. *Social psychology.* New York: Free Press, Macmillan. A beautifully written series of essays on a wide range of topics in the broad area of social behavior.

Festinger, L. 1957. *A theory of cognitive dissonance.* Evanston, Ill.: Row, Peterson. The monograph that first set forth the idea of dissonance.

Festinger, L., Riecken, H., and Schachter, S. 1956. *When prophecy fails.* Minneapolis: University of Minnesota Press. A readable account of the sect that waited for the end of the world and what its members did when the end did not come.

Freedman, J. L., Sears, D. O., and Carlsmith, J. M. 1981. *Social psychology.* Englewood Cliffs, N.J.: Prentice-Hall. An undergraduate text that emphasizes current experimental investigations.

Jones, E. E., Kanouse, D. E., Kelley, H. H., Nisbett, R. E., Valins, S., and Weiner, B. 1972. *Attribution: Perceiving the causes of behavior.* Morristown, N.J.: General Learning Press. A bit dated, but still one of the major classics in attribution theory and research. Not for casual reading.

Milgram, S. 1974. *Obedience to authority.* New York: Harper & Row. The original studies and Milgram's attempts to interpret them are all here in eminently readable form.

CHAPTER 12

The Individual and Society: The Contributions of Sigmund Freud

Overview

The preceding chapter discussed the effects of human culture on patterns of social perceptions and social behavior. The present chapter now turns to the views of Sigmund Freud, whose work addresses the question of how a culture is transmitted from one generation to the next through each person's childhood experience. This chapter begins with a discussion of Freud's theories about the nature and origins of human personality. About one-half of the chapter is devoted to Freud's theories and their development, emphasizing the idea of unconscious conflict and psychosexual development. The second half of the chapter is a reexamination of these views in light of various modern critiques. The major criticisms of Freud's theories of human personality concern his views about the nature and origins of unconscious conflict, including a challenge from the neo-Freudians who regard such conflicts as based on cultural and social factors rather than biological ones. A related critique comes from cultural anthropologists who deny Freud's claims that the conflict patterns he observed in his patients were universal to all humans. In a similar vein, critics have found little evidence for the long-lasting effects of various childhood rearing patterns that a Freudian approach might lead one to expect; nor is there much evidence of a universal Oedipus complex, independent of culture. In a way, this debate can be regarded as yet another extension of the nature-nurture controversy, with Freud arrayed on the side of "nature" and the neo-Freudians and cultural anthropologists on the side of "nurture."

Summary of the Main Topics

THE ORIGINS OF PSYCHOANALYTIC THOUGHT

The chapter begins by sketching the origins of Freud's psychoanalytic theories. It points out that Freud was in some ways a modern Hobbesian. Like Hobbes, he thought that people are savage brutes whose primitive drives for pleasure have to be held in check by society. But unlike Hobbes, he believed that this taming process is accomplished by internalized prohibitions established during childhood socialization. The internalized checks don't always succeed completely. Sometimes, the internal dam is broken and various forbidden thoughts and wishes come through and must then be held in check once more. The result is continual, mostly unconscious conflict between primitive unacceptable urges and the internalized dos and don'ts set up by society.

This section also describes how Freud's views on socialization grew out of his observations of hysteria and hypnosis, and it traces the early development of psychoanalysis (see also Chapter 19, pp. 665-71, and Chapter 20, pp. 695-98).

UNCONSCIOUS CONFLICT

This section takes up Freud's theory on the nature and development of human personality. It focuses first on unconscious conflict. Freud distinguished among three subsystems of personality: id, ego, and superego. The text describes each of these antagonistic subsystems and, more important, the unconscious conflicts produced when they clash.

Internal conflicts are caused by anxiety associated with prohibited thoughts or acts, usually in childhood. To get rid of this anxiety, the child inhibits the forbidden materials. She does so by repression, permitting neither act nor thought to enter consciousness. Even so, the forbidden id-produced materials tend to surface again. This produces new anxiety which in turn prompts further mechanisms of defense, including displacement, reaction formation, rationalization, and projection.

While much of Freud's work was based on the study of neurotic patients, he argued that evidence for unconscious conflict can also be found in normal persons. Here the text takes up slips of the tongue, lapses of memory, and, most of all, dreams.

Second, this section focuses on the origins of these internal conflicts, more specifically, the child's psychosexual development. Freud proposed that all persons go through a largely similar sequence of significant emotional stages in their childhood development, that most of these involve infantile sexual urges, and that these childhood events of the past shape the individual's present. Here, the text takes up the three stages defined by the erogenous zones through which the child gains primary gratification at that period (oral, anal, and phallic) and how at each stage, socialization frustrates some of these gratifications.

The text then turns to that aspect of the theory of psychosexual development that Freud himself regarded as the most important—the family triangle of love and jealousy and fear that is at the root of internalized morality and out of which grows the child's identification with the parent of the same sex—the Oedipus complex.

A REEXAMINATION OF FREUDIAN THEORY

This section forms a major part of this chapter and introduces the student to some post-Freudian ideas on socialization. There is general agreement that there is something like unconscious conflict, as Freud supposed: that people often deceive themselves and fight off all efforts to discover that they do. But the actual evidence is not as solid as one might wish. With regard to dreams, there is little doubt that these often pertain to important and conflict-related matters in the individual's life. What is not clear is whether they are, as Freud believed, a means of disguising forbidden wishes rather than for expressing them in another form.

The evidence is much more negative on Freud's theories of emotional development. There is little reason to suppose that the various childhood events that Freud regarded as all-important, such as toilet-training, have any long-lasting effects. More important yet are the challenges that have come from neo-Freudian analysts who argue that unconscious conflicts have much more to do with social and cultural factors than with the biological (usually sex-related) matters Freud stressed. A similar point is made by cultural anthropologists who argue that personality patterns characteristic of our culture are not universal. (Child-rearing practices and their effects on social development are discussed further in Chapter 16.)

PSYCHOANALYTIC INTERPRETATION OF CULTURE, MYTH, AND LITERATURE

In Freud's view, psychoanalytic interpretations apply not only to individuals, but also to the cultural products they produce. He therefore tried to apply his theories to the interpretation of various cultural phenomena, such as religion, folklore, myth, and literature. These are subject to many criticisms, but they are nevertheless of considerable interest, in part because of their great influence outside of psychiatry and psychology (e.g., among literary critics).

Discussion Topics

1. *The history of a still hardly understood phenomenon—hypnosis.* A good discussion topic is the odd way in which the winds of scientific fashion shifted with regard to the phenomenon we call hypnosis: from animal magnetism to studies of somnambulism, from the belief that it is a species of sleep to the view that it is a close relative of hysteria, from Freud's attempt to use it as a technique to probe for hidden memories to his abandonment of the method; from

its status as a still ill-understood phenomenon to some moderns who regard it as some artifact of "role playing."

Some relevant references are:

Fancher, R. E. 1979. *Pioneers of psychology.* New York: Norton, pp. 170–217. A very readable account of the history of hypnosis from Mesmer to Freud's early days.

Orne, M. T. 1959. The nature of hypnosis: Artifact and essence. *Journal of Abnormal and Social Psychology* 58:277–99. This is an important paper that discusses the enormously difficult question of whether hypnosis is in some sense "real" rather than unwittingly posed or acted.

Orne, M. T., and Hammer, A. G. 1974. Hypnosis. Article in 15th ed. of the *Encyclopedia Britannica.* An excellent brief account of what we know and don't know about the phenomenon, written by leading experts in the area.

2. *Unconscious conflict and the mechanisms of defense.* The concept of unconscious conflict and its associated defense mechanisms is crucial to Freud's view of human nature. But what is the evidence that such phenomena truly exist?

One possible source of evidence comes from the reports of clinical practitioners, many of whom claim that they have observed just such conflicts in their patients. (After all, this was the basis for Freud's original claims.) But is this evidence acceptable? The text discusses some of the possible problems. For example: Can we always trust what the patients report? Can we always trust the practitioner's perception of the patients' reports? And, finally, can we always trust the practitioner's interpretation of the patients' reports? While these are serious questions, the clinical practitioner can turn around and reply that, whatever the limitations of this sort of evidence, it is firsthand, and somehow real. They will argue that those who have not been there (say, in psychoanalysis) simply can't judge, for they have not experienced the sudden recovery of memories that so often occurs in therapy sessions (or at least so they say).

Given the problems of inferring unconscious conflicts from clinical observations, one may try to find evidence for them through laboratory experimentation. The text discusses some of the major lines of research in this area. Further discussion of this can be obtained from the following:

Eriksen, C. W. and Pierce, J. 1968. Defense mechanisms. In Borgatta, E. F., and Lambert, W. W. *A handbook of personality theory and research.* Chicago: Rand McNally, pp. 1007–40. A sound, thorough review of experimental work (especially relatively modern work) on defense against anxiety in perception and memory.

Eysenck, H. J., and Wilson, G. D. 1973. *The experimental study of Freudian theories.* London: Methuen. This book contains a number of articles trying to find experimental evidence for various aspects of Freudian theory, together with fairly lengthy and often rather harsh critiques of these articles. Written from a strongly antipsychoanalytic perspective.

Rapaport, D. 1971. *Emotions and memory.* New York: International Universities Press, pp. 41–103. A review of experimental studies trying to get at repression and related memory phenomena. Emphasizes some of the earlier work. Sympathetic to psychoanalytic point of view.

3. *Attempts to reformulate psychoanalytic concepts into behavior theory terms.* A number of psychologists believe that one of the problems with psychoanalytic theory is that it is so vaguely formulated that it is not clear just what it asserts. As a result, there's no way of telling how a given psychoanalytic hypothesis can possibly be shown to be false. To remedy this situation, some have tried to reformulate psychoanalytic concepts in other, more precisely stated terms.

One approach toward this end tried to translate psychoanalytic concepts into terms derived from behavior theory. The idea was that certain acts or thoughts (e.g., hitting your father) become connected to fear by conditioning until eventually the very idea of, say, hitting one's father, leads to intense anxiety. Since anxiety (here, a synonym for learned fear) is aversive, its reduction is necessarily reinforcing. As a result, any reaction that will block out the forbidden act or thought will be learned. This might explain reaction formation (if you hug and kiss the father, you're not likely to hit him at the same time), or repression (if you push down the thought of hitting the father just as it comes up, there will be a reduction in anxiety).

(For futher discussion of this general approach to the reformulation of psychoanalytic concepts, see Dollard, J., and Miller, N. E. 1950. *Personality and psychotherapy.* New York: McGraw-Hill. An ambitious attempt to deal with various psychoanalytic matters—unconscious conflict, neurosis, psychoanalytic therapy—within the framework of behavior theory.)

4. *Psychoanalysis and the nature-nurture controversy.*   The nature-nurture issue is a persistent theme that runs through many of the chapters of this book, and it has been suggested as a general topic for class discussion in previous contexts (e.g., at the end of Chapter 5, on sensory processes). It is quite appropriate here too. But where exactly does Freud stand on this issue? The answer is by no means simple. On the one hand, Freud seems to emphasize the role of learning, especially early learning, for he is quite insistent that certain childhood experiences are crucial in determining the future course of our emotional lives. Thus weaning, toilet training, and, above all, the various quasi-sexual encounters of the family drama are all-important in determining our adult personality. To this extent, Freud seems to come down on the side of nurture. But in other regards, he writes like a nativist. In contrast with the neo-Freudians, Freud insisted on the importance of innately given biological universals—all humans go through oral and anal stages, all suffer thorugh the pangs of the Oedipal situation, and so on. Here, he surely sounds like someone who regards nature as more important than nurture.

Is this a contradiction? Probably not. One thing to point out is that Freud was interested in human *development.* In this regard (and some others) he resembles Piaget, who also takes an intermediate position in the nature-nurture debate (see Chapter 14). Both Freud and Piaget insist that there are some vital biological givens (in emotional development for the one, in cognitive development for the other). Both also believe that the environment changes the developing infant, who then brings a new psychological structure to his next encounter with the environment.

Demonstration

A class exercise in keeping a dream diary.   A worthwhile project is a class diary kept over, say, seven to ten days. All students are asked to perform a task as soon as they wake up in the morning: they have to write down any dream they can recall which occurred during the preceding night. Be sure to remind the students of this task at every class meeting during the period of the exercise.

Each student scores his or her own dreams so as to answer the following questions:

(a) Was there any evidence that a given dream contained *day residues* (that is, fragments of the previous day's events that were woven into the dream)?

(b) What proportion of the dreams seemed to relate to current, emotionally laden preoccupations? If so, did the dream deal with these matters directly, or in some symbolic fashion?

(c) Did the number of dreams remembered seem to increase over the period the diary was kept? Patients in psychoanalytic therapy often report that they seem to dream more as the analysis proceeds. In fact, of course, they do not. For we know that all of us dream repeatedly every night, remembering only a fraction of the dreams we actually had (see Chapter 3, p. 77). So what changed was presumably the number of dreams that were remembered. What may have happened is that the patients recognized the therapist's interest in their dreams, which may have made them more proficient at rehearsing these dreams on awakening. If so, one might expect a similar increase in the number of dreams reported during the period the diary was kept by the class. More dreams should thus be recalled on the last two days of the diary period than on the first two days.

For other demonstrations in this manual that deal with dreams, see Chapter 1 (Demonstration 1) and Chapter 3 (Demonstration 4).

Selected Readings

GENERAL WORKS

Fancher, R. E. 1973. *Psychoanalytic psychology.* New York: Norton. A good readable overview.

Francher, R. E. 1979. *Pioneers of psychology.* New York: Norton. (Already mentioned in Chapters 2 and 5.) See pages 170–249. A readable description of the history of hypnosis, the early studies of hysteria, and the psychoanalytic movement.

Freud, S. 1977. *Introductory lectures on psychoanalysis.* Trans. by Strachey, J. New York: Norton. Beautifully written lectures for the general public, in which Freud tried to explain his general views.

Hall, S. 1966. *The meaning of dreams.* New York: McGraw-Hill. Interesting account of work on dream content, emphasizing the author's contention that dreams express, rather than disguise, inner motives and conflicts.

Jones, E. 1976. *Hamlet and Oedipus.* New York: Norton. The classic attempt to explain a work of literature in psychoanalytic terms.

CLASSICS
Freud, S. 1900. *The interpretation of dreams.* In Strachey, J., trans., *The standard edition*, vols. 4–5. New York: Norton, 1976. This is the work that Freud himself regarded as his best.

REFERENCE WORKS
Eriksen, C. W., and Pierce, J. Defense mechanisms. In Borgatta, E. F., and Lambert, W. W. 1968. *A handbook of personality theory and research.* Chicago: Rand McNally. See pages 1007–40. An authoritative review of experimental work on mechanisms of defense in perception and memory.

Hall, C. S., and Lindzey, G. 1978. *Theories of personality*, 3rd ed. New York: Wiley. The best undergraduate text in the field (see Chapters 1, 2, and 4).

CHAPTER 13

General Issues
in Development

Overview

Up to now, we've concentrated on two main approaches to explanation in psychology. One is concerned with mechanism—trying to understand how something works. The other focuses on function —what something is good for. We now consider yet another mode of explanation in psychology. This is the developmental approach—it asks how something came into being. The present chapter lays out some general issues and principles that are central to this developmental approach to psychology. Its two main themes are (1) development as progressive change, and (2) development as an interaction between heredity and environment. Our main examples in this chapter will come from the study of physical (including embryological) and motor development. This will set the stage for the discussion of cognitive development, language acquisition, and social development, which are the topics of the next three chapters.

Summary of the Main Topics

THE CONCEPT OF DEVELOPMENT AS PROGRESSIVE CHANGE

The study of development grew out of various concerns. One came from a general interest in all forms of historical change, especially those that involve the evolution of the species and the growth of the embryo. An early and widely held belief was that the stages of embryological development recapitulate the evolutionary history of the individual's species. This in turn led to the hypothesis that the child's early mental processes mirror the thought patterns of so-called primitive peoples. This general approach was abandoned when it was recognized that the recapitulation theory was in fundamental error and that embryological development is much more accurately described as a process of progressive dif-

147

ferentiation—a change from the general to the particular. A number of developmental psychologists believe that this differentiation principle can also describe many aspects of human development, such as motor development, perceptual development, and the development of the emotions.

SOME CHARACTERISTICS OF DEVELOPMENT

Development can be considered as growth. The section first takes up prenatal growth, from early stages of rapid cell division to later ones during which nerve cells mature and begin to make complex interconnections with each other. The section continues with a brief description of growth after birth. It suggests that the continually increasing complexity of the nervous system may be one of the reasons why the child's mental capacities increase during this time. A striking feature of human growth is that it proceeds at a very slow rate from a very immature form at birth. The long dependency that results from this provides the conditions under which human culture can flourish: in the many years it takes children to reach physical and intellectual adulthood, they have the opportunity to master much of the preceding generations' accumulated knowledge of the world around them.

This section continues by describing in more detail the sensory and motor abilities with which the newborn is equipped. On the motor side, newborns have a set of early reflexes, such as grasping and rooting. It is not until several months later that the infant is able to engage in more voluntary, directed motor behavior. The infant's sensory capacities are more sophisticated from the start. For instance, she can discriminate brightness and color, and pitch and loudness. (The more controversial issue of what, if any, interpretations the infant makes of such sensory information is discussed in Chapter 14.)

Although there is variability in age at onset and rate of progress, many aspects of development are characterized by an orderly progression of events, in which certain events necessarily precede others. Examples of motor development, from holding one's head up to walking, and of language acquisition, from cooing to adult-like utterances, are used to illustrate such relatively invariant sequences in children's development.

THE INTERACTION OF HEREDITY AND ENVIRONMENT

What produces the many changes that constitute development? This question has led to debates that echo the nature-nurture controversy we have encountered in so many previous chapters (e.g., Chapters 4, 5, 6, 9, 10, and 12). But most current developmental psychologists are agreed that the development of the individual cannot possibly be understood by considering either heredity (that is, nature) or environment (that is, nurture) standing alone. Instead, they insist that development is produced by the *interaction* of both. Much of the rest of the chapter discusses just what is meant by such an interaction.

The chapter briefly discusses the mechanisms of genetic transmission, including explanations of chromosomes and genes, the process of meiosis, dominant and recessive genes, genotypes and phenotypes, and polygenic inheritance. It discusses how these mechanisms introduce variability into inheritance, as well as how they determine an individual's specific genetic makeup. The inheritance of behavioral, in addition to physical, attributes is illustrated by a description of the recessive gene that causes phenylketonuria, which leads to severe brain damage if the individual is not placed on a special diet soon after birth. This example also makes the point that phenomena that have a genetic cause can often be altered by environmental intervention. The chapter explains how studies comparing identical and fraternal twins can be used to determine whether a behavioral attribute has a genetic basis. (Experimental designs for twin studies are further discussed in Chapter 17.)

How does the environment affect development? The first thing to realize is that what constitutes an individual's environment changes continually. In early embryonic development the environment of a given cell is the other cells it makes contact with; at a somewhat later stage, the embryonic environment includes hormone conditioning. Similar effects continue after birth, since the same physical environment can produce radically different effects at different ages. The fact that what matters at one point in life may not matter at another leads to a discussion of the hypothesis that there are critical periods for certain aspects of development, as illustrated by the emergence of bird song.

Just as the environment influences the individual, so, too, does the individual shape his or her environment. An example is the way in which even newborns are treated differently depending upon their sex.

The chapter closes with a discussion of the relation between maturation—the genetically programmed, inevitable unfolding of behavior patterns—and environmental experience. Some early achievements, like sitting and walking, seem to be relatively unaffected by the presence or absence of specific experience. Other aspects of development, however, seem to require at least some general environmental experience and will not develop properly under conditions of deprivation.

Discussion Topics

1. *The humanitarian background of developmental psychology.* In discussing the origins of developmental psychology, the text stressed the eighteenth and nineteenth centuries' philosophical and intellectual preoccupation with historical change and progress. But there were some additional reasons why questions about childhood became of greater central concern.

One reason is that children seemed to have assumed more emotional importance to their parents in the last two hundred years than they had for some centuries before. The main reason was that more children managed to survive beyond infancy. According to one eighteenth-century account, about a third of all children born in rural France or England were dead before they reached the age of fifteen. Since each child might well die early, parents often chose not to become too deeply involved with any one of them before their survival was assured. In 1770, following the death of a daughter who died ten hours after birth, an English mother commented coolly: "One cannot grieve after her much, and I have just now other things to think of" (Stone, 1979, p. 57). Given these grim mortality figures, eighteenth-century parents may have counted themselves lucky enough if their children just managed to live into adulthood. Only two hundred years later, parents generally took this for granted and could therefore afford the luxury of worrying about the details of the child's rearing and education, for what mattered to them was just what kind of an adult this child would become.

Another reason for the greater concern with children was the growth of a more humanitarian attitude. To some extent, parents have always cared about their own children. But a concern for those of others has varied from one historical period to another. One of the low points in human compassion was reached in the wake of the Industrial Revolution in England from about 1750 to 1850, when the children of the poor often led lives of squalid misery. Some were abandoned as infants, "adopted" by thieves, later caught stealing, and then hanged from the gallows regardless of their youth—in one case at six years of age. Others were taken from poorhouses by chimney sweeps who forced them to ascend dangerous and narrow chimney flues. Some fell and suffered serious injuries; others got stuck and died. When the children refused to climb further, their masters forced them to go by pricking their bare feet with pins or applying lighted straws (Bayne-Powell, 1939).

The situation was no better in industry. In the coal mines boys and girls of six or even five years of age pulled carts filled with coal and minerals by means of a chain tied to a girdle round their bodies. Since most of the tunnels were much too low to stand up in, the children had to crawl on all fours, unable to straighten their backs for their entire work periods, sometimes for sixteen hours a day (Cooper, A. A., 1898, in Kessen, 1965).

Such conditions gradually led to cries for reform. A number of child labor laws were passed in England during the nineteenth century. The initial victories were modest: in 1842, Parliament passed a law that barred women from all underground mine employment and set a minimum age of ten for such work when performed by boys. But as the century wore on, the reforms became more far reaching. Child labor laws were eventually followed by various education acts, which by 1890 established free and compulsory elementary education in Western Europe and most of the states of the U.S. By then it was generally accepted that child development was a proper concern, not just of the parents, but of the community at large.

Considerations of this sort led to an ever-greater interest in a scientific understanding of what children are really like, of how they develop and how they can —and ought to—be educated and reared.

For some relevant background, you may want to look at:

Bayne-Powell, S. 1939. *The English child in the eighteenth century.* New York: E. P. Dutton.

Kessen, W. 1979. The American child and other cultural inventions. *American Psychologist* 34:815-21.

Stone, L. 1979. *The family, sex, and marriage in England 1500-1800.* New York: Harper and Row. (Harper Colophon Books.)

2. *Some other extensions of recapitulation theory.* The text briefly notes that the (quite erroneous) recapitulation theory had far-reaching effects, many of which went considerably beyond the original phenomena of embryological development which it was meant to explain. Some of these effects strike us as simply a bit odd. One was on primary education. Thus some nineteenth-century educators proposed that educational curricula in the early grades should model themselves on the historical sequence of human cultures.

To fashion this theory into concrete form, some curricula were set up that began with stories about the Nomadic Period in the first grade, Greek myths in the second, stories about chivalry in yet later grades, and so on.

Of course, recapitulation theory is false. But it's worth noting that even had it been true, such applications to educational practice don't follow at all. Suppose it were true that a human embryo goes through successive stages in which he is first a worm, then a fish, then a reptile, and so on. Does this mean that his mental development *after birth* will go through the successive *cultural* stages of human civilization, from hunter-gatherers to nomads to farmers to members of a technological society? The extension makes no sense, for it implies that at bottom all development—whether in evolution, in embryo, in mental growth after birth, and in human historical epochs—are ultimately alike. The idea is absurd on the face of it.

Recapitulation theory had much more serious effects than the misguided applications to educational theory it gave rise to, for its views were often used to buttress racist arguments. There is little doubt that the primitive-as-child argument was used by various politicians to justify racist views and policies, and to justify colonialism and sexism. For example, Stephen Gould (the author of a book that discusses the recapitulation doctrine) quotes one author after another:

> . . . "The intellectual traits of the uncivilized" claimed Herbert Spencer, "are traits recurring in the children of the civilized" (1895, p. 293). Lord Avery compared "modern savage mentality to that of a child" (1870, p. 4), while the English leader of child study stated: "As we all know, the lowest races of mankind stand in close proximity to the animal world. The same is true for the children of the civilized races" (Sully, 1885, p. 5). (In Gould, 1977, pp. 128-30.)

Here, as in so many other cases, we have evidence that scientific theories can have effects that spill much beyond the walls of their laboratories. Scientists live in a real world, and their ideas can affect that world, often in ways the scientists might not have anticipated or desired. (For further details, see Gould, S. J. 1977. *Ontogeny and phylogeny.* Cambridge, Mass.: Harvard University Press.)

3. *How widely can the differentiation principle be applied?*   Some early developmental psychologists regarded differentiation as the theoretical cornerstone that underlies all development, whether of physical anatomy (as exemplified by embryology) or mental function. A prime example was Heinz Werner (1890–1964), an influential German developmental psychologist whose book *Comparative Psychology of Mental Development* (1948, rev. ed., New York: International Universities Press) is still regarded as a classic.

According to Werner, earlier stages of mental life are always more diffuse than later ones. He believed that children don't really differentiate various aspects of their feelings and perceptions, but seem to experience them instead as an unanalyzed, rather diffuse whole. One of his many examples is a two-year-old who was angry at his mother. When asked whether his mother was good, he answered "No, she's sour." To Werner, this suggested some lack of differentiation between a (presumably unpleasant) taste sensation and the quality of his own (presumably no less unpleasant) anger.

Werner's belief in the essentially diffuse nature of early thought led him into several further directions. One concerned *synaesthesia*—the tendency of a particular stimulus (e.g., light of 510 nm) to evoke not only the sensation that normally corresponds to it (here, green) but also some second sensory experience that is appropriate to another stimulus entirely (e.g., a tone). Well-documented examples of synaesthesia do occur in some adults: an example is color-tone synaesthesia in which a person has a mental image of a certain color whenever a particular piano key is struck. The reason for such effects is still unclear; some authors suspect that it is based on some prior association between the relevant experiences. But according to Werner such phenomena are much more than a laboratory curiosity, for he sees them as a remnant of an earlier state during which the individual sensations are not as yet fully differentiated. In his view, synaesthesia is the common experience of childhood, not the rare exception. As an example, he quotes such observations as a three-year-old on sniffing a green leaf: "That leaf smells green," and then, when sniffing a purple leaf, "That smells red." Another example concerns a six-year-old who seemed to believe that open eyes make for better hearing, as he told his mother: "Now open your eyes, for you won't hear what I'm saying."

Werner's idea is certainly interesting, but is it true? Ask the students to point to the weak link in the argument, and many of them will probably see it. The problem is surely that Werner took the children's statements at face value. Just what does a three-year-old mean when he says "This leaf smells green?" Does he mean that it produces a synaesthesia-like experience in which leafy smells and green color are somehow merged, or does he merely mean that the leaf smells like some other green things he has recently smelled (e.g., recently mown grass, etc.)? Or does he perhaps mean nothing at all about smell sensations? He may not have an appropriate vocabulary to describe his smell experiences (nor for that matter, do many adults). He hasn't read the text chapter on sensory processes, so he doesn't know terms like *fruity* and *fragrant* (see Chapter 5, p. 149). Under the circumstances, all he can do is to say "This smells . . ." and then he's stuck for a word, and shifts to *green*, because that's the only adjective that seems relevant at all.

Similar objections can probably be leveled against too liberal an interpretation of a statement like "mother is sour." This may well be a metaphor rather than a description of a diffuse mental experience. When we say that "such-and-such a politician is a fox" we don't mean to suggest that our perception of his craftiness is somehow merged with the red coat of a fox; we merely have used a figurative way of calling him shrewd and cunning.

The students no doubt will come up with other equally plausible interpretations of these and similar statements. Such statements may not describe what the children experience but may be merely a reflection of the fact that the child's ability to describe his own experiences is as yet severely limited.

None of this proves that Werner's analysis is necessarily wrong. All it does is to suggest that it may not be right. But if so, can the students suggest a more appropriate way of testing the children so that we can find out? Suppose they had been present when the little boy said that "The one leaf smells green and the other smells purple?" What might they have done to determine whether the boy had a genuine synaesthetic experience in which the color green and the green, leafy smell (perhaps a fruity, fragrant odor) had merged into one diffuse whole? One possible means might be to make them sniff these leaves with their eyes closed. Would they still describe the sensory experience as green or red? This test is by no means foolproof, but it's at least a start. By asking the students to suggest still different tests, they will learn just how difficult it is to make assertions about what goes on in a young child's mind by relying on the child's as yet quite inadequate command of the language.

This general discussion suggests that the notion that development goes from a more diffuse to a more differentiated state can serve as a rough outline of the general direction of mental growth. But it must be specified very much more precisely before it can be usefully applied to any particular problem in development.

(For further examples, see Werner, H. 1948. *Comparative psychology of mental development*, rev. ed. New York: International Universities Press, especially pp. 59-93.)

4. *Is there a relationship between thought in children and thought in so-called "Primitive Man"?*   Until the middle of this century, a number of developmental psychologists believed that there was some correspondence between the (pre-

sumably primitive) thought processes of young children and the thought patterns of preliterate people (who were often called "primitive" as well). This idea came from various sources. As already mentioned in the text, one was an extension of recapitulation theory, which argued that the development of the child recapitulated the history of the human species (with preliterate peoples cast in the role of our early progenitors; see Chapter 13, pp. 446-47). A rather different line of argument came from an uncritical extension of the differentiation principle. Examples are again taken from Werner. As we saw before, Werner felt that since the child's mental experience was relatively diffuse she was unable to distinguish between emotion and various physical sensations. As an example, he quoted a four-year-old who expressed her joy at a present of new clothes: "Oh, Mother, I'm so glad! . . . I'm happy right in the bottom of my stomach."

Werner gave many examples to suggest that preliterate peoples have similar primitive emotional experiences. Thus the Arandas of Australia say of a woman who has suffered an important loss "Her bowels long for it," Melanesians express shame by saying "My forehead is biting me," and a tribe in the Congo describes a man's courage by saying that "His heart is hung fast to his ribs."

Here, as in the previous discussion topic, the weakness of the argument is clear enough. The metaphorical language proves nothing about the actual experience—whether of the child or of the preliterate peoples. The best guess is that both the child and the preliterate man know that emotion has bodily concomitants, and refer to it, for sharper—and perhaps poetic—effect. After all, much the same is true of many expressions in English. There is a recent advertisement of a popular American brand of vodka with the slogan: "Eat your heart out, Russia!" Does this advertisement indicate a diffuse, childlike mentality? The best guess is that we shouldn't take certain linguistic expressions literally. The preliterates undoubtedly don't either.

All in all, there is simply no evidence that indicates that people in preliterate societies have more primitive minds than those who ride in jet planes and automobiles. They may well have more primitive modes of transportation, but their minds—being human—are no better and no worse than those of all other humans.

5. *The developmental landscape.*   The British biologist C. H. Waddington proposed a useful metaphor for embryological development that may give rise to an interesting discussion of development in general. He suggested that developing tissues in the embryo can be likened to a ball that rolls down a mountainous slope with many valleys (see the diagram below). Initially, the ball can run down any one of the valleys. Each valley branches into two or more separate valleys, each of which branches off again. As the ball enters one valley, it may take one or another of the branches, but the further down it rolls, the fewer the number of pathways that are still available for its course. Since the ball cannot roll uphill, it can't retrace its course, and its possible routes become more and more circumscribed the further down it rolls.

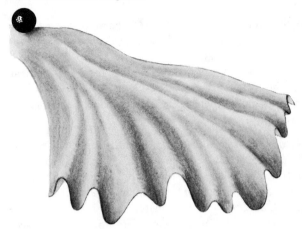

What holds for the ball also holds for developing cells in the embryo. They are initially quite free to become one or another kind of tissue (say, ectoderm or endoderm), but once they have differentiated, their further developmental course is more limited. At this point, they have passed one branching point in the developmental landscape. From here on, they can, so to speak, choose to become skin or neural tissue. After this, their choice becomes more limited again, and so on, until embryological differentiation is complete. Seen in this light, every step along the path narrows further options, as the possible pathways become fewer and fewer.

Is the developmental landscape a reasonable metaphor for development after birth as well as before? One can make a case that it is. As the infant grows, he encounters developmental pathways. He develops an attachment to his mother (or other caregiver, see Chapter 16) which then determines the extent to which his affections can branch out to other persons. He develops early skills—of loco-motion, of perceptual differentiation, of language—which again branch out and lead to further accomplishments. Seen in this light, all of us can be likened to balls rolling down a developmental landscape. Initially our developmental potentialities are very many—limited only by some broad genetic constraints. But as development proceeds, our options narrow further and further (for better or for worse) until we finally reach the bottom of the mountain where all op-tions stop—death.

One can also make a case that this metaphor has its limitations when applied to development after birth. Is it really true that human development can never be retraced, in the sense in which a ball cannot possibly roll uphill? Is it really true that what happens in early childhood has irreversible effects on later life? Some theorists, such as Freud, certainly thought that it does. To some extent, this is probably true. There is some reason to believe that it is difficult to become a first-class athlete or musician if the relevant skills are not acquired rather early in life. But there is also reason to believe that some early deficits (for example, inadequate maternal attachment) can be overcome, for example, by special therapeutic interventions (see Chapter 16, pp. 531–34).

To date, the final verdict is not yet in. Waddington's developmental landscape is a fitting metaphor for embryological development. Whether it is a good description of development thereafter is as yet an open—and a very interesting —question.

6. *The influence of the prenatal environment.*   Some of the points made in the text about the interaction between genetic factors and the environment can be further illustrated by a discussion of prenatal influences on development. Of particular interest are the effects of so-called teratogens. These are environmental agents such as radiation, drugs, maternal diseases, and maternal diet that can adversely affect the development of the fetus; they can produce various malformations and deviations in physical and/or mental development.

Whether a particular teratogen will affect the developing fetus depends on a number of factors. One is the developmental stage of the embryo or fetus. In general, the embryonic stage (from two weeks to about two months) is most vulnerable to teratogenic effects. Just what organ systems are affected depends on their stage of differentiation. The eye is most vulnerable from twenty-four to forty days after conception, the heart from twenty to forty days, the legs from twenty-four to thirty-six days, and so forth. These different periods of vulnerability reflect the time when these various organ systems begin and end their prenatal development. These differences underscore the fact that genetic and environmental factors interact. Whether a particular organ system is affected by a teratogen (for example, by German measles), depends on the state of its development, which in turn depends on the rate at which that system matures, a rate that is dictated by the genes. In effect, this is yet another demonstration of a critical period—a period during which some environmental agent has a particular effect. If the agent is introduced before or after that period, it does not act adversely (at least on that particular organ system).

Whether a teratogenic agent affects the developing embryo depends on yet another factor—the genotype of the mother or of her unborn child. The drug thalidomide results in malformations of the infant's limbs if it is present at a particular time of the embryo's development. But this effect doesn't always occur. Some mothers are fortunate. They may have been exposed to thalidomide (or German measles, or some other teratogen), but their babies are born without defect. This suggests that there are some genetic predispositions of the mother (or her offspring, or both) that make for decreased vulnerability—one more indication of an interaction between environmental and genetic factors.

(For further discussion of teratogenic agents and their effects, see Hetherington, E. M., and Parke, R. D. 1979. *Child psychology: A contemporary viewpoint.* New York: McGraw-Hill.)

Demonstration

Lack of differentiation in adult motor behavior. Infant motor behavior is relatively undifferentiated. An example discussed in the text is the development of grasping, which begins with uncoordinated reaching movements of the whole hand, continues with later separation of thumb and fingers, with separate movements of the individual fingers coming still later (see p. 448). Some differentiation depends on the maturation of the appropriate neuromuscular machinery, such as the myelination of the tracts that control the relevant muscle groups. Other aspects of differentiation are acquired through learning.

While behavior is much less differentiated in infancy than at other ages, some failures of differentiation are found even in adults. To get some sense of what lack of differentiation means (with perhaps some appreciation of the infant's plight), students should be asked to perform several tasks.

(1) To begin with, ask them to pat their bellies with the left hand, while rubbing their heads in a circular fashion with the right. Unless this has been practiced previously (and why would anyone have done so?), they will find this task quite difficult. They will have considerable trouble in separating (that is, differentiating) the actions of both arms. It will seem as if both arms want to pat or both want to rub, and the proper separation of the two will come only with some repeated practice.

(2) As a second demonstration, ask them to bend the little fingers of one hand without moving the fourth finger (that is, the ring finger) in the process. Most people find this extremely difficult, if not impossible—another demonstration of a failure of differentiation. Here, too, practice will generally improve performance, but only after a while.

Selected Readings

ON HISTORICAL BACKGROUND
Gould, S. J. 1977. *Ontogeny and phylogeny.* Cambridge, Mass.: Harvard University Press. The first six chapters (in particular Chapters 4, 5, and 6) are a fascinating discussion of the background of embryological theories (especially recapitulation theory) and their impact on subsequent thought.

Ariès, P. 1962. *Centuries of childhood.* London: Jonathan Cape. A fascinating (if somewhat speculative) discussion of the origin of our modern concept of childhood.

REFERENCE WORKS
Hofer, M. A. 1981. *The roots of human behavior.* San Francisco: Freeman. A

well-organized paperback that describes how biological factors shape animal and human development.

Hetherington, E. M., and Parke, R. D. 1979. *Child psychology: A contemporary viewpoint.* New York: McGraw-Hill. A good undergraduate text with a thorough treatment of the biological and prenatal factors that shape development.

CHAPTER 14

Cognitive Development: Thought

Overview

This chapter continues the discussion of human development begun in the previous chapter. But where Chapter 13 concentrated on physical growth and motor behavior, the present chapter focuses on the growth of the mind—on cognitive development. This intellectual growth will allow the child to gradually become master at the trade that all adults are already masters of: understanding the world. The question is how the child charts the path by which he eventually comes to understand what adults take for granted.

The chapter begins with a discussion of the theories and discoveries of the Swiss psychologist Jean Piaget, whose conceptions have affected all subsequent accounts of cognitive development. According to Piaget, all mental growth involves major qualitative changes as the child passes through several mental stages: specifically, the period of sensory-motor intelligence, the preoperational period, the period of concrete operations, and the period of formal operations.

In many ways, Piaget shares some of the fundamental assumptions of such British empiricists as Locke and Berkeley. As they do, he believes that the child starts life with little more than a set of disconnected sensory impressions and a limited repertoire of built-in motor reactions. Initially, there are no concepts of space, time, number, or causality. There is no concept of external objects that exist whether the child looks (or touches or manipulates) them or not. Nor is there an initial separation of the self and the outer world, including other people. All of these notions that adults take for granted come with increasing cognitive development.

While similar to the British empiricists in granting relatively little to the child's initial endowment, Piaget sharply differs from them in his views of how the child moves from her modest starting point to achieve adult intellectual functioning. Unlike the empiricists, Piaget does not believe that we achieve mental adulthood through more and more associative learning. He argues instead that our adult mental functions grow out of the continuing interaction between

159

the maturing intellectual capacities of the child and her environment. As development proceeds, there is a gradual shift from the concrete here-and-now to increasingly abstract conceptions of what the world is like and how one can think about it. The initial jumble of sensory impressions and motor reactions of the sensory-motor period gives way to a world in which there are mental representations (or ideas); during the period of concrete operations, the disconnected representations of the preoperational period are superseded by mental operations that organize these representations. At the same time, the egocentrism of the preoperational period gradually gives way to an increasing awareness that others have a different perspective from the child's own. As the child finally enters the period of formal operations, she becomes capable of ever more abstract mental processes in which she can think not just of what is but of what might be.

Piaget's general position has been criticized on two major counts. One concerns Piaget's descriptions of the facts of mental development, the other challenges his conception of its causes.

With regard to the facts, a number of recent studies of infants suggest that Piaget has seriously underestimated the intellectual capacities that represent the starting point of mental growth and that such basic concepts as space, time, causality, and objects may have primitive (and perhaps built-in) precursors in early life. Studies of preschoolers suggest that their intellectual abilities have also been underestimated and throw some doubt on the concept of discrete stages of mental growth analogous to the stages of embryological development.

The chapter concludes with a discussion of the causes of mental development, contrasting theories based on maturation, specific learning, and Piaget's concepts of assimilation and accommodation. A final section deals with recent attempts to think of the child's mental growth in terms of information processing. In contrast to Piaget, proponents of this general approach argue that the difference between the child and the adult is in large part a matter of different levels of expertise. In their view, cognitive development occurs as memory capacity, strategies for remembering and problem solving, and various metacognitive abilities improve.

Summary of the Main Topics

PIAGET'S THEORY OF COGNITIVE DEVELOPMENT

The chapter begins with an exposition of Piaget's theories of cognitive growth. According to Piaget, all humans pass through the same sequence of developmental stages. The first is the period of sensory-motor intelligence (roughly birth to two years), during which the infant develops the concept of object permanence and acquires increasingly complex mental representations.

The next stage is the period of preoperational thought (roughly two to seven years), during which the child's representations (that is, ideas) become ever more numerous, rich, and complex, but are not yet organized by a set of mental rules (which Piaget calls operations). As a result, preoperational children manifest a number of characteristic cognitive deficits: they fail to conserve quantity and number, they fail to take proper account of other people's perspective (egocentrism), and they are rigidly concrete in their moral judgment.

At around age seven, children begin to acquire a set of mental operations by means of which they can begin to relate and order their representations. As a result, they become more and more successful at conservation tasks, lose their preoperational egocentrism, and so on. But for quite a while, these operations are still relatively limited and concrete. In the later stages of this period of concrete operations (about seven to eleven), a child may know that the addition of one to a particular even number makes that number odd but cannot understand that this principle can be generalized to any even number whatsoever. This kind of abstraction is achieved during the period of formal operations (eleven years on), when children are finally able to entertain hypothetical possibilities and can grasp the kind of mental strategies that underlie scientific thought.

PERCEPTION AND MOTOR ACTION IN INFANCY

The chapter continues by describing some current reevaluations of Piaget's position. One arena of current controversy is the level from which the infant's mental development starts, for many current studies challenge Piaget's belief that the infant's mind is a jumble of unrelated sensory and motor patterns. One line of criticism comes from the finding that there seem to be some very early (perhaps built-in) correspondences between sights and sounds. Another comes from findings that show a remarkable degree of hand-eye coordination in young infants and even newborns. Yet another comes from studies utilizing the habituation method which suggest that, under certain conditions, four-month-olds seem to perceive partially occluded objects in much the same way as do adults—a finding which suggests that some rudiments of an object concept are attained at a much earlier age than Piaget had supposed. Such results give some credence to the nativist view, most recently formulated by the Gibsons, which maintains that many aspects of the perception of objects and events are part of the infant's native endowment.

THE PRESCHOOLER AND THE STAGE CONCEPT

The chapter continues with a discussion of the Piagetian concept of mental stage, as applied to the mental achievements of preschoolers. Piaget uses the term by analogy with embryology. In this context, a stage must be *consistent*—so that its characteristics hold pretty much across the board. A stage must also be relatively *discrete* rather than continuous, so that various cognitive capacities are absent at one age and then emerge, more or less full blown, at some later point. According to various critics, neither of these criteria seem to fit the behavior of pre-schoolers particularly well.

To begin with, there is some evidence that the young child's behavior is not as consistent as a strict stage account would have one suppose. For example, a child who can succeed in one of the tasks characteristic of concrete operations does not necessarily succeed in other tasks that are usually taken as indices of the same stage.

In addition, there is evidence that suggests that the developmental stages are not discrete as originally proposed. Thus children between two and four years of age are much less egocentric than Piaget had supposed, and various cognitive achievements such as number conservation have primitive precursors that appear several years earlier than had been predicted by the Piagetian calendar.

THE CAUSES OF MENTAL GROWTH

The text next turns to theories about the factors that lead to cognitive development. A number of causes have been proposed. One is maturation (that is, nature), another is learning (that is, nurture), or an as yet poorly understood interplay between the two (as in Piaget's twin concepts of assimilation and accommodation). Any account must explain not just why cognitive development occurs, but why it involves qualitative progressive changes that occur in an ordered sequence.

The chapter finally turns to a discussion of recent attempts to apply the information-processing approach to cognitive development. Seen from this perspective, intellectual growth largely reflects the acquisition of new ways of acquiring, retrieving, and transforming information. An example is the development of increasingly better memory performance. In part, this may reflect a maturational process that enlarges the child's memory capacity. But there is good evidence that it also reflects the acquisition and improvement of various memory strategies such as "chunking," various forms of rehearsal, and the development of metacognitive skills (see Chapters 7 and 8). In some ways, the developing child may be likened to an apprentice telegrapher. The apprentice becomes a master by acquiring higher-order concepts (such as conservation of mass and number) that are based on lower-order concepts (such as object permanence).

Discussion Topics

1. *Precursors of number perception in infants.* The text discusses a number of ways in which Piaget seems to have underestimated the intellectual capacities of infants and children. One example concerns tasks that involve number. While Piaget believed that number conservation is not found much before age six, the text describes some studies that find some numerical capacities at ages of three

and four. More recent evidence indicates that the ability to perceive number (and in a sense, to conserve) number may have its origins at about seven months of age. (See Starkey, P., Spelke, E., and Gelman, R. 1983. Detection of inter-modal numerical correspondences by human infants. *Science* 222:179–81).

One study used the preferential looking method that was used to show early links between sights and sounds (see text, pp. 477–78). The infants were seated in an infant chair and were shown two pictures side by side, projected on two screens in front of them. One of the pictures always contained two items (e.g., a pipe and a ribbon) while the other contained three items (e.g., a coin purse, a ring box, and a feather). On some trials, the two-item display was on the left; on others, it was on the right. While the infants were looking at these displays, they heard either two or three drum beats which came from a loudspeaker located midway between the two screens.

The question was which of the displays the infants would look at immediately after they heard the two-boom or the three-boom sounds. The results showed that they tended to look at the display that contained the same number of items as the number of drum beats they had just heard. They would look at, say, a picture of a ball and a flower after hearing two drum beats, but at a picture of a cup, a kitten, and a key after hearing three drum beats.

Studies of this kind suggest that infants have some means that allows them to detect the sheer number of items—regardless of whether the items are perceived by eye or by ear, and regardless of what the items are. To be sure, at this age, their comprehension is still limited to very small numbers. And many questions still remain. For example, it is still unclear whether the infants possess some understanding of the *absolute* number categories of "2" and "3" or whether their comprehension is as yet more relative, such as "more numerous" and "less numerous." But it does appear that some rudiments of numerical abilities are present at a very early age indeed.

2. *U-shaped curves in cognitive development: Knowing more and performing worse.* Since development is progressive growth, we usually assume that this growth manifests itself in various ascending curves: of size, of weight, of vocabulary, and so on. But occasionally, development—especially cognitive development—does not reveal itself by an ascending curve, but rather by a curve that first goes up, then comes down, and only then comes up again—with its last portion shaped like a U (see the diagram below).

An example is provided by language learning. Children who are learning language quickly acquire a number of verbs that have an irregular past, and they use both the past and present tense of these verbs quite accurately. For example, they will say *run* and *ran, eat* and *ate, go* and *went, take* and *took,* and so on. But some time later, they will begin to make errors on some of these verbs by overgeneralizing the regular past ending *-ed* and applying it to them. As a result, they may say *eated, runned, goed, taked,* and so on. Eventually, the U-shaped part of the curve will go up again, and they will come back to what they seemed to know initially. They will then produce the irregulars that adults use, such as *ran, ate,* and *went.* (For a more detailed discussion of this phenomenon, see Chapter 15.)

What accounts for such up-and-down curves in cognitive development? They seem to be based on the acquisition of a general rule, which at first is over-applied. Take the case of the irregular verbs. At first the child simply learns various words: *run, ran, eat, ate,* and so on. But he seems to learn them as individual items, without seeing any particular relation between them. With time he learns a rule: *-ed* means past tense. Having acquired the rule, he applies it across the board, and so he necessarily makes some errors using *runned* instead of *ran,* and so on. On the face of it, this seems like a step backwards, and it leads to a downhill part of the curve. But the backward step is only apparent, for the child has mastered something new with far-reaching effects: a general rule about the past tense. With time, he'll apply the rule where it is appropriate and take account of the exceptions. Thus up-and-down curves in development do not really disprove the general principle that development involves progressive growth.

An interesting recent study found U-shaped curves of development in a block-balancing task. Children were asked to balance small wooden blocks on a narrow metal strip so that they wouldn't fall. Three kinds of blocks were used. Type A consisted of narrow wooden planks whose center of gravity was identical to their geometrical center. Type B were blocks that were rather oddly shaped; they consisted of a narrow plank that had a cube glued to their top at one end. For these blocks, the center of gravity was necessarily displaced toward the cube and away from their geometrical center. Type C was the toughest block of all. This looked just like a block of Type A, but it was invisibly weighted with metal that was hidden within one side of the plank. Of course, the center of gravity here was also not identical to the geometrical center (see the diagrams below).

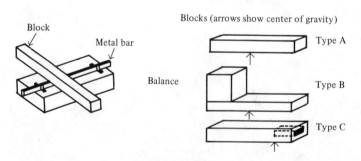

Block

Metal bar

Balance

Blocks (arrows show center of gravity)

Type A

Type B

Type C

The authors found an interesting progression in the block-balancing efforts with ages that increased from four-and-a-half to nine-and-a-half years. At around six, the children became moderately successful at this task. They tried to balance the block by placing it on the scale at one point, holding it with one finger, then adjusting it back and forth until it seemed to balance. Sometimes it did. But children a year older did not do as well. What happened is that these children hit on the—sometimes correct—principle that the geometrical center is the best point of balance. Once they placed the block there, they no longer corrected it. As a result, it fell down when the blocks were of Types B and C, leading to a downhill part of the developmental curve. Older children performed much better. They also used the geometrical center, but they then checked to see whether it was indeed appropriate for the block in question. (See Karmiloff-Smith, A., and Inhelder, B. 1977. If you want to get ahead, get a theory. In Johnson-Laird, P. N., and Wason, P. C., eds., *Thinking: Readings in cognitive science.* New York: Cambridge University Press.)

In the block-balancing experiment, as in the acquisition of irregular past-tense verbs, the drop in performance seems to be associated with the initial acquisition of some general principle. At first, the principle is applied imperfectly. As a result, there is a temporary decline in performance. But even when imperfectly understood, the principle represents the beginnings of genuine intellectual insight. The techniques the child used earlier may have worked more often, but when they worked, it was on a hit-and-miss basis, without real understanding. When the principle is finally understood—together with its exceptions—the child has really mastered the task.

3. *Some similarities between Piaget's and Freud's conceptions of the ego.*
The text briefly touches on an interesting similarity between Piaget's conception of early cognitive development and Freud's theories of early ego development (see text, p. 472). This similarity is worth a bit of elaboration.

There are obviously many differences between these theorists. Freud's concern was with the child's motives and desires where Piaget's was with his thought processes. But in some ways their general conceptions are similar. For both Freud and Piaget believed that the young organism is initially so utterly self-centered that he doesn't even comprehend the distinction between his own self and the rest of the world.

According to Freud, at the start of life the infant is little more than a seething cauldron of biological urges—the id, screaming for immediate satisfaction. The notion that there is an external world that must be somehow dealt with so that these urges can be satisfied comes in at a later point when the so-called pleasure principle is opposed by the reality principle. Freud's ego is a mental agency that is developed as the id's demands for immediate satisfactions are repeatedly denied by external reality; the ego's job is to reconcile the two somehow. Note that at first the infant has no real conception that this external world exists independently of himself. Initially, he cries when he is hungry or needs a diaper change, and since his cries are generally answered, he believes that his wishes are automatically ministered to by various agents (that is, his mother, father, or other caregiver) who have no independent will of their own. The realization that the external world, and other people in it, exist independently of himself comes later. One of the consequences of this realization is the formation of the ego.

Piaget's views on these matters have much in common with Freud's. For Piaget also believed that initially there is no real distinction between the self and other persons, or between the self and the external world. As Piaget saw it, this distinction grows out of continued intercourse with the real, external world. But for quite a while, the differentiation is far from perfect as shown by the child's egocentrism, which persists through the preoperational period.

At bottom, both Freud's and Piaget's views come from their insistence that there is no initial—and perhaps built-in—conception of external reality. In this view they differ from many contemporary theorists who regard some initial rudimentary conception of a real, external world—with objects and events that exist independently of the child—as something that all humans come equipped with. To the extent that such theorists—for example, the Gibsons—believe that some crude awareness of external reality is part and parcel of the infant's native endowment, they have little difficulty in accepting that some similar distinction between self and other is also given in early infancy.

Demonstrations

1. *A demonstration of liquid conservation in children.*   Children's failures on the classic Piagetian conservation tasks make compelling class demonstrations. If you have access to children of the appropriate ages and if the classroom situation is conducive to it, you may want to bring the children into class. Otherwise, you might consider videotaping their performance on conservation tasks and showing the videotape in class. Students with access to children may also do this as a project outside of class.

The procedure for the conservation of liquid quantity is as follows. Fill two identical glasses with equal amounts of a colored liquid. (Kool-aid is good because children are familiar with it and the colors make it easy to see.) Ask the child whether there is more Kool-aid in one glass or in the other, and add or pour off a bit until the child is satisfied that there is as much Kool-aid in one glass as in the other. Now place a new glass, noticeably taller and narrower, on the table. While the child is watching, pour the entire contents of one of the original glasses into the new glass and place it next to the other glass with Kool-aid in it (see figure below). Ask the child, "Is there more Kool-aid in this glass or in this one?" as you point to the shorter, fatter glass and the taller, narrower one. Children of about four or five years will insist that there is more Kool-aid in the taller glass, because the liquid reaches a higher level. Young children fail

to see that if the two original glasses had equal amounts of Kool-aid, the new
taller glass must have the same amount, since the quantity was completely transferred. Children of about age seven or older will say both glasses must have the
same amount in them, and will often point out that you could pour it back into
the original shorter glass and see that the levels are again the same. In Piaget's
terms, the older child is not misled by the change in appearance because she
understands that the transformation is reversible.

2. *Metacognition in adults.*   One important difference between children and
adults is that children are deficient in metacognition—knowing that one knows
(see text, pp. 491–92). An example is metacognition of memory (sometimes
called metamemory). Adults generally know whether some piece of information
is in their memory store, even if they can't retrieve it at the moment. A demonstration is memory monitoring. In a memory-monitoring task, a subject is asked
to recall something. If she is unable to come up with the answer (for example, to
a question such as "What is the capital of Peru?"), she is asked whether she
thinks she might do better on a recognition test on which she has to pick the
correct answer from among a list of alternatives. Adults are rather good at monitoring their memory in this way. In effect, they can predict their own performance on a later recognition test on items they couldn't recall. In contrast,
children do much more poorly. They don't seem to know what they can and cannot remember.

The demonstration below illustrates memory monitoring.

Part A.   The students are told that they will hear a list of fairly infrequent
words. Their job is to indicate which of the following three alternatives best
describes what they know about the word (these alternatives should probably
be written on the blackboard or on a transparency projected overhead):

    a. I know the meaning of the word, and I recall it right now. If asked, I
       could provide a rough definition.

    b. I think I know the meaning of the word, but I can't recall it right now.
       I believe that if I were given a choice of alternatives, I would be able to
       pick out the correct one.
    c. I don't know the meaning of the word. I believe that if I were given a
       choice of alternatives, I would not be able to pick out the correct one.

The list of words follows. They should be read aloud, one word at a time,
with enough time (say, eight seconds) between words to allow the students to
indicate which of the three choices applies to each word. (The difficulty of the
items on the list may have to be adjusted to suit the background of the students
in the class. The words should be generally hard, but not totally unfamiliar.)

1. laconic	7. mercurial
2. garrulous	8. quiescent
3. senescent	9. veracious
4. onerous	10. recalcitrant
5. exegesis	11. exculpate
6. imbroglio	12. impecunious

Part B. The next step is to give the students a multiple-choice recognition
test for the items they just saw. The choices follow. (These choices are probably
best presented in written form, perhaps on a handout. But in a pinch, they could
probably be read aloud. In the list below the correct alternative is in italic type.)

1. laconic
   a. lazy
   b. drowsy
   c. *concise*

2. garrulous
   a. *pointlessly talkative*
   b. ill-tempered
   c. difficult to manage

3. senescent
   a. eclipsed
   b. *aging*
   c. ready to bloom

4. onerous
   a. *burdensome*
   b. obscure
   c. weighty

5. exegesis
   a. religious ceremony

      b. surgical procedure

      c. *critical explanation of a text*

6. imbroglio
   a. secluded place
   b. cooking device
   c. *an embarrassing misunderstanding*

7. mercurial
   a. hot to the touch
   b. *unpredictably changeable*
   c. increasing rapidly

8. quiescent
   a. *at rest or quiet*
   b. cooperative or agreeable
   c. guilty

9. veracious
   a. *true or factual*
   b. greedy
   c. difficult to prove

10. recalcitrant
    a. shy or aloof
    b. easily convinced
    c. *obstinately defiant*

11. exculpate
    a. unearth or discover
    b. *to clear from some alleged guilt*
    c. to explain in a clear manner

12. impecunious
    a. haughty
    b. *poor*
    c. unimpeachable

After the students have gone through the multiple-choice test, present the correct alternatives, and ask the students to score themselves. The next step is to determine the accuracy of their memory monitoring. To check this, they will have to compare their judgments in Part A of the demonstration with their recognition scores in Part B. We are only interested in words whose Part A rating was either "b" (can't recall it but would be able to recognize it) or "c" (can't recall it and would not be able to recognize it). Ask each student to calculate the proportion of "b" words that he or she recognized correctly (the number of "b" words recognized correctly divided by the total number of all "b" words) and the proportion of "c" words recognized correctly (the number of "c" words recognized correctly divided by the total number of all "c" words). The accuracy of memory monitoring is then revealed by looking at the difference between these two proportions. If memory monitoring were perfect, a student's recognition score for "b" words would be 100 percent; that for "c" items, would be 0 percent (ignoring guessing). Ask students to indicate whether their "b" proportion was higher, equal to, or lower than their "c" proportion. A simple show of hands will probably indicate that virtually all students have higher "b" than "c" proportions—a demonstration of memory monitoring that is characteristic of most adults but not of young children.

(For further discussion of memory monitoring, see Hart, J. T. 1967. Memory and the memory monitoring process. *Journal of Verbal Learning and Verbal Behavior* 6:685-91. For a general discussion of metacognitive processes in memory and their development in children, see Flavell, J. H., and Wellman, H. M. 1977. Metamemory. In Kail, R. V., Jr., and Hagen, J. W., eds., *Perspectives on the development of memory and cognition.* Hillsdale, N.J.: Erlbaum, pp. 3-34.)

3. *Adults' naive beliefs about the motion of objects.*   According to Piaget, the failure of young children to conserve mass or liquid quantity is an indication that they are still at a preoperational level of thinking. But according to some more recent investigators, it may simply reveal that the child has not as yet achieved an adequate understanding of the way the physical universe works. He has probably seen toy clay being molded and liquids being poured, but he hasn't had much of a chance to think about these observations. As a result, he fails the conservation tests. But this failure only shows that he has not yet reached a level of appropriate expertise. In effect, he holds a set of rather naive "theories" about the way the physical world is constructed; with time, he will adopt the more sophisticated (and more accurate) theories held by adults.

This general way of thinking finds some support in the fact that if we provide appropriate tests, even adults show that they too hold theories about some aspects of the physical world that can also be regarded as naive, at least when contrasted with the way in which physicists think about such matters. Some recent studies show that many adults (including the majority of college students, sometimes even those who have had a course in physics) hold mistaken beliefs about the paths that moving objects follow. As an illustration, consider two problems that were posed to these subjects which you might want to give to your own students.

Problem 1.   Consider a metal tube curved into a spiral. In the center of the spiral is a metal ball that is shot out of the tube at a very high speed (see Diagram I below). What is the path the ball will take as it leaves the tube (ignoring air resistance)? Choose among alternatives 1 and 2 pictured in Diagram II below. In the figures, the spiral tube is seen from the top, and the path of the ball is indicated with a dotted line.

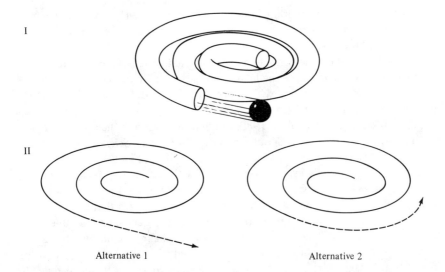

Alternative 1   Alternative 2

Problem 2. Imagine someone who is rapidly twirling a metal ball attached to a string above his head, as shown in Diagram I below. What path will the ball take when it suddenly breaks off the string? Choose among alternatives 1 and 2 shown in Diagram II below. In the figures, the circular path is shown from above,

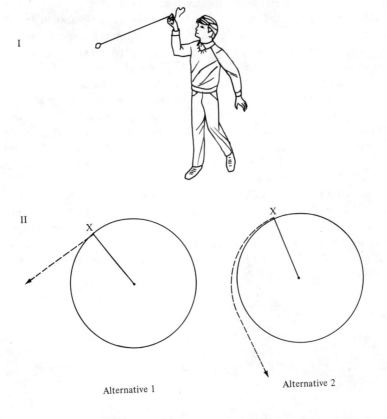

Alternative 1   Alternative 2

with the direction of the twirling indicated by the arrows. The point at which the ball breaks off is indicated by the letter X, and the path of the ball after it breaks off is shown by the dotted line.

For both problems, the correct choice is alternative 1. But a considerable number of the students chose the incorrect alternative. In problem 1, the incorrect alternative was chosen by 51 percent of the subjects; in problem 2, the proportion who chose the incorrect alternative was 30 percent. (See McCloskey, M., Caramzza, A., and Green, B. 1980. Curvilinear motion in the absence of external forces: Naive beliefs about the motion of objects. *Science* 210:1139–41.) Why did so many adults choose incorrectly?

It appears that merely everyday experience with moving objects does not necessarily make for a correct solution. Interviews with the students after they had completed the task indicated that many of them believed that an object that is forced to move in a curved path (that is, traveling in a curved metal tube or twirling around on a string) acquires a "force" that makes it continue to follow a curved path for a time after this force is removed (that is, after it is shot out of the tube or breaks off the string). The authors argue that the students had developed a theory rather similar to that held by medieval thinkers—the notion that objects acquire an "impetus" that makes it continue a path it once followed. This theory is false (and is at odds with modern theories of motion). But the theory seems somehow reasonable; after all, it was held for centuries before modern science analyzed the problem of motion successfully.

If adults hold naive theories in fields in which they are novices, shouldn't one expect children to exhibit naive theories in many other areas? For children are novices in many more areas than are adults. It may be that when we ask them to solve problems, they can't help but attack them with their own naive theories. Where such naive theories come from, whether they are universal (that is, found in all children of a certain age and in all cultures), and how they are modified and abandoned are questions that are still unanswered. But the fact that adults (including some college students who had a course or two in physics) also hold naive incorrect theories about some aspects of the physical world should provide a certain perspective (and some sympathy) on the plight of five- and six-year-olds who are asked to solve certain Piagetian problems.

(For more on the role of naive theories in children's learning, especially in the domain of biology, see Carey, S. 1985. *Conceptual change in childhood.* Cambridge, Mass.: MIT Press, which explores the development of biological conceptions in children's thought. For additional reading on adults' naive theories about physics, see McCloskey, M. 1983. Naive theories of motion. In Gentner, D. and Stevens, A., eds., *Mental models.* Hillsdale, N.J.: Erlbaum.)

Selected Readings

CLASSICS

Piaget, J. 1952. *The language and thought of the child.* New York: Humanities Press. Difficult to read, but for those who want to get their Piaget at first-hand.

Gruber, H., and Voneche, J. J. 1977. *The essential Piaget.* London: Routledge and Kegan Paul. An excellent selection of original writings with introductions.

REFERENCE WORKS

Flavell, J. 1985. *Cognitive development*, 2nd ed. Englewood Cliffs, N.J.: Prentice-Hall. An eminently readable paperback introduction to the field by a major figure in the area.

Gardner, H. 1982. *Developmental psychology*, 2nd ed. Boston: Little, Brown. A well-written, good undergraduate text that devotes considerable space to cognitive development.

CHAPTER 15

Cognitive Development: Language

Overview

This chapter begins by stating that language is a prime case of a complex behavior whose learning requires both innate predispositions (only humans can learn it) and environmental support (children in France learn French, while children in England learn English). The problem of learning language is posed by the fact that appropriate language use is creative; the words and sentences that are learned in one context can be applied to new contexts by the successful language user. It is shown that the appropriate knowledge cannot be acquired through such simple learning mechanisms as imitation, reinforcement, and correction. Rather, the process of language learning is highly organized in terms of innate dispositions in the child; and a variety of social, cognitive, and more specifically linguistic supports from the environment are shown to affect the course of learning. Much of language design is shown to evolve from the requirements of its young learners, and hence language learning affects how languages change over historical time. It is concluded that, though many language details differ from community to community, much of the explanation of learning lies in the fact that humans are "linguistic animals."

Summary of the Main Topics

IS LANGUAGE LEARNING THE ACQUISITION OF A SKILL?

The main burden of this section is to show that certain simple learning principles such as imitation, reinforcement, and correction do not explain the course of language learning. This is because children say many things they haven't heard—including many that they are negatively reinforced for saying— and because parents rarely correct their children on matters of grammar. In many societies, correction of grammar is altogether absent from the teaching situation, and yet children in those societies learn their languages as rapidly as do middle-class American children.

THE NORMAL COURSE OF LANGUAGE LEARNING

Here, we take an excursion through the various stages of language learning, from babbling and single words all the way through to complex sentences. It is shown that the child brings many useful biases into the learning situation, for example good discrimination of and attentiveness to phonetic contrasts. In addition, mothers seem to be adapted to provide a special kind of baby talk ("Motherese"), which is particularly liked and well-discriminated by the young learners. This special kind of language serves social-affective ends as well as being useful for strictly linguistic-teaching purposes. As she develops, the child seems to become more and more inclined to organize the language data she hears in terms of general principles, instead of learning each part of the language piece by piece. This bias toward discovering general regularities often leads the child to temporary overgeneralizations, in which she extends rules beyond their real scope in the adult language she is hearing. The language learning scenario seems to follow a quite regular course, regardless of the language the children are learning and regardless of the particular culture and the particular child-rearing procedures within which they are raised. In all cases, they acquire their native tongues within about the same time period: one-word speech at about one year, two-word speech at about two years, and complex speech between the third and the sixth years of life.

LANGUAGE LEARNING AND LANGUAGE CHANGE

Learning is shown to be related to language itself, in the sense that languages change in part in response to the biases of the learner. What is hard to learn disappears from the language, while what is easy to learn remains part of the language through the generations.

LANGUAGE LEARNING IN CHANGED ENVIRONMENTS

We next take up the question of how language fares under changed environmental conditions, including the cases of wild children, isolated children, and deaf and blind children. It is shown that young children can recover even from extreme maltreatment, provided they are rehabilitated and exposed to normal language environments during childhood. Furthermore, both blind and deaf children acquire language well if their environmental circumstances are otherwise normal.

LANGUAGE LEARNING AND CRITICAL PERIODS

In this section, we consider the "critical period" hypothesis, which argues that children are better at first language learning than are adults. Some evidence that children learn language more easily than adults is presented. Thus the difference between first language learners and (adult) second language learners is discussed as a possible case of "changed endowment." Since the adult may have passed the period of maximum sensitivity to language, he acquires a new language more slowly and less well than child learners.

THE NECESSARY CONDITIONS FOR LANGUAGE LEARNING

The chapter closes by reemphasizing the intermix of native endowment and environmental input that yields language learning.

THE GROWTH OF THE MIND

A brief coda to the chapter brings its findings together with the prior chapters on child development. Again the moral drawn is that neither extreme "innatism" nor extreme "environmentalism" can explain cognitive development. It is the interaction of innate predispositions with information from the environment that, in the end, turns the child's mind into the mind of an adult.

Discussion Topics

1. *The acquisition of language principles: Singular and plural in English.*
Both the text and a previous chapter in this manual discussed the fact that children learn the general principles whereby plurals are formed in English (see text, pp. 505-506, and this manual, Chapter 9, Demonstration 1). Young children evidently learn that words which end with a voiced consonant (such as *g, b,* or *d*) take the sound *z* to form the plural, while those which end with an unvoiced consonant (such as *k, p,* or *t*) take the sound *s.* They learn this as a general principle that can be applied to new words that they have never heard before. Proof comes from the fact that when they are told that a cartoon figure is called a *wuk,* they call two such figures *wuks*; when told the figure is called *wug,* they call two of them *wugz*—using the unvoiced *s* sound in the first case, the voiced *z* sound in the second. (See Gleason, J. G. 1958. The child's learning of English morphology. *Word* 14:150-77.)

One might suppose that the plural sound principle is just a consequence of the way our vocal tract is built. Perhaps we are unable to follow a voiced consonant with an *s* or an unvoiced one with a *z.* That is not the case as shown by words such as *presence.* At the end of this word a voiced consonant (*n*) is followed by an unvoiced one (which is pronounced as *s*). This shows that English speakers are able to say *n + s* at the end of a word. But if the idea "plural" is involved, and if the consonant that ends the root or stem of the word is voiced, they always say *z* rather than *s* (for example, *buttons*). Children as young as three honor this *s/z* distinction when they form plurals. It is curious that such young children go to the trouble of learning the meaningless (and pretty boring) idea that *s* and *z* are used after different sounds in English plurals. The child's parents would understand her perfectly well if she used only one of the two sounds—say, the s—to indicate the plural. The fact that she uses both, and comes to use them properly, shows that children learn very abstract and formal facts about their language even if they do not clearly contribute to meaningfulness. Perhaps the child is simply "built to acquire" rules and principles of language.

2. *Morphological effects in the writing system.* So far our discussion has focused on language as it is spoken. What about the way it is written and read? Let's go back to the use of plurals. As we all know, in English the morpheme "plural" is written down (that is, spelled) in one way, regardless of the voiced/ unvoiced opposition. (The fact that the "plural" morpheme is spelled—and pronounced—differently when a word ends in an s or z, as in *kisses* or *buzzes* is another matter.) We write an "s" even if the spoken plural is "z" (for example, we write *cats* and *dogs*, not *catz* and *dogz*). And it is quite easy to teach young readers/writers to do the same, though they sometimes err along the way.

What explains the fact that there is a systematic alternation in speech (s vs. z) that is completely ignored in writing? The answer has to do with the nature of writing. In English, as in most modern languages that have a writing system, writing is a way of transcribing sound into a visual form. But this transcription is by no means perfect. The English writing system (its orthography) often transcribes morphemes (the units of meaning) rather than phonemes (the units of speech sound). To the extent that this is so, English orthography is more systematic than it might appear to be at first glance. Consider the word *bomb*. This is pronounced *bom*, without the final *b*, but nevertheless the written form of the word is *bomb* and not *bom*. Now take the word *bombadier*. Here the word is written just as it is pronounced, with two *b*s. How can we explain this? Here as before the answer is that English orthography is often more true to morphemes than to phonemes. It is clear that the same morpheme—*bomb*— is contained in both words (a *bombadier* is someone who drops a *bomb*). In many cases English orthography is faithful to this fact rather than to facts about phonemes. The orthography is quite systematic in its own way. While it is a relatively poor transcription of phonemes, it is a relatively good transcription of morphemes. (For a discussion, see Chomsky, N. 1970. Phonology and reading. In H. Levin and J. P. Williams, eds., *Basic studies on reading.* New York: Basic Books.)

3. *Overgeneralization.* The phenomenon of overgeneralization is our best evidence of how children set out to create an orderly and regular language, even though the "rules" (or principles) that govern adult speech are sometimes quite limited and full of exceptions. An example that is discussed in the text (see pp. 505-506) is the overuse of the regular rule that adds "-ed" to form the past tense. Such overgeneralizations lead the child to say *holded* rather than *held*, *runned* rather than *ran*, and so on. (For a useful discussion of this overregularization, see Kuczaj, S. A. II, The Acquisition of regular and irregular past tense forms. *Journal of Verbal Learning and Verbal Behavior* 16:589-600.)

Another overregularization made by children (and occasionally by adults!) has to do with creating verbs from nouns. For example, a child says to another child who is hitting him in the head with a Woodstock doll: "Don't Woodstock me or I'm going home!" And a sign on a beer carton, presumably written by an adult, reads "Litter-basket your empties!" (that is: Put your empties in the litter basket). The class might be asked to collect (or invent) such forms (e.g., "I 707-ed to England last summer"). They might be asked why they think some of these forms sound childish and others sound fine. According to some authors, the inventor has to be careful that the listener understands the present topic of conversation, for otherwise such novel expressions are hard to understand. There is reason to believe that children are not as sensitive as adults to what their listeners may know or infer from the present context of conversation; that is why they create more such new forms than adults do. (For discussion, see Clark, E., and Clark, H. 1979. When nouns surface as verbs. *Language* 55:767–811. Clark, E. 1982. The young word maker: A case study of innovation in the child lexicon. In Wanner, E., and Gleitman, L., eds., *Language acquisition: State of the art*. New York: Cambridge University Press.)

4. *Learning new words.*   How are words learned at various ages? College students are continually required to learn new words—usually in technical contexts (e.g., biological terms). Such new terms take some time and a good deal of conscious effort to acquire. It may be that word learning is a bit easier in childhood.

This suggestion comes from a study which showed that nursery school children can learn a new color term after just one exposure. In a play school, two trays were placed on a table or shelf. One of the trays was red, the other was olive-green. The experimenter asked a child to "get the chromium tray . . . not the red one . . . the chromium one." (The word *chromium* was chosen on the reasonable supposition that the children had never heard it before.) Children who could already apply color terms correctly consistently retrieved the tray that the experimenter had called "chromium" even though they had never heard that particular word before. They evidently supposed it was a color term (since it was contrasted with the word *red*). When tested a few weeks later, some of the children still remembered what "chromium" meant (as used by the experimenter). When asked, they pointed to color samples that were olive-green. Others retained partial information; they remembered that "chromium" indicated a color, but they had forgotten which particular color it indicates. All in all, these results are quite impressive. It appears that children can infer the meaning of a word from just one presentation, and they may recall that meaning a week later. (For more details, see Carey, S. 1978. The child as word learner. In Halle, M., Bresnan, J., and Miller, G. A., eds. *Linguistic theory and psychological reality*. Cambridge, Mass.: MIT Press.)

5. *"Good" and "bad" English.*   It is sometimes said that the young learners are ruining the language. One could discuss some recent changes in English,

carried out and used by the younger generation (and still hated by the older generation). Ask the class whether they think that in these respects the language is "getting worse" or "just plain changing." Examples are:

(a) Extension of the suffix -*wise*. This formerly appeared in only a few words, such as *otherwise* and *drop-wise*. Now it appears widely. It is used to convert a noun to an adverb (e.g., "She hunched dog-wise on the floor"). In earlier English, one could convert a noun to an adverb only by first converting the noun to an adjective (e.g., *dog, doggish*) and then converting that adjective to an adverb (*doggishly*). Another method is to use the long expression "In a doggish manner." Why might the children of this generation have created this new piece of morphology? Is it "bad" for English?

(b) Another example is the insertion of *of* in structures where it never previously appeared. For example, young speakers will often say "I didn't have so good of a time there" where most older speakers say "I didn't have so good a time there."

(c) Yet another popular new case is the use of *like*, e.g., "I like went for a walk." It often seems to express doubt, as in the locution "I more-or-less (or sort-of) went for a walk." Is this new locution "bad for the English language"? Why might the younger generation have created this form?

Demonstration

Word frequency of regular and irregular verbs. The text discusses the relation between overgeneralization and language change (pp. 507–10). To simplify the problem, let's only consider the question of past and present tenses. In the course of language learning, children have to learn a considerable number of verbs. When the verbs are regular, they pose less of a problem to the child's memory. She only has to learn the present tense, for once she has acquired the -*ed* (at about three years of age), she can form the past tense by simply adding the -*ed*. Her task is much harder for the irregular verbs. For these, she must learn the present and past tense separately, since there is no ready rule by means of which she can derive the past tense form from the present. As a result, she must learn both *go* and *went*, both *speak* and *spoke*, and so on. This naturally puts a certain load on the child's memory. This is one reason why she sometimes overgeneralizes, and overapplies the -*ed* rule (e.g., saying *holded* instead of *held*).

At the time it is made, the child's overgeneralization is a language error. But what happens if the child persists in this overgeneralization (and if other children in the same community do the same)? Eventually the child becomes a parent, and when she does, she will use this new, overgeneralized form when talking to her child (for example, saying *holded*). But now this use is no longer an error because the entire adult community uses the same form. The child's overgeneralization error has led to a change in the language: the regularization of an irregular verb.

If such a process is at work in English, we should expect a tendency toward the regularization of irregulars, as we look over historical time. In fact, there is evidence for such a tendency, for quite a few English verbs that are now regular were once irregular. Some examples (followed by their old past tense in parentheses) are *abide* (*abode*), *glide* (*glode*), *help* (*holp*), and *bide* (*bode*).

We should also expect such regularization effects to be much more frequent for irregular verbs that are rarely encountered because such infrequently encountered verbs are the ones for which the memory problem is most acute. The situation is quite different for very common irregular verbs such as *go, do,* and *make* (and their irregular past tenses *went, did,* and *made*). These are heard very often, so that their special forms are easily memorized. Such very common verbs should be less likely to be overgeneralized. As a result, we would expect such common irregular verbs to stay irregular over the passing generations.

Overall, irregular verbs should be more common (that is, frequently encountered) than regular verbs. They are the ones that resisted the tendency toward regularization, and the fact that they are so often heard is one of the reasons why they did. The regular verbs would include quite a few that were once irregular, but being less common, did not survive the regularization tendency. The following demonstration is meant to illustrate this fact.

The students are presented with ten sets of four synonyms (taken from a thesaurus) shown below. For each of the sets, the students should decide which of the four is "the most common, the most frequently encountered," and which is "the least common, the least frequently encountered" verb. A simple show of hands should suffice.

The next job is to compare the verb judged to be most frequent with the one judged to be least frequent. In the majority of cases, the most frequent will be an irregular verb (here indicated by italics), the least frequent will be a regular verb.

The list is presented below:

Set 1	*Set 3*
a. *bite*	a. *eat*
b. chew	b. devour
c. gnaw	c. gulp
d. munch	d. ingest
Set 2	*Set 4*
a. *drink*	a. collapse
b. imbibe	b. drop
c. swallow	c. *fall*
d. sip	d. topple

Set 5	*Set 8*
a. part	a. converge
b. *go*	b. join
c. *leave*	c. *meet*
d. move	d. unite

Set 6	*Set 9*
a. *hit*	a. acquire
b. slap	b. grasp
c. smack	c. seize
d. *strike*	d. *take*

Set 7	*Set 10*
a. *build*	a. edify
b. create	b. inform
c. *make*	c. instruct
d. produce	d. *teach*

The results will show that irregular verbs tend to be more frequent than regular verbs. Thus *bite* will be judged to be more frequent than *chew, gnaw,* and *munch.* This and other irregular verbs managed to remain irregular precisely because they are more frequent—they are encountered so often that they are less likely to give rise to errors of overgeneralization in childhood. As a result, they stay irregular from one generation to the next.

Selected Readings

GENERAL WORKS
De Villiers, J., and DeVilliers, P. 1978. *Language acquisition.* Cambridge, Mass.: Harvard University Press. A fairly simple exposition for undergraduates.

Gleitman, L. R., and Wanner, E. 1984. Current issues in language development. In Bornstein, M. H., and Lamb, M. E., eds., *Developmental psychology: An advanced textbook.* Hillsdale, H.J.: Erlbaum. A recent review of facts and theories in the field of language acquisition.

CLASSICS
Bloom, L. 1970. *Language development: Form and function in emerging grammars.* Cambridge, Mass.: M.I.T. Press.

Brown, R. 1973. *A first language: The early stages.* Cambridge, Mass.: Harvard University Press.

REFERENCE WORKS ON SUBAREAS IN LANGUAGE ACQUISITION
Bowerman, M., 1976. Semantic factors in the acquisition of rules for word use and sentence construction. In Morehead, D. M., and Morehead, A. E., eds., *Normal and deficient child language.* Baltimore: University Park Press. Studies of overgeneralization of meaning and syntactic forms.

Carey, S. 1982. Semantic development. In Wanner, E., and Gleitman, L. R., eds., *Language development: State of the art.* New York: Cambridge University Press. A classic discussion of the acquisition of word meaning by children.

Slobin, D. I. 1977. Language change in childhood and in history. In Macnamara, J., ed., *Language learning and thought.* New York: Academic Press. An interesting discussion of the relation between the child's development and the history of language change.

Snow, C., and Ferguson, C., eds. 1977. *Talking to children: Language input and acquisition.* New York: Cambridge University Press. A collection of papers on the role the mother's speech plays in the language acquisition of their children.

REFERENCE WORKS ON READING
One major issue in this area—of interest to psychologists as well as educators—is whether learning to read is like learning to talk, and whether fluent reading is like fluent comprehending. Does reading a sentence or a word require as a component process that the word or sentence be converted into some phonological form, or could reading be "immediate," a direct translation from print to meaning? For some pertinent references see:

Gibson, E., and Levin, H. 1975. *The psychology of reading.* Cambridge, Mass.: MIT Press. An early discussion.

Rozin, P., and Gleitman, L. R. 1977. The structure and acquisition of reading. In Reber, A., and Scarborough, D., eds., *Toward a psychology of reading.* Hillsdale, N.J.:Erlbaum. This chapter presents a general review of the major psychological issues in the area.

Seidenberg, M. S. 1985. The time course of phonological code activation in two writing systems. *Cognition* 19:1-30. A recent interesting discussion.

REFERENCE WORKS ON LANGUAGE IN SPECIAL GROUPS

In the blind

Fraiberg, S. 1977. *Insights from the blind.* New York: Basic Books.

Landau, B., and Gleitman, L. R. 1985. *Language and experience: Evidence from the blind child.* Cambridge, Mass.: Harvard University Press.

In the deaf
Goldin-Meadow, S. 1982. The resilience of recursion. In Wanner, E., and Gleitman, L. R., eds., *Language acquisition: The state of the art.* New York: Cambridge University Press. A discussion of "home sign"—an invented version of sign
language developed by deaf children who are not exposed to sign language.

Klima, E., Bullugi, U., et al. 1979. *The signs of language.* Cambridge, Mass.: Harvard University Press. A series of important papers on the manual languages of the
deaf, discussed from the point of view of psychology.

In retarded persons
Fowler, A. E. 1986. Down's syndrome language: Syntax and morphology. In
Cicchetti, D., and Beeghley, M., eds., *Down's syndrome: The developmental
perspective.* New York: Cambridge University Press.

In isolated children
Curtiss, S. 1977. *Genie: A psycholinguistic study of a modern-day "wild child."*
New York: Academic Press.

CHAPTER 16

Social Development

Overview

Like the preceding chapters on motor and cognitive development, this chapter on social development makes the point that the scope of an individual's universe increases as development proceeds. From the earliest bond with the first caregiver to the complex social interactions of family, friends, school, the workplace, and the community, the number and variety of a growing child's social relations increase dramatically. The child's social perceptions, thoughts, and skills grow, too, and this chapter examines current ideas about the course this development takes.

The chapter begins with the nature and role of attachment in infancy. Important questions in this section include what accounts for attachment in the first place, how crucial is early experience for later development, and whether the effects of the absence or disruption of attachment on subsequent development can be reversed. Harlow's studies of attachment phenomena in monkeys and studies of children reared in impersonal institutions provide data and examples for the discussion.

The chapter next takes up several theories of childhood socialization, including theories based on reinforcement (e.g., Freudian and behavior theories), social learning theory with its emphasis on modeling and imitation, and cognitive developmental theory, which focuses on children's capacity for understanding. This section also examines the effects of various child-rearing practices and parental attitudes.

Having discussed some hypotheses about how socialization takes place, the chapter takes a look at some of its products. First, moral reasoning and behavior are examined, then the development of gender identity, gender role, and sexual orientation.

Summary of the Main Topics

SOME GENERAL CHARACTERISTICS OF SOCIAL DEVELOPMENT

The most striking aspect of the pattern followed by social development is its continued expansion. Whether this expansion is accomplished by a regular, orderly progression, as in motor and cognitive development, is still a matter of speculation, since few psychologists have attempted to chart the course of social development in a comprehensive, detailed way. Freud's theory of psychosexual development was one of the first attempts to describe stages of social development. Although few psychologists today accept the substance of Freud's theory, many are pursuing the questions he raised about how the child first becomes attached to the mother and whether early childhood experience is the primary determinant of later personality and social development.

ATTACHMENT

The infant's attachment to the person who takes care of him (usually the mother) starts off the process of social development. In Freud's theory, the mother's satisfaction of the infant's bodily needs produces the infant's attachment to her. More recent work, including studies of infant monkeys, suggests that the infant is attached, not because the mother feeds it, but rather because she comforts it. According to some theorists, infants have a built-in fear of the unfamiliar, and they become attached to the mother because she is familiar to them.

Experiments with birds suggest that the mechanism of imprinting is what fixes the infant's attachment on a mother-object, and that the attachment can only be formed during a critical period. The text describes studies on motherless monkeys and institutionally reared human children that suggest that when no proper attachments are formed, there may be a serious impairment of later social development. Further studies with monkeys and adopted children, however, indicate that these impairments can be at least partially reversed with appropriate interventions.

CHILDHOOD SOCIALIZATION

The chapter continues by comparing several theories of how human socialization comes about. The social learning theorists' view holds that observational learning is the most important component underlying the socialization process in humans. This approach emphasizes the effect of modeling, both upon the acquisition of new responses and on the performance of responses that are already known. It is at odds with the idea that socialization is simply a process of molding, as suggested by the theories of Freud, Pavlov, and Skinner.

Still another approach to socialization is that of cognitive developmental theory, which goes beyond the social learning theorists' opposition to blind molding. Cognitive developmental theory emphasizes the role of understanding rather than imitation. Thus, instead of regarding the child's observational learning as caused by, say, vicarious reinforcement, cognitive theorists believe that the child's motive for imitation is an attempt at understanding, where successful imitation is its own reward. What a child understands about the situation he imitates changes over time, as his general mental development proceeds. This progressive intellectual growth affects not only the way in which the child comprehends the physical world around him, but also the way in which he thinks about social situations.

The text also takes a look at how various patterns of child rearing affect the socialization process. Specific practices, such as different models of weaning or toilet training, do not seem to have long-term effects. The general home atmosphere, on the other hand, does lead to long-term differences in children's behavior. The text summarizes the findings of studies that have divided parental patterns into three types: autocratic, permissive, and authoritative-reciprocal. The outcome was best for children of authoritative-reciprocal parents. Children of autocratic and permissive parents had characteristics similar to each other, many of which were less favorable.

The text goes on to explore the role the child herself plays in the process of socialization. From birth, children have different temperaments, which may, in turn, cause parents to treat them differently. It is likely that during socialization the child's behavior affects the parents', just as the parents' behavior affects the child's.

THE DEVELOPMENT OF MORALITY

An important aspect of social development is learning to govern one's moral conduct. Part of this involves internalizing the prohibitions of one's culture. According to Freud's theory, internalization of prohibitions comes with the development of the superego. Freud's theory predicts that harsh punishment would lead to stronger superego development and greater internalization. The evidence, however, does not support this. More recent theorists have argued that children's behavior fits the principle of minimal sufficiency, which states that internalization is greatest when there is just enough pressure for a child to behave a certain way but not so much that she feels she was forced to do so.

In addition to ensuring that prohibitions are obeyed, morality involves positive moral action and altruism. Several studies have demonstrated empathic responses in young children. Empathy may be a necessary precursor of altruism; however, even in adults it is possible to find strong empathy without altruistic action accompanying it. The chapter ends its discussion of the development of morality by describing Kohlberg's theory of stages of moral reasoning.

THE DEVELOPMENT OF SEX ROLES

Socialization affects both how we see ourselves and how others see us. As an illustration, the text considers sex roles. The discussion includes our sense of gender identity, our gender role, and our sexual orientation. The text considers how each of these develops through the interplay of various socializing factors and of our biological makeup. Particular attention is paid to certain psychological differences between the sexes (e.g., in the aggression and in the pattern of intellectual aptitudes) and to the effect of socially imposed sex roles as observed in cases of sex reassignment in early childhood.

The text next turns to the three major theories of sex typing: psychoanalysis, social learning theory, and cognitive developmental theory. The first theory emphasizes the sex drive, the second stresses cultural learning, and the third focuses on the child's cognitive growth and the resulting awareness of his or her gender identity.

The chapter continues with a discussion of homosexuality and points out that there is no convincing evidence that it implies any personal disturbance or neurosis. The origins of homosexuality are not well understood, but whatever its causes, this sexual orientation (no less than heterosexuality) is a fairly stable condition that can be changed only with difficulty, if at all.

DEVELOPMENT AFTER CHILDHOOD

Development does not end with childhood. A few authors, most notably Erikson, have attempted to document stages of development through the life cycle. The text considers the period of adolescence in some detail, emphasizing the role culture plays in defining the length of adolescence and the degree of turbulence in the transition to adulthood. The chapter closes with a discussion of the question of whether there are true universal stages of development in adulthood.

Discussion Topics

1. *Attachment.*   The text describes the great importance of the young offspring's early attachment to the mother (or other caregiver) in animals and humans. There is good reason to believe that failure to form such an attachment or its disruption has adverse effects. The question is whether these effects—as indeed any adverse effects of early experience—are irreversible. It is widely believed, by both laypersons and various psychological theorists (especially psychoanalysts)—that such early experiences are extremely difficult if not impossible to reverse. But is this really true? The text discusses this question at some length (see pp. 529-34), and it may be a good starting point for further classroom discussion.

For some relevant material see the following:

Clark, A. M., and Clark, A. D. B. 1976. *Early experience: Myth and evidence.* New York: Free Press. A series of papers that question the all-importance of early experience in humans.

Moltz, H. 1960. Imprinting: Empirical basis and theoretical significance. *Psychological Bulletin* 57:291-314; Bateson, P. P. G. 1979. When do sensitive periods arise and what are they for? *Animal Behavior* 27:470–86. Both bear on the question of whether imprinting is reversible.

2. *What can we conclude from studies on the effects of different forms of child rearing?* The text considers the effects of different child-rearing patterns on subsequent personality development (see pp. 539–41). Most of our evidence comes from correlational studies. These studies are usually in the following form:

Situation A: The interaction of parents and children are observed in one condition and rated (say, for the degree to which the parents are strict and auto-cratic).

Situation B: The children are observed in a different situation, away from their parents (say, when playing with other children).

Situation C: Ideally, the children are observed some years later (for example, in interactions with their peers).

Suppose the results show clear-cut correlations. For sake of argument, let's assume that (1) the stricter the parents are as rated in Situation A, the more aggressive are the children as rated in Situation B, and (2) the more aggressive the children are as rated in Situation B, the more aggressive they will be when rated years later in Situation C. Does this allow us to conclude that parental strictness leads to aggressiveness which then persists for years later?

What methodological questions can be raised about the way strictness or aggression is rated? What other conclusions could be drawn from this kind of evidence? What are some of the factors the psychologist has to keep in mind when interpreting results of this sort?

3. *Is there a difference in male and female moral development?* According to Carol Gilligan, Kohlberg's analysis of moral reasoning misses an important point (Gilligan, 1982). In her view, the moral reasoning of men and women cannot be properly compared by using the same scale and the same items because women approach moral issues from a different perspective than men do. She argues that female morality springs from different childhood experiences which emphasize connectedness to others. This connectedness leads women to judge the moral value of an action according to the effect that action has on people. In contrast, men grow up with a sense of their separateness, which leads them to devise systems of social rules to reconcile the inevitable conflicts that must arise between themselves and other, separate, persons. As a result, they judge the moral value of an action by how it fits in with a broad social rule.

To what extent can Gilligan's argument be maintained? The data suggest that the difference is by no means as great as she had maintained, for when educational and class differences are controlled, men and women score pretty much the same on Kohlberg's test. (See Damon, W. 1983. *Social and personality development.* New York: Norton.) But her position is very stimulating even so, and it may lead to interesting class discussion. (See Gilligan, C. 1982. *In a different voice.* Cambridge, Mass.: Harvard University Press.)

4. *What do various aspects of development have in common?* By now, the text has dealt with all facets of development: physical and motor development (Chapter 13), cognitive development (Chapter 14), the development of language (Chapter 15), and social development (Chapter 16). To what extent are these different aspects of human development interrelated? A number of theorists believe that at least some of them are intimately intertwined. According to Piaget, cognitive development is a continuation of the development of motor reactions, for as we have seen, according to Piaget, thought grows out of internalized action (see pp. 470–71). In addition, Piaget's approach involves concepts that are social by their very nature; an example is egocentrism (p. 475). Another theorist who regards cognitive and social development as interrelated is Kohlberg, for his (as well as Piaget's) interpretations of imitation, moral development, and the development of gender identity are tied up with his views of the child's developing cognitive capacity (pp. 538–39, 545–47, 557). On the other hand, these issues are by no means settled, for other theorists suspect that there are different domains of human thought and action that are at least partially independent and governed by different laws; for example, language and thought. (See Fodor, J. 1983. *The modularity of mind.* Cambridge, Mass.: Bradford Press.)

Such questions cannot be settled in an introductory course (nor any further course, no matter how advanced it may be), for they are still a matter of continuing debate. But they should provide material for an interesting discussion.

Demonstration

Sex stereotypes. There is no doubt that men and women are perceived to be different in many psychological regards, many of which, at least on the face of them, seem to have little to do with the biological distinctions between the sexes (see text, pp. 548–55). A number of demonstrations will make the same point.

(1) One is to ask the students to rate themselves on a number of adjectives. For each adjective, they are to indicate how descriptive this is of them by using a 5-point scale, in which 1 means "virtually never," 2 means "rarely," 3 means "sometimes," 4 means "often," and 5 means "very often or always." The adjectives are listed below (they are adapted from Bem's androgyny scale). Read the adjectives aloud and ask the students merely to note their number and to place the rating next to it:

1. self-reliant
2. yielding
3. defends own beliefs
4. cheerful
5. independent
6. shy

7. athletic
8. affectionate
9. assertive
10. easily flattered
11. competitive
12. loyal

13. analytical	19. makes decisions easily
14. sympathetic	20. compassionate
15. forceful	21. self-sufficient
16. sensitive to others' needs	22. gullible
17. willing to take risks	23. dominant
18. understanding	24. soft-spoken

To score the list, simply ask the students to add up their scores on all the odd-numbered items and all the even-numbered items separately. Then ask them to substract the odd-item sum from the even-item sum. The results will indicate some differences in how the two sexes perceive themselves. All the odd items are adjectives that tend to be applied more to males than to females; the reverse is true for the even items. A show of hands will demonstrate whether this holds for the members of the class by indicating whether the women show a difference in favor of the even items, the men for the odd items.

(2) The preceding demonstration shows how the subjects perceive themselves. Another demonstration will get at how they see men and women in general. Use the same adjectives with the same rating scale, but ask the subjects to rate how each adjective describes "men in general" and "women in general." Each subject will therefore give two ratings for each of the adjectives. This permits a number of interesting comparisons. (a) We can ask whether there is a tendency to exaggerate sex differences when subjects try to describe "men in general" or "women in general." To test whether this is so, ask the subjects to add up the odd-item sums and the even-item sums as they did before and to compute the difference between them. Is this difference larger than it was before, when the subjects rated themselves rather than men and women in general? (b) Another question is whether this tendency to exaggerate sex differences—assuming it exists—is greater for men than women. We might ask how women rate men, how men rate women, how they rate themselves. This is done simply by looking at the results separately for the two sexes. Do women rate men the way men rate themselves as a group? How about men rating women, compared with women rating themselves?

(3) A third demonstration of sex stereotyping does not involve an experiment. It merely requires a walk to a drugstore that sells birthday cards. Ask several students to look at birthday cards entitled "To a baby boy" and "To a baby girl" and report on the different themes in the cards.

The preceding demonstrations show that men and women perceive themselves differently and have certain broad stereotypes of men and women in general. But are these alleged differences really there? Some probably are; others are most likely fictions. If some turn out not to be there (for example, the famed intuition of women), then one might ask how and why the stereotype ever arose.

The next question concerns such differences as actually exist. It is probably true enough that—on the average—men are more assertive than are women. But if so, why is this true? As so often, we are again faced with another facet of the nature-nurture controversy. Are men constitutionally more assertive (on the average) than women, and if so, why? Is the effect cultural or learned? If so, what leads to such cultural patterns?

There are no pat answers to any of these questions. They involve serious social and political issues. They also raise difficult questions of psychological fact and theory. For some useful source material, see the following:

Maccoby, E. E., and Jacklin, C. N. 1974. *The psychology of sex differences.* Stanford: Stanford University Press. This provides an authoritative review of what differences have and have not been found in a large number of relevant studies as well as a discussion of their possible sources.

Maccoby, E. E., ed. 1966. *The development of sex differences.* Stanford: Stanford University Press. A good collection of papers on the subject.

Selected Readings

GENERAL WORKS

Money, J., and Ehrhardt, A. A. 1972. *Man and woman, boy and girl.* Baltimore: Johns Hopkins University Press. A fascinating account of the biological and social factors that determine gender role and gender identity, much of it based on the authors' studies of children born as hermaphrodites who were then surgically and hormonally turned into persons whose outer sex did not correspond to their chromosomes.

CLASSICS

Bandura, A., and Walters, R. H. 1963. *Social learning and personality development.* New York: Holt, Rinehart and Winston. The classic statement of the social learning position.

Kohlberg, L. 1966. A cognitive developmental analysis of children's sex-role concepts and attitudes. In Maccoby, E. E., ed. *The development of sex differences*, pp. 82–171. Stanford: Stanford University Press. One of the best illustrations of the cognitive developmental approach to socialization, applied to the problem of sex-role acquisition.

REFERENCE WORKS

Barnouw, V. 1963. *Culture and personality.* Homewood, Ill.: Dorsey Press. A good, if somewhat dated, review of the work on the relations between culture and personality from the pioneering studies of Benedict, Malinowski, and Mead to more contemporary approaches.

Cairns, R. B. 1979. *Social development.* San Francisco: Freeman. A text that emphasizes the biological aspects of social development.

Damon, W. 1983. *Social and personality development.* New York: Norton. A good undergraduate text that considers social development from its origin in infancy to its later stages in adolescence.

Flavell, J. H., and Ross, L., eds. 1981. *Social and cognitive development.* New York: Cambridge University Press. A collection of papers that deal with the relations between cognitive and social growth.

Maccoby, E. E. 1980. *Social development.* New York: Harcourt Brace Jovanovich. A well-organized discussion of the child's social development, with particular emphasis on the parent-child relationship.

Williams, J. H., ed. 1985. *Psychology of women: Selected readings*, 2nd ed. New York: Norton. A collection of readings on the topic of sex roles and their relation to psychology.

Zigler, E. F., Lamb, M. E., and Child, I. L. 1982. *Socialization and personality development*, 2nd ed. New York: Oxford University Press. A good, concise review of facts and theories in the field of socialization. It also includes a dozen important research papers in the area.

CHAPTER 17

Intelligence: Its Nature and Measurement

Overview

The previous chapters have been primarily concerned with the nature of humankind, not with particular men and women. In the next four chapters, the emphasis changes. The concern is now with individual differences as a topic in its own right.

The present chapter discusses the differences in cognitive ability, in what is usually called intelligence. The chapter begins by asking how mental tests in general (and intelligence tests in particular) are constructed, and once constructed, how they are evaluated. It then turns to the much more difficult question of what the psychological processes are that underlie differences in intelligence performance.

The last topic is intelligence-test performance considered in light of the nature-nurture controversy. This last section of the chapter first asks to what extent one can attribute differences in such test performance to genetic rather than to environmental factors. It concludes by considering group differences in intelligence-test performance, such as those found between American blacks and whites.

Summary of the Main Topics

MENTAL TESTS

The chapter begins with a brief discussion of the basic phenomenon that underlies the study of individual differences—variability. To explain what this really means requires some elementary concepts of statistics such as frequency distribution, mean, variance, normal curve, and correlation. This primer in statistics lays the groundwork for discussing mental tests in general and intelligence tests in particular.

The text then turns to the general topic of assessing psychological traits or capacities on which people differ by the use of mental tests. Among the topics dealt with are the ways in which tests are constructed, evaluated, and standardized. Special attention is paid to the indices that measure a test's effectiveness—reliability and validity.

The text then turns to an important application of some tests—as selection devices. All such selections will depend upon the choice of a cutoff score below which applicants will be rejected. How this cutoff score is chosen depends in part on the relation between the test and the criterion, and also on the payoff matrix that determines the cost of different kinds of errors.

INTELLIGENCE TESTING

In this section, the text describes various steps in the development of intelligence tests from Binet's work with children to Wechsler's adult scales to various group tests. It describes diverse measures: from mental age (MA) to intelligence quotient (IQ, as a ratio of mental age to chronological age) and deviation IQ. It finally turns to an important area of application—mental retardation.

THE NATURE OF INTELLIGENCE

After reiterating the difficulty in determining what intelligence is, the text considers the psychometric approach as a possible way to discover an answer. The results of intelligence tests reveal certain patterns that can tell us something about the structure of mental abilities, for example, whether intelligence is one unitary ability or is composed of several abilities that are unrelated. Analyses of this kind have led to two main theories of the structure of intelligence: (1) Spearman's view that there is one general intellectual factor and (2) group-factor theory's view that there are several different capabilities that compose intelligence.

The relation between intelligence-test performance and age is the next topic. Studies of intelligence in later life suggest that for some—though not all—facets of test performance there is a drop after middle age. Several authors believe that there is an important distinction between two kinds of intellectual abilities —fluid intelligence, which declines with age, and crystallized intelligence, which does not.

While these psychometric considerations tell us something about the structure of intelligence, they do not speak to the processes which underlie intelligence. In an attempt to address this issue, a number of information-processing theorists have begun to look for correlations between differences in people's ability to perform various cognitive operations and performance on intelligence tests. The cognitive correlates approach has concentrated on simple cognitive abilities, such as the speed with which one can look up something in memory. Other investigators have attempted to relate intelligence-test performance to higher-order cognitive components like analogical reasoning. A third information-processing approach has attempted to explain differences in intellectual functioning in terms of differences in the use of various cognitive strategies. Retarded people and young children, for example, are less likely than normal adults to rehearse and organize material they want to remember. Such attempts to understand the processes underlying intelligence are still tentative, however, and we are still far from having a general theory of intelligence.

HEREDITY, ENVIRONMENT, AND IQ

The chapter next turns to one of the most vehemently debated facets of the nature-nurture controversy: the relative contribution of hereditary and environmental factors in determining differences in intelligence-test performance. It takes up certain prerequisites to this discussion such as methods for assessing the role of genetic factors, and the concept of heritability. It then looks at the evidence for a genetic contribution to within-group differences in intelligence-test performance, concluding that the evidence indicates that such a genetic contribution does exist. It finally ends with a discussion of between-group differences, focusing on IQ differences between American whites and blacks. A key point in this discussion is that differences that exist *within* groups may have quite different causes from differences that exist *between* groups. The chapter ends by observing that while the evidence is not as yet conclusive, it tilts toward an environmental interpretation of between-group differences.

Discussion Topics

1. *Reliability and validity.* Students may get a better understanding of the meaning of these two crucial terms if they think of two situations.

(a) One is the case when the test has excellent reliability but poor validity. Is the test useful? This case is discussed in the text, and the answer is pretty obvious. The test may be useful for something but not for whatever it is supposed to measure. Consider a yardstick, measuring inches from head to toe. Is it a useful test? It surely is a fine test of height. But it obviously is a poor test (in fact, an absurd test) of, say, mechanical aptitude. It will not correlate with, say, success in a training program for machinists. Thus, if validity is low, a test is useless to measure that characteristic, no matter how high its reliability may be.

(b) What about the reverse case? Suppose a test of, say, mechanical aptitude has low reliability. Can it have high validity? Here the answer is no. For it turns out that the validity of a test can never be higher than its reliability. The reason is that both reliability and validity (at least, predictive validity) are ultimately correlation coefficients. The validity coefficient of a test is its correlation with some validity criterion (e.g., the correlation between the test score and performance in a school for machinists). The reliability coefficient of a test is also a correlation, specifically, the correlation of a test with itself (e.g., a test-retest correlation, in which one correlates the test scores obtained by the same person when the same test is taken twice). We now refer to a simple rule of test construction, namely, that a test cannot correlate with any other index any better than it can correlate with itself. But if so, validity (which is a correlation between a test and some external criterion) cannot be greater than reliability (which is the correlation between the test and itself). As a result, a test of zero reliability cannot have more than zero validity.

2. *The nature–nurture controversy as it applies to intelligence testing.* The nature–nurture controversy is a continuing thread that runs through many of the topics discussed in this book: sensory processes, perception, language and language acquisition, motor and cognitive development and certain aspects of human socialization, especially where it concerns Freud's theories (that is, Chapters 5, 6, 9, 12, 13, 14, and 15). We run up against it once again in the present chapter, where we consider heredity and environment as they affect performance on intelligence tests. But it cannot be emphasized too strongly that it has some different implications in this present context. (Some were already mentioned in previous discussion topics of this manual, for example, in Discussion Topic 1, in Chapter 5.) Two major differences should be mentioned:

(a) One is that the nature-nurture debate in the realm of testing concerns differences between people rather than aspects of psychological functioning that concern all human beings. When psychologists ask whether, say, the perception of form is learned or innately given, they ask whether experience or built-in structures are responsible for the fact that all sighted adults (whose brain is intact) see circles and triangles—they are not discussing individual differences at all. Or if they debate the nature-nurture issue in the field of language, they are asking whether there are some innate, species-specific characteristics that allow virtually all human beings to speak (or sign) and comprehend at an early age. In short, in all the preceding discussions, the question was not what accounts for the differences between people. It was rather what caused certain characteristics that they all share (e.g., form perception, language), whether these samenesses are produced by a common human endowment or by a common environment. The issue is very different when we turn to the nature-nurture issue in the context of intelligence testing. For here the question concerns the factors that make for *differences* between people. It is therefore perfectly possible to be a nativist in the realm of perception or language and accept the "nurture" position of the nature-nurture controversy when discussing differences in intelligence-test performance.

(b) A second point relates to the fact that discussions of such individual differences concern differences that exist in *populations.* The debate about the relative contribution of heredity and environment in the context of intelligence testing (that is, the heritability of IQ) concerns the relative contribution of these factors in a given population. Suppose we look at six sextuplets and ask about the differences in their IQ. Here, the heritability is necessarily zero—whatever differences exist have to be due to environmental factors, since all six have the same genes. Conversely, if we imagine a population in which every person had

the identical environment from birth on, then the heritability must be 1.00—
it has to be since there are no environmental variations.

3. *Methodological problems in determining the relative contributions of heredity and environment to IQ differences.*   The text discusses twin studies and
studies of adopted children as methods for estimating the role of genetic factors
and takes up some of the methodological problems with these methods. The following material is a further discussion of these problems:

(a) Twin studies. (1) Can we be sure that the twins are really identical or
fraternal? There are ways of assessing this objectively, such as looking at blood
types, but not all studies have done an adequate job of checking this out. (2)
Can we be sure that environmental factors are the same for identical and fraternal twins? The usual belief is that they are—after all, they were born at the same
time, etc. But one can argue that identical twins are much more similar in the
environment they encounter than are fraternal twins. After all, identical twins
look alike and are therefore treated more equivalently. This point is hard to re-
fute, though some attempts in this direction have been made (see p. 602). One
possible way of dealing with it is to look at identical twins reared apart compared to such twins reared together, but these studies face still different problems (e.g., whether the environments of the reared-apart twins are all that
different).

(b) Adoptive children. Here, an important criticism concerns selective place-
ment. The adoption agency (which knows who the child's biological mother is)
generally tries to place the child with adoptive parents whose background resembles that of the biological mother. This criticism has difficulty explaining why
the correlation between child and biological parent should be greater than that
between child and adoptive parent, but a number of statistical arguments can be
raised even so.

The text has tried to weave a path through these complicated methodological
issues and tried to reach the most plausible conclusion on the data available.
Nevertheless, there is still considerable room for argument.

(For a discussion of these matters, written from a strongly environmentalist
bias, see Kamin, L. 1974. *The science and politics of IQ.* New York: Wiley.
Perhaps the most vehement debate yet published on the topic is that between
Leon Kamin, a thorough-going environmentalist, and H. J. Eysenck, a no less
thorough-going hereditarian. See Eysenck, H. J. versus Kamin, L. *The intelligence controversy.* 1981. New York: Wiley.)

Demonstration

Positive and zero correlation.   To provide two quick examples of correlation,
one positive, the other zero, two relations will be determined: that between a

person's weight and his height, and that between his own weight and the height of a classroom neighbor.

The first step is to ask all students to get a partner (the person next to them or in front of them). The members of each partnership pair will then exchange information about each other's height.

After this is done, the experimenter determines the class medians for height and weight. This is a simple procedure, requiring shows of hands to "Are you above 5′5″?" "Are you below 5′ 5″?" "Are you above 5′6″?" and so on, until the number of persons above and below the number seem about equal. This done, each student classifies himself according to the outline below.

The first classification concerns his (or her) own weight and own height:

A: above class median for height, below median for weight
B: above class median for height, above median for weight
C: below class median for height, below median for weight
D: below class median for height, above median for weight

A simple show of hands will indicate how many students are in each of the four categories here described. These can now be tabulated in a simple 2 × 2 table. An example of a likely outcome is shown below:

	below in weight	above in weight
above in height	5	15
below in height	15	5

This hypothetical result indicates a positive correlation: by and large, people who are taller than average will also be heavier than average, while people who are shorter than average will also weigh less than average. All positive correlations show this pattern: by and large, there will be more people in the so-called ++ and - - cells (that is, above average on both measures, or below average on both measures) than in the +- and -+ cells. In the negative correlation, the reverse is true. Here, more cases will be found in the +- and -+ cells than in the other two, for a negative correlation means that an increase in one variable goes along with a decrease in the other.

The final step is to show the pattern for a zero correlation. Here, the scatter diagram is a circle (see Chapter 17, p. 575). The result is that the number of cases in the ++ and - - cells will be just about equal to those in the +- and -+ cells. There simply is no relationship between the variables such that being above the mean in one has anything to do with being above the mean in the other variable.

To demonstrate this, ask the students to classify themselves once more using the previous categories A, B, C, and D, but with one difference. This time they are to use their *own* weight and their *partner's* height. Thus a classification of "A" now means "above the class median for my *neighbor's* height, below the class median for my *own* weight," and so on. By going through the same procedures as before, we again end up with a 2 × 2 tabulation. In all likelihood, this will now show virtually no correlation. There may be some bias in classroom seating patterns (perhaps tall and heavy people tend to sit together with other tall and heavy people), but this is unlikely to be very strong.

Selected Readings

GENERAL WORKS
Francher, R. E. 1979. *Pioneers of psychology.* New York: Norton, especially pp. 250–96. (Already mentioned in Chapters 2, 5, and 6.) See the chapter on Francis Galton and the psychology of individual differences, which forms the historical background to the study of mental testing.

REFERENCES TO MENTAL TESTING AND INTELLIGENCE
Butcher, H. J. 1973. *Human intelligence: Its nature and assessment.* London: Methuen. Readable, sound paperback text.

Cronbach, L. J. 1970. *Essentials of psychological testing*, 3rd ed. New York: Harper & Row. An authoritative text on all branches of mental testing.

Resnick, L. B., ed. 1976. *The nature of intelligence.* Hillsdale, N.J.: Erlbaum. An excellent collection of papers on the possible nature of human intelligence.

Sternberg, R. J. 1977. *Intelligence, information processing and analogical reasoning.* New York: Wiley. A difficult but important book that shows how the author's "componential approach" might be applied to one particular intellectual task, analogical reasoning.

Sternberg, R. J., ed. 1982. *Handbook of human intelligence.* New York: Cambridge University Press. A compendium featuring papers on virtually all aspects of intelligence by many of the major figures now working in the field.

REFERENCES TO INTELLIGENCE AND THE NATURE-NURTURE ISSUE
Block, N. J., and Dworkin, G., eds. 1976. *The IQ controversy.* New York: Pantheon Books. A paperback collection of a number of articles on the IQ controversy, ending with an important summary article by the editors.

Jensen, A. R. 1969. How much can we boost I.Q. and scholastic achievement? *Harvard Educational Review* 39:1–123. (Reprinted in *Environment, heredity and intelligence*, a monograph which can be obtained from the Harvard Educational Review.) This is the widely debated Jensen report which added new fuel to the nature-nurture controversy, especially as it pertained to IQ differences between American blacks and whites.

Kamin, L. J. 1974. *The science and politics of I.Q.* New York: Wiley. A sharp attack on the assertion that IQ is to a great extent inheritable, together with an analysis of the social and political views that led to a bias in this direction. This is an important and controversial book.

Leohlin, J. D., Lindzey, G., and Spuhler, J. N. 1975. *Race differences in intelligence.* San Francisco: Freeman. A good, comprehensive paperback review and discussion of the evidence which is as balanced and objective as one could possibly hope for, considering the controversial nature of the issues. The best overall treatment of the topic currently available.

CHAPTER 18

Personality Assessment

Overview

Whereas the preceding chapter concerned differences in cognitive abilities, the present one asks how one can assess differences in personality. The chapter considers the major methods for assessing personality traits and asks whether such traits are essentially constant over time and across situations.

Summary of the Main Topics

METHODS OF ASSESSMENT

This chapter takes up two major approaches to the problem of describing and assessing different personalities. First, it takes up several structured and objective tests: the Minnesota Multiphasic Personality Inventory (MMPI) and the California Psychological Inventory (CPI). The MMPI assesses the degree of correspondence between a person's responses and those of a criterion group made up of psychiatric patients distinguished on the basis of diagnostic category. The CPI uses normal persons as criterion groups. The logic underlying the internal construction of both MMPI and CPI is discussed, as are their predictive validity and construct validity.

A second approach to assessing personality is by way of projective tests, such as the Rorschach inkblot test and the Thematic Apperception Test (TAT). Unlike objective tests, these tests are said to have the advantage of tapping personality attributes of which the subject himself may be unaware. The text considers their validity as well as an additional measure, their incremental validity.

TRAITS VERSUS SITUATIONS

Neither of the above approaches has fared too well in validity studies. One reason may be that what the tests are trying to assess—a set of stable personality traits—just isn't there. The discussion of this disquieting possibility is the next major topic of the chapter. It takes up Walter Mischel's critique of trait theory, considers an extreme alternative, situationism, and turns to an intermediate view which stresses trait-situation interaction. The evidence indicates that there is indeed something constant about the way an individual behaves, and to this extent the concept of personality differences is upheld. What is missing is a set of categories according to which different personalities can be classified, to indicate which person can be categorized along with others whose behavior is in some respects equivalent.

THE SEARCH FOR A TAXONOMY

This introduces the final theme of the chapter: the search for an adequate taxonomy of personality attributes. A number of efforts toward this end are described, including factor-analytic approaches (e.g., Cattell's trait terms or Eysenck's neuroticism and extraversion-introversion dimensions) and classifications based on biological considerations (e.g., Sheldon's somatotypes).

Discussion Topics

1. *Projective techniques.* The driving force behind the development and acceptance of projective techniques has been psychoanalytic thinking. Since psychoanalysis began with the premise that much of what we are we hide from our very selves, its practitioners were obviously disinclined to accept methods of assessment (such as the MMPI) that were based on a person's self-evaluation. They preferred some method that could peer behind the veil of self-deception that the person had drawn around him. The basic idea is that you have to have an ambiguous situation that will circumvent these defenses and the projective techniques were thought to be that.

The question is whether the tests really perform the function they were meant to: whether they really penetrate the person's mask (even assuming that he has one, as Freud supposed). And to evaluate this, one needs some means of assessing these tests' validity. (Let's assume the reliability is acceptable.) We can't simply take a given clinical practitioner's word for it. Many will say, "It works for me." But this proves little. For all we know, clinicians are as capable of self-delusion as their patients are. Or perhaps the test helps a particular clinician interpret his interview better than he would have without it—but the way it helps is idiosyncratic to him and may not be easily communicated to others. If so, we are still left with a clinical tool, but not with a test that can be evaluated.

The ultimate answer has to be some kind of validity test. The most obvious is some index of predictive validity, though it's by no means clear just what the validity criterion should be. Should it be a psychiatric interview? Behavior as judged by friends and family? And so on. Nor is it clear that a moderate predictive validity coefficient is adequate. As some clinicians point out (see pp. 620-

21) what we really want is incremental validity—some increase in our ability to predict that goes over and above the various interviews that have to be performed anyway, at least in clinical practice.

(For further discussion, see Sundberg, N. D. 1977. *Assessment of persons.* New York: Prentice-Hall, Chapter 9, on projective techniques.)

2. *Other methods of assessment.*   The primary focus of the text is on assessment methods using personality tests. But there are other ways of assessment that have been utilized. One concerns the basic identifying data (they are sometimes called "face sheet data" to indicate what would be on the top sheet of the patient's case record). These would include personality tests. It might be worth discussing the importance of certain other data as they bear on assessment. Among these are the basic identifying data about the person: sex, age, occupation, education, marital status, and (in the case of patients) reasons for referral. They also include data provided by the case history: the basic life history, its major crises, etc. The evidence to date suggests that just knowing the minimal identifying data allows one to make more predictions than anything else. If we also add the case history, then various personality tests add little more incremental validity.

Why are the basic identifying data (the basic facts that one might tell a census taker, plus a bit of one's history) so very important in predicting later behavior? One argument is that they say much about the overall social situation in which a person finds himself—his income, his home, his fellow workers, and so on—and these have much to do with the way we behave, a point raised insistently by Mischel (see text, pp. 621–23). For further discussion of these matters, see the following sources:

Kostlan, A. 1954. A method for the empirical study of psychodiagnosis. *Journal of Consulting Psychology* 18:83–88. This article shows that basic identifying data are most important in predicting judges' descriptions of the patients.

Potkay, C. R. 1973. The role of personal history data in clinical judgment: A selective focus. *Journal of Personality Assessment* 37:203–13. This article says that personal history data are at least as effective as materials derived from psychological tests.

Sundberg 1977, Chapters 3 and 4.

3. *Lying scales on personality inventories.*   Objective personality tests such as the MMPI are sometimes attacked on the grounds that one can fake anything one wants to, since the tests are self-inventories in which a person answers questions about himself. Who is to stop him from lying—from making himself appear either more or less personally adjusted than he actually is? The text describes some of the attempts to meet these objections in the construction of the MMPI— the development of several validity scales which give an indication of how well the person can be trusted (see p. 614). For further discussion see the following:

McKinley, J. C., Hathaway, S. R., and Meehl, P. E. 1948. The MMPI. VI. The K scale. *Journal of Consulting Psychology* 12:20–31.

Sundberg 1977, pp. 181–86.

Yonge, G. D. 1966. Certain consequences of applying the K factor to **MMPI** scores. *Educational and Psychological Measurement* 26:887–93.

Demonstration

Beliefs in the relation between body build and personality. The text discusses some of the controversies that surrounded Sheldon's particular hypotheses about the relation between body types and personality (see Chapter 18, pp. 632–34). Sheldon's original claims were certainly overstated, but there may nevertheless be a core of truth to the general notion.

Whether the notion is correct or not, there is little doubt that people believe that it is. A demonstration of this phenomenon is described below, but the demonstration requires that students *have not yet* read Chapter 18. It might be worth doing on the first day of class.

The demonstration is as follows: The students are asked to make judgments about the personality traits of three persons, A, B, and C, shown below (who correspond to the somatotypes of extreme endomorphy, mesomorphy, and ectomorphy, respectively).

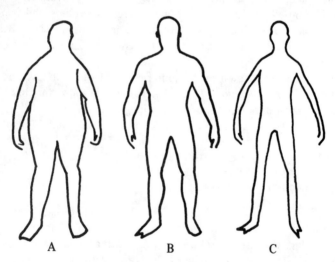

A   B   C

(These are presented on a slide, overhead projector, or a mimeographed stencil for handouts.)

The instructions are as follows: "Here are three silhouetted male persons, A, B, and C. I am going to read you a number of personal characteristics. Your job is to decide to which of the three the characteristic most likely applies. Do this by numbering each characteristic as I read it, then writing an A, B, or C next to it. Try to guess, but if you can't decide, indicate with an *X*. Are you ready?"

The list of characteristics follows. After each of them is the answer that would follow from Sheldon's system.

1. loves polite ceremony (A)
2. self-assertive (B)
3. troubled sleep, generally fatigued (C)
4. overly fast in his reactions (C)
5. insensitive to other persons' feelings (B)
6. sociable (A)
7. takes risks (B)
8. always wants affection and approval (A)
9. prefers to be alone (C)
10. when troubled, wants to act (B)
11. socially inhibited (C)
12. slow to react (A)
13. energetic (B)
14. self-conscious (C)
15. loves comfort (A)

A simple way of scoring the results is to tell the subjects the answer Sheldon would have expected. Ask the students to score their agreement with Sheldon by indicating a + whenever their judgment fit his, and a − whenever it did not. Then ask them to tally their total number of pluses. A score of 5 is chance; a class mean much above this suggests either (a) that Sheldon's or some similar view is correct or (b) that there are popular stereotypes that, correct or not, fit Sheldon's view and that these are held by many persons.

(For further discussion see Hall, C. S., and Lindzey, G. 1978. *Theories of personality*, 3rd ed. New York: Wiley. Chapter 13, pp. 477–522.)

Selected Readings

REFERENCE WORKS

Cronbach, L. J. 1970. *Essentials of psychological testing*, 3rd ed. New York: Harper & Row. (Already mentioned in Chapter 17.) An authoritative general account of the principles of test construction and test evaluation in all areas where mental tests are employed.

Feshbach, S., and Weiner, G. 1982. *Personality.* Lexington, Mass.: Heath. A good, readable undergraduate text in personality with good discussions of personality assessment and the trait-situation controversy.

Hall, C. S., and Lindzey, G. 1978. *Theories of personality*, 3rd ed. New York: Harper and Row. (Already mentioned in Chapter 12.) The classic book on the subject, with good chapters on the factor-analytic approach (using Raymond Cattell's version of that approach as an illustration) and Sheldon's somatotype theory.

Mischel, W. 1968. *Personality and assessment.* New York: Wiley. A provocative book which raised the possibility that there might be no such thing as stable personality traits.

Sundberg, N. D. 1977. *Assessment of persons.* New York: Prentice-Hall. A readable introduction to personality testing.

CHAPTER 19

Psychopathology

Overview

The preceding chapter looked at differences in human personality traits. The present chapter considers conditions in which the differences from the norm are so extreme, cause so much pain, and are so harmful to the individual and/or society, that they are regarded as pathological.

There are two main themes around which much of the discussion is organized. The first concerns the nature of mental illness itself, how it can be diagnosed, and the extent to which it can be regarded as a pathology—an underlying disturbance whose outer manifestations are various symptoms. A second theme concerns the origin (or causes) of such mental disorders, with particular attention to the extent to which they seem to be produced by psychological rather than biological factors.

A useful framework for discussing the origin of many mental disorders is the diathesis-stress conception, which holds that many of these (as well as many nonpsychiatric diseases) are produced by an interaction between some environmental stress and a predisposition (which may be genetic) toward the disorder. Here, as in the next chapter, the text incorporates the terminology of DSM-III, the most recent diagnostic manual of the psychiatric profession.

Summary of the Main Topics

DIFFERENT CONCEPTIONS OF MADNESS

The chapter begins with a brief, historical survey of different conceptions of madness: insanity as demonic possession, as a condition requiring incarceration, and as a disease that may be somatogenic or psychogenic.

THE PATHOLOGY MODEL

The chapter then presents an outline of what is here called the pathology model. As the term is used in the text, this model holds that most mental disorders can be analyzed in much the manner in which diseases in general can be analyzed, and this quite apart from any decisions about the somatogenic or psychogenic nature of the condition. In terms of this pathology model, symptoms are regarded as the outer manifestations of an underlying cause (the pathology), which in turn is determined by more remote causes such as hereditary predispositions (diatheses) and environmental precipitating factors (stressors).

There are a number of different approaches to psychopathology that can usually be regarded as subcategories of the pathology model (as the term is employed in the text). One is the medical model, which assumes that the underlying pathology is organic. Another is the psychoanalytic model, which assumes that the symptoms are psychogenic and that the underlying pathology is a constellation of unconscious conflicts typically rooted in early childhood experience. Yet another is the learning model, which sees the underlying pathology as some form of maladaptive learning.

The next topics constitute the bulk of the chapter: the descriptions of the major forms of psychopathology. Each of these disorders is described within the framework of the pathology model. In some cases (e.g., schizophrenia), the most probable underlying pathology—as it appears today—seems to be organic. In other cases (e.g., phobias), the underlying pathology seems to be psychological.

SCHIZOPHRENIA

The first major disorder taken up is schizophrenia. Its main symptoms are disorders of thought and attention, social withdrawal, disruption of emotional responding, and in some cases, the construction of a private world accompanied by delusions and hallucinations.

One question about the pathology is how best to characterize the schizophrenic's underlying psychological malfunction. Many authors believe that it is fundamentally a disorder of thought, based on an inability to focus mentally in space and time. A different question concerns the cause of this psychological deficit. This is widely believed to be an expression of an organic pathology. Evidence comes from studies which show that the incidence of what appears to be schizophrenia is roughly the same in different cultures, from genetic studies which show that it has a substantial heredity component, and from the fact that a certain class of drugs, the phenothiazines, have a specific therapeutic effect on schizophrenic symptoms.

AFFECTIVE DISORDERS

Schizophrenia appears to be a disorder of thought. Affective disorders, on the other hand, are characterized by a disturbance in a person's mood. Here, the text takes up mania and depression. Affective disorders may be bipolar, with recurrent swings from one emotional extreme to the other, or unipolar, in which the mood extreme is of one kind only, generally depression. According to one view, affective disorders, especially the bipolar ones, are produced by an organic pathology, a belief bolstered by evidence that such conditions have a genetic component. One hypothesis has it that there is a defect in the supply of certain neurotransmitters, perhaps norepinephrine and/or serotonin. Other investigators stress the role of psychogenic factors, such as cognitive outlook, especially in cases of reactive depression. An influential example of a psychogenic approach is the learned helplessness theory of depression.

ANXIETY DISORDERS

In some mental disorders both the symptoms and the underlying pathology appear to be psychological rather than organic. Among disorders of this kind (which formerly were all grouped together under the collective label "neuroses") are the anxiety disorders. This diagnostic category includes phobias, generalized anxiety disorders, and obsessive-compulsive disorders. In all of these disorders, extreme anxiety figures prominently, but the way in which it is manifested differs. In phobias, there is an irrational fear of some specific external object or event; in generalized anxiety disorder, the patient's anxiety is not focused on anything in particular but is all-pervasive; in obsessive-compulsive disorders, the patient's anxiety is aroused by some internally produced, irrational thought.

Practitioners with a psychoanalytic orientation believe that these various disorders are behavioral manifestations of defense mechanisms that are meant to ward off intolerable anxiety brought on by unconscious conflict; in their view, the defenses are typically inadequate so that some of the anxiety breaks through anyway. (See also Chapter 12 for a more detailed discussion of the psycho-analytic interpretation of such disorders.) In contrast, behavior therapists follow the general approach of behavior theory (see Chapter 4) and believe that such disorders are produced by various conditioned fear reactions. Despite these different orientations, there is general agreement that the anxiety disorders are largely based on stressful learning experiences in the individual's past.

CONVERSIONS AND DISSOCIATIVE DISORDERS

There is another group of disorders in which both symptoms and the under-lying pathology seem to be psychological rather than organic. These are con-versions and dissociative disorders. In conversion disorders (formerly called con-version hysteria), the patients develop what on the surface seems to be a bodily ailment but which on closer examination turns out not to be somatically genuine (for example, a patient with "paralyzed" legs who runs out of a hospital ward in a fire; see the discussion of hysteria in Chapter 12, pp. 414–15). In dissocia-tive disorders, the patients may develop psychogenic amnesia, fugues, or in extreme cases, multiple personalities. These disorders are as yet not clearly understood. Psychoanalysts regard them as defense reactions to unconscious conflict; behavior theorists believe they are conditioned reactions; yet others suspect that they represent some form of unconscious playacting.

PSYCHOPHYSIOLOGICAL DISORDERS
Psychophysiological disorders (psychosomatic disorders) are physical maladies (e.g., asthma, essential hypertension, ulcers) that have psychological origins. This section takes up essential hypertension and describes how it is brought about by the continued arousal of the sympathetic nervous system in people exposed to prolonged environmental stress. Diathesis and stress factors probably combine to determine which psychophysiological disorder, if any, a person will have.

THE SOCIOLOGICAL CRITIQUE OF THE PATHOLOGY MODEL
The chapter ends with a contemporary critique of the pathology model which takes a sociological perspective, arguing that the fact that disordered people are regarded as deviant is no less—and perhaps more—important than whatever disorder they may actually have. This orientation has led to labeling theory which, in one extreme version, asserts that mental illness is a myth. The chapter argues that while labeling may worsen a patient's condition, labeling theory has little to say about how that patient's condition arose in the first place and does little to alter the view that many mental disorders reflect genuine pathologies. But granting these reservations, labeling theory seems to have had some salutary effects, such as focusing attention on certain abuses, as in commitment procedures. It has also highlighted the problem of how psychopathology is to be defined. One example concerns conditions in which mental disorder and criminality overlap, as in antisocial personalities (formerly called "sociopaths").

Discussion Topics

1. *The idea of the madwoman as witch.* The text discusses various conceptions of madness held at different periods. Some simply reflect the level of scientific sophistication of the period. Others are an expression of broader social and cultural conditions of the time. An example is the notion of madness as a form of demonic possession and witchcraft. The text briefly describes the period of the witchcraft trials which claimed the lives of many deranged persons, as well as those of religious dissenters and of victims of an informer's malice and greed (see pp. 639-40). What is not mentioned is the enormous streak of pathology in the persecutors. It seems that some of the witch-hunters' persecution frenzy was fired by a fear of their own suppressed sexuality, which was then projected out upon the innocent females they accused. The extent to which the witch-hunters went to protect themselves against the devil—ever ready to use his female ally, the witch, to seduce and damn the faithful—defies description. The accused witch was shaved from head to toe, since the devil could hide in her hair; she had to face away from her interrogators lest they be tempted by seeing her from the front; and so on. The major treatise that prescribes the proper methods for deal-

ing with the poor women who were accused of witchcraft is an amazing document: a grotesque mixture of psychopathology (violent reaction formation and projection), hatred and fear of women, and simple pornography. (For more details, see Zilboorg, G., and Henry, G. 1941. *A history of medical psychology.* New York: Norton.)

2. *Changing fashions in psychopathology.*   The incidence of various forms of psychopathology appears to change over time. An example is conversion disorder (see this chapter, p. 670, and also Chapter 12, pp. 414–15). Various instances of this—psychogenic paralyses and sensory deficits—seemed to be fairly common in Charcot's Paris and Freud's Vienna during the latter part of the nineteenth century and its end. But these conditions are encountered much less frequently today. The exception is in less developed, usually more rural areas of the world, where they are still found rather often. The question is why.

(a) One possible explanation is a change in the social climate. Especially in urban, middle-class settings, the general attitude toward child rearing is more relaxed and much less prudish. That such a change has taken place is hard to deny. Attitudes toward toilet training are much less coercive than they used to be. The same holds even more strongly for reactions toward the child's expression of early sexuality. An example is the attitude toward masturbation, which was once held to be a major cause of insanity and was often severely punished and prevented by extreme measures of all kinds. (See Hare, E. H. 1962. Masturbatory insanity: The history of an idea. *Journal of Mental Science* 108:2-25.)

That there has been a change in social views on this and related matters is unquestionable. As a result, the repressive forces that psychoanalysts believe to underlie hysteria would not be as severe. The effect would be a decline in the numbers of persons suffering from conversion disorders and other related disorders. It would be pleasant to suppose that this decline is accompanied by a general decrease in the number of neurotically disturbed persons. But this is probably not so. Today's neuroses are not less numerous than they were in the days of Freud and Charcot; they are simply more subtle and elusive. They involve the entire character structure of the person rather than a set of particular symptoms—a general, and presumably maladaptive, way of coping, rather than a set of particular defense mechanisms that keep anxiety at bay. (For an interesting description along these lines, see Shapiro, D. 1965. *Neurotic styles.* New York: Basic Books. A Harper Torchbook paperback.)

(b) There may be an additional factor that accounts for the decline in the number of persons with conversion disorders. And that is simply an advance in the state of our general medical (especially neurological) knowledge. No doubt, there are some cases that are bona fide conversion reactions. But not all may be. For it is all too easy to say that a patient's complaints are "simply psychological" when we don't understand them in terms of organic pathology. It may well be that some of Charcot's and Freud's patients suffered from some neurological disorder, such as multiple sclerosis, whose full symptom patterns were not yet understood. These patients undoubtedly suffered from various emotional side effects and were therefore readily diagnosed as hysterics. Had the diagnosis been made fifty or a hundred years later, when much more was known about various organic conditions that might produce symptoms of the kind Freud and Charcot observed, the diagnosis might have been different. Some evidence in line with this view is provided by a study by Slater and Glithero of conversion reactions. Within nine years, 60 percent of these persons had died or developed various serious organic symptoms, usually of a neurological sort. Their earlier diagnosis as having conversion disorders was presumably a reflection of the fact that at the time their symptoms were still rather subtle and not yet recognized as an indication of the underlying organic illness. (See Slater, E., and Glithero, E. 1965. A follow-up of patients diagnosed as suffering from hysteria. *Journal of Psychosomatic Research* 9:9–13.)

3. *The essential psychological deficit in schizophrenia.* Most authors agree that one of the main characteristics of schizophrenia is a pervasive thought disorder. The best examples come from case histories. For examples, see the following: Bleuler, E. 1911. *Dementia praecox, or the group of schizophrenias.* English translation by Zinkin, J., and Lewis, N. D. C. New York: International Universities Press, 1950 (still a classic and the best source of case material). Rosenhan, D. L., and Seligman, M. E. P. 1984. *Abnormal psychology.* New York: Norton, pp. 463–504. White, R. W., and Watt, N. F. 1973. *The abnormal personality,* 4th ed. New York: Ronald Press, pp. 432–40, 449–54 (good case descriptions).

Additional material may be found in the following accounts and novels, though these stress emotional and interpersonal difficulties in addition to noting the odd thought patterns: Vonnegut, M. 1975. *The Eden express.* New York: Bantam Books (an autobiographical account that describes the illness so to speak, from within). Sechehaye, M. 1951. *Autobiography of a schizophrenic girl.* New York: Grune and Stratton. Greenberg, J. 1964. *I never promised you a rose garden.* New York: Holt, Rinehart and Winston (a Signet paperback novel).

What is the underlying feature of the thought disorder? A widely held view is that it is some inability to attend selectively and to maintain a set over some time period. Some examples are provided by the patients themselves, who report that they are "always taking in too much at the one time, and then . . . can't handle it and can't make sense of it" or that they simply "have too many thoughts . . . might think about something, let's say that ashtray and just think, oh! yes, that's for putting my cigarette in, but . . . would think of it and then . . . think of a dozen different things connected with it at the same time." (See McGhie, A., and Chapman, J. S. 1961. Disorders of attention and perception in early schizophrenia. *British Journal of Medical Psychology* 34:103–16.)

4. *Experimental models of psychopathology.* One way that psychology can help in the understanding of psychopathology is to bring to bear the facts and theories it has gathered in other, nonclinical realms and then to apply these to

the topic of mental disorder. One example comes from the animal laboratory, where a number of authors have suggested that this or the other facet of fear conditioning may provide us with a model for, say, depression, phobias, or for various anxiety disorders (see this chapter, pp. 663-64, 666-67, and also Chapter 4). Another example is the suggestion that various hallucinogenic drugs mimic some of the thought disorders found in schizophrenia. (Some of the issues that one has to face if one wants to develop a model of this or another form of psychopathology based on laboratory studies are discussed in Abramson, L. Y., and Seligman, M. E. P. 1977. Modeling psychopathology in the laboratory: History and rationale. In Maser, J. D., and Seligman, M. E. P., eds. *Psychopathology: Experimental models.* San Francisco: Freeman, pp. 1-26.)

Demonstration

How one might become hypertense.   This demonstration is similar to one described at the end of Chapter 3 in this manual (Demonstration 3), but its purpose is quite different. Begin by asking the students to feel for their heartbeat and determine their heart rate by counting the number of beats during a one-minute interval indicated by the experimenter. The students are now asked to become amateur "method actors" who have to imagine themselves in a situation in which they are violently angry but feel totally impotent, totally unable to do anything about it. On the contrary, what they have to do is to try not to show their anger. Give examples that might trigger this reaction. It might be a supercilious instructor who has just given them an unfair grade. Or perhaps they were accused of cheating, but can't defend themselves. Or perhaps they are badgered and insulted by an overbearing boss (or athletic coach, or whatever) and are unable to retaliate. Or they are threatened by a vicious bully who has a weapon and will use it if the victim gives him the slightest provocation. As these scenes are described to the subjects, it is crucial to paint them very concretely, so that the subjects can "feel in it." After a while, the experimenter asks the subjects, "How many of you can really imagine yourself in the scene, and how many really feel the impotent anger?" Go on, describing the scenes as concretely as possible, and ask them to put themselves into the victim's shoes, until enough of them say, yes, they do feel in it.

When this occurs, ask them to measure their heart rate again. This will almost certainly rise as the sympathetic emergency reaction takes over. When this is ascertained, explain the point. What the subjects have just experienced is what many people experience for years or decades. Their sympathetic nervous system is overactivated, over and over again, the heart pumps too quickly, the arteries contract too much—without ever discharging into motor action. The feeling of impotent anger is bad enough. But it also leaves its toll on the body in the form of various psychophysiological disorders, of which hypertension is one.

Experimental studies have shown that cats kept in cages and forced to listen to barking dogs for days on end (all the while spitting and back arching and hissing but unable to escape or fight back) develop hypertension. The subjects felt what the cats must have felt, but only for a few minutes (and only in imagination at that).

Two Case Histories

A discussion of mental disorders becomes much more concrete if it is supplemented with case histories. Some case material has been included in the text's chapter on psychopathology (Chapter 19), but because of lack of space, the cases were only presented in a fragmentary way. To supplement this lack, two complete case histories are presented below—a case of an obsessive-compulsive disorder, and a case of schizophrenia. (Both are taken from Spitzer, R. L., Skodol, A. E., Gibbon, M., and Williams, J. B. W. 1983. *Psychopathology: A case book.* New York: McGraw-Hill.)

These cases are provided to give the student a concrete sense of what information clinicians gather and how they organize and evaluate it. Each case is presented in two parts.

(1) The first part is a case summary, which begins with a statement of the problems that brought the patient in contact with the mental health system, followed by the context in which these problems developed, changed over time, and interfered with the patient's life or that of others. (The cases are quite real, but all names and other identifying information have been altered to make identification impossible.) This in turn is followed by the patient's personal history, and a description of the treatments the patient received and the results of that treatment.

(2) The second part is a discussion of the case prepared by the authors of the case book, which notes the most likely diagnosis, discusses theories about the etiology (that is, the origin) of the disorder, possible treatments, and probable prognosis (that is, most probable outcome).

Just how these case histories will be used for class discussion can only be decided by each individual instructor. Some might want to have the students read the case material before looking at the authors' discussion, and make guesses about the diagnosis, possible treatment, and so on. Others may prefer a different approach.

The two cases follow.

THE CASE OF TED

Clinical case material

Ted is a thirteen-year-old referred to a midwestern inpatient psychiatric research ward because of "senseless rituals and attention to minutiae." He can spend three hours "centering" the toilet paper roll on its holder or rearranging his bed and other objects in his room. When placing objects down, such as books or shoelaces after tying them, he picks them up and replaces them several times until they seem "straight." Although usually placid, he becomes abusive with family members who try to enter his room for fear they will move or break his objects. When he is at school, he worries that people may disturb his room. He sometimes has to be forced to interrupt his routine to attend meals. Last year he hid pieces of his clothing around the house because they wouldn't lie straight in his drawers. Moreover, he often repeats to himself, "This is perfect; you are perfect." He makes a gesture of head bowing, hand saluting, and sniffing. When outside, as in a movie house, he points his gestures in the direction of the house. To him, the gesture is a form of tribute to the "perfection" of his room. It's "like letting me know the room is straight."

There is little other thought activity during his compulsive behavior. His attitude and resistance fluctuate; he knows it takes time from his other interest— film making and projecting. He can get through his rituals quickly if he wants to do something else. Otherwise he is quite slow about them. He has little interest in school or socializing, and doesn't appear overly concerned about his condition. Because he spends the whole day in compulsive arranging and gesturing, he has not been able to attend school and is being tutored at home by his father.

Until he started kindergarten, his parents saw him as an average child who was cheerful and outgoing. His early development had been normal except for head banging as a toddler. Upon entering school, however, his teachers saw him as "withdrawn." He could not tolerate contact sports or anyone touching him. He was also quite apathetic, just "sitting there."

He always had a fear of water, in spite of the fact that no untoward incident had ever occurred. He could not go any further than ankle deep without panicking and protesting strongly, and could only dangle his feet over the edge of a pool.

At ten he also began fearing contamination with germs. He needed to know who had prepared his food before eating. He picked up his food with paper if his hands were not washed and placed the last piece of food back, fearing it was "drugged." At eleven he began to wear two layers of clothing, even in sweltering heat, so he would avoid "catching pneumonia." The teacher was disturbed because he spent too much time washing his lips and mouth with his own smuggled-in mouthwash and soap. Again, he feared germs were entering his mouth. On reflection, he always acknowledged that these habits and thoughts were unreasonable. Paradoxically, he could also go without taking a bath for many days unless his parents forced him. He kept the same clothes on, slept in his socks, stayed in his pajamas all day, and neglected his chores unless great pressure was exerted on him.

Throughout grade school he remained aloof from other children. Although his parents sensed he had affection for them, he never overtly expressed it. He would kiss his parents in a polite way when he had to leave them.

When Ted was eleven the family spent two years in biweekly family therapy with a psychologist with no discernible change. School officials became progressively concerned about skin irritation and chapping from his cleansing rituals; hospitalization was suggested at age twelve because he spent all his free time doing them.

In his first hospitalization he received an antipsychotic drug for a week, without effect other than sleepiness. An elaborate behavior modification system was established in which all privileges required payment in points. These were earned for time spent not performing rituals and for compliance with ward routine. Most rituals and excessive cleansing were quickly suppressed on this regime. He was slowly desensitized to water and could duck his head under water, a feat of which he was proud.

After eight weeks of hospitalization he was discharged, and his parents were asked to keep a detailed diary of his compulsive behaviors. They noticed that he was now more responsible, bathing, and doing chores without prodding. His teachers reported more participation in class activities and no time lost doing rituals. The staff of the hospital trained the parents to continue behavior modification techniques. Three weeks later they relinquished this approach as "difficult and unnatural" and Ted's compulsive activity recurred.

The family history contains no individuals with this disorder. One uncle did have repetitive facial grimacing (tics) and was severely socially isolated. At age sixteen he walked out of school after giving a class presentation and "remained in bed for two years." Despite a very high IQ he remained a farm hand on the family property. He became an alcoholic in his twenties and died of it in middle age. He carried a diagnosis of schizophrenia. None of the immediate family is unusual in any way. Ted's father is rather placid but successful in a management career, and participates in community activities. One full sibling and three half siblings (from a previous marriage of his father) are without behavioral difficulties.

When examined on admission to the research ward, Ted's mental status was normal except for mild emotional flattening and quiet speech. He was friendly and likable, with a shy but attentive manner. There was no evidence of thought disorder or delusions. His compulsions were associated with a "feeling." He said he "knows" nothing will happen if his objects are rearranged, but has difficulty resisting his "feeling" indefinitely. The feeling is at first weak but increasingly compelling, turning into irritation if it is denied its outlet.

Follow-up. On admission to the research ward Ted began receiving an experimental antidepressant drug that had been reported effective in adults. It helped dampen the urgency felt behind the compulsions and feelings of irritability or frustration if they are blocked. Three weeks after admission his absorption in rituals and resistance to discontinuing them for the sake of other activities had lessened. However, he still spent his spare time (two to three hours per day) doing his usual routines.

A program of behavior therapy involving increasing exposure to intolerable messiness and "dirt" and the prevention of compulsive responses was planned. Despite the 75 percent chance of eventual success, Ted stated he was not willing to subject himself to such stress.

Instead, ward privileges and his money allowance were tied to the attainment of progressively more difficult goals such as decreasing tardiness because of involvement in rituals, decreasing rearranging and gesturing in public, and the toleration of disorder outside of his immediate bed area and closet space. Social skills and friendship-making lessons were added once this approach was established.

By the time of discharge, Ted was never late to classes and activities. He initiated conversations more often to socialize rather than to ask for something. He no longer gestured in public, but occasionally did so when he thought no one was looking at him. He stopped being verbally abusive when interrupted in his rituals or when his belongings were moved. He quietly rearranged them on his own.

These methods were shared with the parents, and at discharge they were referred to a psychiatric clinic in their home area. There a child psychiatrist in conjunction with a psychologist interested in behavioral techniques helped his parents extend and continue the above approach at home. His parents remarked that they preferred this behavioral program to the previous program that involved earning points for good behavior, because it made use of natural rewards, such as giving him his allowance. In addition, they appreciated the simplicity of this program, which did not require them to keep any records.

Ted returned to public school, where he did average work. The teachers were to report any tardiness or public compulsive behavior to his parents, in addition to using usual school disciplinary measures. His parents were to decrease his allowance and/or restrict an activity in response to relapse. However, this rarely happened. By three months after discharge Ted continued doing his rituals in private in his spare time, and continually thought about them. He reported the absence of a buildup in frustration when prevented from doing so. His parents stated he was not verbally abusive when they entered his room, and he regularly did things with another boy outside of school. However, he remained aloof from most other people.

Discussion

Psychopathology and Diagnosis. Ted's life is dominated by his obsessions and compulsions. Obsessions are recurrent, persistent ideas, thoughts, images, or impulses that are experienced by the individual as alien and senseless. That is, the individual recognizes that these thoughts are not voluntarily produced, but seem to invade consciousness against his will. These thoughts, as in Ted's case, frequently involve the idea of contamination. Other common obsessions involve thoughts of violence, such as of hurting one's child, and doubt about whether one has done something, for example, hurt someone accidentally, or neglected to do something, such as turning off the stove.

Obsessions frequently, as in Ted's case, are the stimulus for compulsions—repetitive and seemingly purposeful behaviors performed in a stereotyped fashion and designed to produce or prevent some future event. The compulsions are not, in fact, realistically connected with what they are designed to prevent, or they are clearly excessive in relation to their purpose. In Ted's case, the obsession about contamination leads to a variety of compulsions, all designed to avoid illness: he spends inordinate amounts of time washing his lips and mouth; he wears two layers of clothing to avoid catching pneumonia; he picks up his food with paper. His compulsions arranging his room are related to obsessions about "perfection."

Adults with obsessions and compulsions invariably recognize that the symptoms are senseless and, at least initially, make some attempt to resist them. Resisting, however, leads to increasing anxiety until eventually the symptom cannot be resisted any longer.

The world "compulsive" is often used loosely to describe any behavior that is repetitive, driven, or excessive, such as gambling, certain forms of sexual behavior, and overeating. The technical term "compulsion," however, is used only to describe behaviors that are not in themselves pleasurable (as is gambling, sex, and eating) and that are designed to avoid some future dreaded event.

Similarly, the word "obsessive" is often used loosely to describe brooding and rumination about some unpleasant thought, regardless of its content. The technical term "obsession" is used only to describe thoughts that are both intrusive and senseless. The parent who cannot help worrying about his sick child may be said to be brooding, but does not have an obsession. On the other hand, the parent who everyday cannot help having the thought that he may have run over one of his children as he backed his car out of the garage on the way to work has an obsession.

Obsessions and compulsions range from mild superstitions ("Step on a crack, you'll break your mother's back."), which normal individuals may have, to a crippling condition such as Ted's. They may also be seen as symptoms of other disorders, such as a major depression or schizophrenia. When, as in Ted's case, they are the predominant disturbance and significantly interfere with functioning, the diagnosis of *obsessive-compulsive disorder* is made. Obsessive-compulsive disorder is considered an anxiety disorder, since the symptoms have the function of warding off anxiety, and anxiety is experienced when the individual resists the symptoms.

Etiology. Psychoanalytic theory explains the symptoms as the result of the ego's attempt to keep aggressive impulses from reaching consciousness. Thus the parent who worries that he has run over his child may be turning a wish to hurt his child into the "senseless" fear that he has in fact hurt the child. Ted's compulsion to have his room neatly arranged might be a defense against the anxiety that is caused by his wish to be defiantly messy. His refusal to bathe or change his clothes might be evidence that he is indeed ambivalent about how neat and clean he wants to be.

Learning theory proposes that an obsession originates in an association between an anxiety-producing event and a neutral thought. A compulsion develops when an individual discovers that performing a particular act is associated with diminishing anxiety. The reduction in anxiety reinforced the act, and the individual is therefore likely to repeat it. More recently, electroencephalographic and neuropsychological data suggest that subtle dysfunction of the frontal-temporal lobe of the brain may be associated with the disorder. All of these proposals are hypotheses for which conclusive evidence is not yet available.

Course and Treatment. Obsessive-compulsive disorder tends to be a chronic condition. Treatments ranging from psychoanalysis to electroconvulsive therapy have been used, without notable success. In Ted's case, both drugs and behavior therapy were used. The behavior therapy consisted of techniques designed to control the symptoms, regardless of their etiology. This combination of treatments seems to have helped Ted temporarily. Whether the effects will be lasting remains to be seen.

Prognosis. Ted's history suggests that his improvement may be short-lived unless his parents are able to continue to use the behavioral approach when he returns home. Even with treatment, the early onset and severity of the symptoms do not bode well for the future.

THE CASE OF HAROLD

Clinical case material

Harold Jameson is a single twenty-eight-year-old black man who has been attending a day hospital in a community mental health center. Three days after his therapist left for vacation, he appeared in the emergency room of a local hospital complaining that he was confused, depressed, and fearful. He had been hearing voices and "seeing colors," and requested admission to the inpatient unit because he was afraid to go home.

The first indications of Mr. Jameson's illness occurred when he was nineteen. He had graduated from high school and was studying voice and working in a music store. He precipitously left the Catholic church, in which he had been raised, and became passionately involved with a fundamentalist Christian group. He spent all his free time at church, going on weekend retreats and entering into "consecrations" that involved fasting and abstaining from sex and alcohol. He soon began to feel that his employer was treating him like a slave, and quit his job. He claimed to be "the ambassador of Christ" and became preoccupied with what he felt was his special mission. On a visit to the World's Fair, he upset his mother by making bizarre gestures, standing and staring for long periods, and laughing and crying to himself. The next day he went to work at a new job but walked out after an hour. He was picked up by the police in Macy's, where he had shoplifted some clothing in a very obvious manner, claiming that he was not stealing because "everything belongs to God."

Admitted to the city hospital, he was agitated and unable to sleep; he heard the voice of God and saw the face of the Devil. He was transferred to a state hospital where he remained for three months, and was treated with antipsychotic medication.

After being discharged he resumed his voice lessons and found a part-time job as a custodian. He functioned relatively well for nine months, but then had a recurrence of the same symptoms and was rehospitalized.

During the intervening eight years, Mr. Jameson has been hospitalized seven times for periods ranging from two weeks to three months. Most of these episodes of illness have begun with increasing preoccupation with religion, followed by agitation, delusions, and hallucinations, until finally Mr. Jameson would begin talking in a manner that did not make sense, and he would be brought to the hospital by his family or associates. Mr. Jameson apparently had stopped taking his medication prior to several of these admissions, because he felt he was well and did not need it any longer.

During his last few hospitalizations there were other complicating factors. Mr. Jameson had begun to drink heavily and smoke marijuana, and this, combined with his history of illness, made it more difficult for him to get jobs. He spent some time in a vocational rehabilitation program, but for most of the past three years has been either in a day hospital or just "hanging out."

Two of his previous hospitalizations were apparently precipitated by specific events: his father's hospitalization for medical problems and his therapist's leaving. On admission both of these times he was depressed, not sleeping or eating, and had made suicide gestures by taking increased doses of his medication. He also heard voices telling him to kill himself. During these hospitalizations he received antidepressants as well as antipsychotic medication.

Mr. Jameson is the second son of a middle-class family living in Harlem. His father was a printer until severe arthritis made it impossible for him to work. Even when he was working, the father was a "binge drinker" who was frequently abusive and violent with his wife and children; during his eight years on disability his binges have merged into one another, and he is nearly always somewhat intoxicated and hostile. Mrs. Jameson is an anxious, timid woman who works as a secretary for the Red Cross. She was at home with the children until the patient was eleven. She then spent three years in and out of psychiatric hospitals for unknown reasons. (The children were placed in a Catholic home

during this time.) Since the patient was fourteen she has been working full-time
at her current job. Mr. Jameson has a brother two years older who was the "bad
boy" of the family. He is a heroin addict, and has been living away from home,
on welfare, since he was eighteen.

Mr. Jameson describes his early years as "happy." According to the family, he
walked and talked "at the normal times." He was pleasant and friendly, probably
overly obedient, and clearly had an intense relationship with his mother, who
counted on him to fulfill some of her own unrealized dreams. He was an average
student, but because of his musical talent got a lot of recognition from peers and
school personnel. He received a music scholarship on graduation from high
school.

Mr. Jameson claims to have had close friends during his high school years, but
became more isolated as he grew older. He had his only serious girl friend at
eighteen, but she left him because he refused to continue a sexual relationship.
(This was prior to his becoming involved with the fundamentalist church. Join-
ing the church was part of his attempt to "purify" himself.)

When not acutely ill, Mr. Jameson is an engaging, alert, somewhat obsequious
young man who speaks in an ornate and convoluted manner, using many multi-
syllabic words, and sometimes making up his own words. The following is a verbatim excerpt from an interview done when he was attending the day hospital:

Q: How do you spend your time?
A: I spend my days by, of course, perhaps shopping in the morning very
quickly for what might be, or what is, rather, my lunch, and from that point I go
to the clinic branch at approximately 9:00 and spend the day there in which I
might be involved with musical programs, or devising basically any kind of
musical forms that I can in order to participate with the O.T. program.

Q: Did you have a group of friends that you hung out with?
A: We found that most of our time was consumed being involved with studies
or tasks that might be assigned or what have you. But after school most of the
coagulations would begin as far as basically about friendships and et cetera.

Mr. Jameson was hospitalized and begun on prolixin—a long-acting, injectable
antipsychotic drug, and within two weeks the delusions and hallucinations had
disappeared and he was no longer anxious. He returned to the day hospital and
resumed treatment with his therapist who had returned from vacation. In the
next five years Mr. Jameson had no further hospitalizations. He stated that the
medication made him feel good, and although he was not able to work, he had
no recurrences of the delusions, hallucinations, and disorganization that had
occurred in the past. He lived with his mother (his father was now chronically
hospitalized), and spent his days at the day hospital, where he organized a
patients' chorus. Mr. Jameson's use of alcohol and marijuana tapered off, to the
point that it no longer seemed to create problems for him. His inability to return
to work or school was, in part, the result of his unwillingness to give up grandi-

ose notions of what was an appropriate job for him. He claimed to be content with his life.

Discussion

Psychopathology and Diagnosis.   There can be little doubt about the diagnosis of schizophrenia in this case. Mr. Jameson has a history of delusions (e.g., he was the "ambassador of Christ") and hallucinations (e.g., he heard the voice of God and saw the face of the Devil), incoherent speech (talking in a manner that did not make sense), bizarre behavior (e.g., laughing and crying to himself in public), and deterioration in his functioning over a period of many years. This clinical picture is characteristic of the illness.

Schizophrenia is subclassified according to the most prominent symptoms of the current episode. Because of the lack of prominence of persecutory delusions (as in paranoid subtype), frequent incoherence and inappropriate or silly affect (as in disorganized subtype), and catatonic behavior (as in catatonic subtype), the most appropriate subtype is undifferentiated. The course of the illness is considered "chronic" because signs of the illness have been present for many years, and "with an acute exacerbation" as evidenced by the recurrence of psychotic symptoms ("hearing voices and 'seeing colors'") that he described in the emergency room.

The only other diagnosis that should be considered for this case is major depression, recurrent, with psychotic features, since several of Mr. Jameson's episodes were characterized by depressed mood along with delusions and hallucinations. However, it does not appear that the full depressive syndrome (that is, a depressed mood accompanied by several other symptoms of depression such as loss of appetite, trouble sleeping, difficulty concentrating, and suicidal thoughts) was present during each episode. In addition, in between the acute episodes the patient was still unable to work and was somewhat socially isolated. These are classic signs of residual schizophrenia, and suggest that diagnosis rather than major depression, which tends to be episodic. Therefore, *schizophrenia* is the primary diagnosis, although there are also superimposed depressions.

The individual with schizophrenia is not immune to other psychological problems; in fact, depression and substance abuse are relatively common in individuals with the disorder. Two of Mr. Jameson's hospitalizations were primarily for symptoms of depression occurring after stressful life events—his father's hospitalization and his therapist's leaving. During these periods he had insomnia, poor appetite, and was suicidal. Severe depressions, such as this, occurring in a patient with chronic schizophrenia are different from major depressions occurring in individuals without chronic psychotic disorder. For that reason, such depressions are diagnosed as atypical depressions. Mr. Jameson also apparently used alcohol and marijuana to excess, perhaps even to the extent of warranting the additional diagnoses of alcohol and cannabis abuse.

Course. As is often the case, the first signs of Mr. Jameson's schizophrenic illness appeared during later adolescence. Since then there has been a typical course of recurrent acute psychotic episodes (referred to as acute exacerbations) with increasing functional impairment between each episode.

Treatment. Mr. Jameson was treated with antipsychotic medication, both to control the acute psychotic episodes and to prevent further episodes. Even when patients are told the importance of continuing to take their medication, they often stop after the acute episode subsides. In Mr. Jameson's case the reason that he often stopped taking his medication is not clear. Some patients do so because they find the side effects very unpleasant. Others may stop because they do not like to think of themselves as ill and requiring medication. In some cases patients may stop taking the medicine as their thinking becomes disorganized with the onset of another exacerbation. Eventually Mr. Jameson was given antipsychotic medication in a long-acting injectable form that only needs to be given every two weeks. This was probably done because of a concern that, on his own, he would again discontinue taking his daily medication. This seems to have been a wise decision, since there have not been any exacerbations requiring hospitalization since that time.

For the last five years, Mr. Jameson's life has revolved around the day hospital. Although it is true that he has not been able to work, marry, and have a family, and certainly has not fulfilled his early promise as a singer, his life is probably considerably better than it would have been if he had lived twenty or thirty years ago. With the help of antipsychotic medication, psychotherapeutic management, and the structure provided by the day hospital, he has been spared a life that in the past might have been spent on the back ward of a state hospital.

Prognosis. The prognosis for Mr. Jameson is certainly not good. It is unlikely that he will ever function very much better than he does currently—barring some breakthrough in the treatment of chronic schizophrenia. A particularly difficult time for him will be when his mother dies and he no longer has a home. Whether he will be able to manage his own household remains to be seen.

Selected Readings

GENERAL WORKS
Bernheim, K. F., and Lewine, R. R. J. 1979. *Schizophrenia: Symptoms, causes, treatments.* New York: Norton. A well-written book about schizophrenia that tries to explain the disorder to the lay audience, including the patient's friends and relatives.

Kaplan, B., ed. 1964. *The inner world of mental illness.* New York: Harper & Row. A number of autobiographical accounts of what mental disorders look like when seen from within.

Siegler, M., and Osmond, H. 1976. *Models of madness, models of medicine.* New York: Harper & Row. Easy-to-read paperback discussion of several conceptions of the major disorders, with a strong preference for the so-called medical model.

Snyder, S. H. 1974. *Madness and the brain.* New York: McGraw-Hill. A popular, well-written book by a leading authority on biochemical factors in mental disorders.

Spitzer, R. L., Skodol, A. E., Gibbon, M., and Williams, J. B. W. 1983. *Psychopathology: A case book.* New York: McGraw-Hill. A collection of fifty-four case studies, covering the entire range of mental disorders, and arranged according to the diagnostic categories of DSM-III. Each case includes a description of the clinical material, followed by the authors' discussion of most probable diagnosis, origin of the disorder, treatment, and probable outcome.

Szasz, T. S. 1974. *The myth of mental illness: Foundations of a theory of personal conduct.* New York: Harper & Row. An influential book that criticizes the pathology model from a sociological perspective.

REFERENCE WORKS

Davison, G. C., and Neale, J. M. 1982. *Abnormal psychology*, 3rd ed. New York: Wiley. A good undergraduate text, written from a behavior theory perspective.

Maser, J. D., and Seligman, M. E. P., eds. 1977. *Psychopathology: Experimental models.* San Francisco: Freeman. A paperback that contains a dozen papers that describe laboratory models of clinical disorders.

Rosenhan, D. L., and Seligman, M. E. P. 1984. *Abnormal psychology.* New York: Norton. A solid undergraduate text written from a broad perspective by two major figures in the field.

CHAPTER 20

Treatment of Psychopathology

Overview

Whereas the preceding chapter described various forms of psychopathology and discussed some attempts to understand how they come about, the present one focuses on attempts to provide treatment and cure. Some of the proposed treatments rely on biological interventions; others are based on psychological means. The chapter describes the various therapeutic efforts, emphasizing those of psychotherapy, and considers the procedures for evaluating their effects.

SOMATIC THERAPIES

This chapter begins with a discussion of somatic therapies. It takes up drug therapy (e.g., the use of phenothiazines for schizophrenia, tricyclics for depression, and lithium carbonate for bipolar affective disorder) and the evaluation of a drug's effectiveness. It also considers other somatic therapies, including psychosurgery and electroconvulsive shock treatment (ECT).

PSYCHOTHERAPY

The next major section is devoted to several kinds of psychotherapy. First, classical psychoanalysis is discussed: free association, resistance, catharsis, and transference are all explained, as are some modern versions of psychoanalysis, which place more emphasis on interpersonal and social problems than on underlying psychosexual matters in the past.

A second approach is taken by behavior therapists whose concern is with unwanted, overt behaviors rather than with hypothetical underlying causes. Many of the behavior therapists' techniques are derived from the principles of classical and instrumental conditioning. Here, systematic desensitization, flooding, and aversive therapy are discussed (see also Chapter 4, pages 116–19). Some off-shoots of behavior therapy are (1) cognitive therapy, which tries to change the way a client thinks about his or her situation and (2) techniques (graded task assignments, modeling, and role-playing) that attempt to advance the client's social education.

A third class of therapies is humanistic therapy. Here, the text describes

Rogers's client-centered therapy—a therapy that is largely nondirective and based on the idea that therapy is a personal growth process.

The psychotherapy section ends with a discussion of some common themes that underlie the various psychotherapies.

EVALUATING THERAPEUTIC OUTCOME

The chapter next turns to the problem of evaluating therapy outcome. It describes some of the methodological difficulties such outcome studies face: finding matched groups that can be compared after equal intervals of treatment and non-treatment, controlling for placebo effects, and so on. The evidence at present evidently suggests that psychotherapies produce a modest effect, yielding somewhat greater improvement rates than would be expected if no treatment were given.

EXTENSIONS OF PSYCHOTHERAPY

A final section considers some recent extensions of psychotherapy. One extension concerns methods, as in play therapy for children and various forms of group therapy. Another extension concerns the therapeutic goals. Once these were simply to cure pathology. With time, these goals were broadened and in many cases include personal growth and the discovery of a meaning in life (e.g., existential therapy).

Discussion Topics

1. *Placebo effects.* One of the most pervasive phenomena in the treatment, not just of mental disorders, but of disease in general, is the so-called placebo effect (see Chapter 20, pp. 690–91). This is the beneficial result brought about by some procedure that has no demonstrable specific effect on the disorder it is supposed to treat (e.g., a sugar pill). Placebo effects are usually rather modest, but they are real enough (even though the sugar pill or the pilgrimage to the holy shrine works only because the patient believes in it). As a result, scientists have to employ special procedures to rule out this placebo phenomenon when they try to evaluate the effectiveness of a given therapy. They want to know whether the therapy has *specific* effects that are unique to it, rather than *nonspecific*, placebo effects that might have been produced by administering sugar pills or by similar means.

Students should realize that the need for a placebo control is not limited to somatic treatments. The evaluation of psychotherapies also requires this control, in order to rule out the possibility that any other kind of treatment might have worked as well if the patient believed in it. (For an example of such a control, see the text, Chapter 20, pp. 707–708.)

A last point. Placebo effects are often considered as a kind of nuisance—something that has to be ruled out to make sure that a given therapy has a specific effect. But it surely is more than this. For the very existence of placebo effects is a fascinating phenomenon. How do they come about? Students with a fear of speaking show some improvement after performing a boring task; surgical patients report relief from pain after taking saline injections. Why? We really don't yet know. One would suspect that placebo effects of this sort should be related to various aspects of "suggestion," as reported in studies of hypnosis, and related phenomena. But thus far not too much is known.

(For some further discussion of placebo effects, see the following: Frank, J. D. 1961. *Persuasion and healing.* New York: Schocken Books. Shapiro, A. K. 1971. Placebo effects in medicine, psychotherapy, and psychoanalysis. In Bergin, A. E., and Garfield, S. L., eds. *Handbook of psychotherapy and behavior change: An empirical analysis.* New York: Wiley.)

2. *Some underlying themes of psychotherapy.* Despite all their divergences, there are some common themes that run through the beliefs and practices of the many schools of psychotherapy, a point stressed in the text (see Chapter 20, pp. 704–705). Just about all schools try to help the patient rid himself of various intense and unrealistic fears. In one way or another, they all regard the therapist's office as a kind of school for remedial interpersonal learning in which the therapeutic relationship serves as the major educational instrument. They all try to help the patient gain one or another kind of self-knowledge. They all agree that whatever therapy consists of, it works gradually. A final point is that since psychotherapy is a socially accepted practice, all of its versions will lead to non-specific, placebolike gains.

The appreciation of these similarities is of great importance, though it is often lost amid polemics which tend to overemphasize the differences between the various schools. (For an incisive discussion, see Wachtel, P. L. 1977. *Psychoanalysis and behavior therapy: Toward an integration.* New York: Basic Books.)

3. *How to design a study of the effectiveness of a particular kind of psychotherapy.* It is probably impossible to design (let alone conduct) a flawless study of the effectiveness of any particular form of psychotherapy. But the sheer attempt will undoubtedly be educational. At minimum, it will convince students of the complexity of the task. All we will do here is to briefly list the various problems such an evaluation study has to overcome.

(a) The first task is to pinpoint the disorder that is to be treated. To begin with, we have to have a way of identifying this disorder by various symptoms or other signs. Are these symptoms overt, visible to the outside? Do we have to rely on the patient's self-evaluation? Can we supplement the observations with physiological indices of some kind (e.g., blood pressure in the case of hypertension)?

(b) We next have to ask how improvement is to be defined. What does it mean to get better? Can this be defined objectively, or do we have to rely on the self-evaluation of the patient and the judgment of the therapist?

(c) Grant that we have settled (a) and (b), we next have to select our patient population. Can we simply look at one population and study it before therapy (say, six months) and after? Surely not, for if improvement occurs, this might have been brought about through mere passage of time (spontaneous improvement) or through the patients' belief that the treatment would help them (placebo effect). Both of these have to be ruled out, which can be done only by comparing before-and-after scores of a treated group with those of an untreated control. Now the problems become harder. For we have to be sure that the treated and the untreated groups are comparable. Can we be sure of that?

(d) Suppose our treated group consists of thirty people who chose that form of psychotherapy, while the untreated group consists of thirty other patients matched in age, sex, occupation, and similar indices. This is not enough, for the treated group chose treatment while the untreated group did not. For all we know, the very act of deciding "I am going into therapy" is itself therapeutic. To control for this, we have to select both groups from among a larger group who said they wanted to be treated. Given this larger pool of persons, one now divides it arbitrarily into two groups—giving therapy to one and not to the other. This was precisely the procedure adopted in Paul's study reported in the text (Chapter 20, pp. 707-709) and also in some later studies that were to some extent patterned on his. (See Sloane, R. B., Staples, F. R., Cristol, A. H., Yorkston, N. J., and Whipple, K. 1975. *Psychotherapy versus behavior therapy.* Cambridge, Mass.: Harvard University Press.) The members of the waiting group are told that they will be treated after some specified period, and indeed they are.

(e) The next step is to devise a placebo. This is far from easy, because it has to be one that makes sense to the patient. (Laying on hands will probably not do in 1986.) Paul got around this problem by giving his placebo group "practice in dealing with aversive situations"—in actuality, solving dull problems. This evidently produced some effect when compared to the results of the waiting group.

(f) In all likelihood, the experimenter will not be satisfied with merely comparing the effects of one therapy with those of the placebo and of the waiting group. There are, after all, several dozen psychotherapies that vie with each other, and it might be useful to see whether any of them are more beneficial than the others (let alone the various controls). As a result, one might want to use several groups in which different therapies are used. If so, it is again essential that the subjects be assigned randomly to each group.

(g) Another problem arises the moment we are considering the therapists. Suppose we find that one form of therapy (call it X) does better than another (call it Y). Does this mean that X is a better therapeutic procedure than is Y? Perhaps the real reason for the difference is in the therapists. Jane Brown ran therapy X; Joe Brown ran therapy Y. Maybe Jane is a better therapist than Joe, and what matters is their personal characteristics (warmth, sensitivity, or whatever) rather than the particular therapeutic method they employ. To test this, Joe and Jane would have to switch therapies: have her practice Y while he practices X. In principle this might work well enough (it did for Paul, who used this approach in his study). But in practice it may be too difficult to employ widely. Behavior therapy, nondirective therapy, and psychoanalysis are different procedures, and to learn how to practice them takes time and effort. Nor is it clear that therapists could switch even if they learned each others' methods. Can anyone imagine Freud practicing Rogerian therapy or see Rogers as a behavior therapist? One possible way of dealing with this is to use a large number of therapists—ten different psychoanalysts, ten Rogerians, and so on. This (quite impracticable) procedure should abolish the effects of different therapists, for they should average out. But will they? For all we know, there are some selective factors that make one clinician become a Rogerian, another an analyst, yet another a behavior therapist, because different therapies may attract different kinds of people. If so, increasing the number of therapists in each group will not eliminate the problem.

4. *Mental health care as a community problem.*   How does the community deal with various problems of mental health? Of particular interest is the question of how the community treats persons who return from mental hospitals. In the days before the widespread use of psychoactive drugs, such people were relatively few. Now they are more numerous, but their discharge does not mean that they are fully restored to normal functioning. They may have been in the hospital for a while and need time to adjust to the world outside. A number of programs have been developed to facilitate such a return to the community, including the so-called halfway house, a midway station between the hospital and the patient's old, "normal" world, which allows a period of readaptation. For a discussion of this and related matters, see the following:

Freeman, H. E., and Simmons, O. G. 1963. *The mental patient comes home.* New York: Wiley. Some problems of the returning patient and some attempts to cope with them.

Raush, H. L., and Raush, C. L. 1968. *The halfway house movement: A search for sanity.* New York: Appleton-Century-Crofts.

White, R. W., and Watt, N. F. 1981. *The abnormal personality*, 5th ed. New York: Wiley. See Chapter 17 on community mental health for an overview.

5. *Family therapy.*   There is an interesting development in psychotherapy which does not focus on the individual as such. Its unit is the family (sometimes a marriage), and its goal is to establish a proper interaction between its component parts. This approach fits in with the emphasis on the situation in which that person finds himself which we noted elsewhere (especially in Chapter 18). If it is really true that people behave, not just because they are *what* they are, but also because they are *where* they are—such as a malfunctioning family system—then some attention to this social system might well be profitable.

In this form of therapy all of the members of the family participate, and the family is treated as a kind of social system. Thus far, there have not been any attempts to evaluate outcomes systematically, but the method appears promising. (For some discussions, see the following: White, R. W., and Watt, N. F. 1981.

The abnormal personality, 5th ed. New York: Wiley. Haley, J. 1973. *Uncommon therapy*. New York: Norton. Chapter 5—marriage and its consequences—and Chapter 7—marriage and family dilemmas.)

   Whether family therapy is a proper approach when one of the members is suffering from a severe mental disturbance, especially schizophrenia, is a subject of considerable debate. (For a negative evaluation, see Siegler, M., and Osmond, H. 1974. *Models of madness, models of medicine*. New York: Harper & Row.)

Selected Readings

GENERAL WORKS
London, P. 1964. *The modes and morals of psychotherapy*. New York: Holt, Rinehart and Winston. A well-written introduction.

CLASSICS
Alexander, F., and French, T. 1946. *Psychoanalytic theory*. New York: Ronald Press. A description of a modified version of psychoanalytic therapy that was very influential.

Rogers, C. R. 1942. *Counseling and psychotherapy: New concepts in practice*. Boston: Houghton Mifflin. The original formulation of humanistic, nondirective therapy.

Wolpe, J. 1958. *Psychotherapy by reciprocal inhibition*. Stanford: Stanford University Press. The classic presentation of behavior therapy based on classical conditioning.

REFERENCE WORKS
Davison, G. C., and Neale, J. M. 1982. *Abnormal psychology: An experimental approach*, 3rd ed. New York: Wiley. (Already mentioned in Chapter 17.) A good undergraduate text oriented toward behavior theory.

Rosenhan, D. L., and Seligman, M. E. P. 1984. *Abnormal psychology*. New York: Norton. (Already mentioned in Chapter 17.) A well-organized, solid undergraduate text in which discussions of therapies and particular disorders are linked within the same chapter.

Wachtel, P. L. 1973. *Psychoanalysis and behavior therapy*. New York: Basic Books. An important book that tries to show what psychoanalysis and behavior therapy have in common, and in so doing, gives a rich insight into what a clinical practitioner really does when he tries to help disturbed people.

White, R. W., and Watt, N. F. 1981. *The abnormal personality*, 5th ed. New York: Wiley. A good undergraduate text with some emphasis on a modern, neo-Freudian psychoanalytic outlook.

A Guide to Audiovisual Materials

James B. Maas
CORNELL UNIVERSITY

Audiovisual materials and computer simulations serve as valuable supplements to lectures and readings. Slides, overhead transparencies, videotapes, films, and the computer, when properly used, can help the student understand and enjoy more the ideas taught in the introductory course. In addition to raising important issues, media can serve as discussion starters, as a means of demonstrating psychological phenomena and documenting crucial experiments and results, and as a rich source of historical and biographical material. They enable the instructor to bring into the lecture hall individuals, events, phenomena, and equipment not otherwise easily accessible. Lastly, appropriate use of media provides a change of pace from the traditional lecture-discussion format.

Successful use of audiovisual materials requires some preparation and followup. The instructor should examine his or her teaching objectives for a given body of material and decide whether media would make the learning process more efficient and effective. Film and slide catalogs should be readily available and materials ordered well before the date of their planned use. Films should be previewed by the instructor, who must ascertain whether the material is worthwhile for student viewing. Does the film impart meaningful information and meet teaching objectives? Does it instruct at the appropriate level? Does the film make appropriate use of the medium? Successful classroom use of films requires that the instructor guide the students' viewing by specifying the teaching objectives beforehand, alerting students to critical concepts. Failure to prepare viewers might result in passive watching or create an expectation of entertainment without educational purpose. It is essential to follow up media presentations with comments and discussion of the material. Good films provoke considerable thought and, often, emotional reaction. It would be a mistake not to capitalize on the interest generated by the use of effective media. Finally, the instructor should prepare examination questions based on the media used.

233

In preparing your film program, add the following to your checklist: Remember to check the projector beforehand to make sure it is in proper condition. Do you have a spare bulb on hand? A take-up reel? Extension cords? Adapter plugs? Can the room be properly darkened? Does the projector lens have the appropriate focal length for the particular classroom? Assigning a teaching assistant or work-study student as projectionist will reduce the possibility that technical problems will interfere with the learning process.

There are thousands of audiovisual materials with some potential for use in introductory psychology courses. Space limitations preclude presenting information on everything that is available. Therefore, I have provided a list of some comprehensive resources (pp. 258–59), some film series and special collections (pp. 259–64), and some computer simulations (pp. 270–71). But first let us take a look at a list of films that have been well received by my own students.

Some Recommended Films for Introductory Psychology

The following films are organized by chapter in *Psychology*, Second Edition. They are recommended to serve as supplements to lectures and the text. The entries do not include all available and potentially useful materials. Rather, they are representative of the films that I have used extensively in the classroom: they have withstood the test of time. For some text chapters there are few recommended materials; certain topics are not suitable for film treatment, and others simply lack effective media explication. The instructor should preview any film before showing it to students, and decide what is most appropriate for his or her particular goals or objectives. Some segments of films are very exciting and useful, while other parts need not be shown. Many films represent specific points of view and any biases should be identified. Whether or not a film will be successful in the classroom will in large measure depend on the context provided. The teacher's introductory remarks and the discussion that follows the film often determine the value of the educational experience.

The producer's name follows the entry's title, after which are noted the year of production, the running time, and "color" or "black and white." Rental sources appear last, in abbreviated form. Full names, along with addresses, are listed at the end of the audiovisual section (see pp. 266–68).

(A larger, but less selective, listing of psychology films by subject matter can be found in chapter 6, "Audiovisual Materials," written by this author for the *Psychology Teacher's Resource Book* and published by the American Psychological Association, 1979.)

CHAPTER 1. INTRODUCTION

Aspects of Behavior. CRM, 1971. 31 minutes, color. CRM/MHF.

This film touches on a variety of areas covered by the study of contemporary psychology. Included are treatments of autism, physiologically based behaviors, ethical issues in psychology, attitude change, and environmental influences. Social psychologists Stanley Milgram, John Darley, and Bib Latané discuss their theories about social problems. The film includes a reenactment of the bystander phenomenon experiments.

Behaviorism and Beyond. CRM, 1974. 20 minutes, color. CRM/MHF.

B. F. Skinner discusses the beginnings of modern behaviorism and presents his interpretation of behaviorism's basic principles.

Learning about Human Behavior. Coronet Films, 1974. 11 minutes, color. Coronet.

This film provides an introduction to psychological study in the areas of development, perception, learning, emotions, intelligence, and social psychology.

Methodology: The Psychologist and the Experiment. CRM, 1975. 30 minutes, color. PSU, CRM/MHF.

This film documents research methodology used in Stanley Schachter's "fear and affiliation" experiment in social psychology and Austin Riesen's physiological experiment on visual motor coordination. It also covers independent and dependent variables, control groups, random assignment to conditions, and use of statistics in research.

Powers of Ten. Pyramid, 1968. 8 minutes, color. P, UC.

This is an animated trip through the universe at a speed that changes the visual scale by a power of ten every ten seconds. It begins with a man lying on a Miami beach, seen from a distance of one meter. After ten seconds he is ten meters away. In ten more seconds we see the city, then most of the state, and onward away from the earth to intergalactic space. Then, in reverse, we return to the man and go within him to the nucleus of an atom. An excellent film to set perspective on the study of man, one *very small* element in the universe.

Search and Research: Psychology in Perspective. Psychological Films, 1962. 30 minutes, b/w. PFI.

Harry Harlow, Carl Rogers, and Rollo May present experimental, psychoanalytic, and existential approaches to psychology. Good historical footage marks the film.

67,000 Dreams. C. G. Jung, BBC, 1972. 30 minutes, color. TLM.

This explains the development of the major theories and concepts of Carl Jung, including discussion of the collective unconscious, the psychology of types, the psyche in space and time, and the importance of myth and intuition to the complete man.

CHAPTER 2. BIOLOGICAL BASES OF BEHAVIOR

Biology and Behavior. Harper & Row Media, 1980. 21 minutes, color. HARM.

Focusing on the nature-nurture controversy, this film includes research foot-age on taste aversion, imprinting, instinctive drift, and tropisms.

Brain: Creating a Mental Elite. Document Associates, 1972. 22 minutes, color. PSU, UC, DA.

This film focuses on three major areas of brain research: chemical stimula-tion, electrical stimulation, and environmental conditioning. It includes discus-sions with brain surgeon Wilder Penfield, and psychophysiologists E. Roy John, Marian Diamond, and David Krech.

Classic Experiments in Behavioral Neuropsychology. Harper & Row Media, 1979. 22 minutes, color. HARM.

This presents experiments in behavioral neuropsychology which show brain behavior interaction in complex species:
1. "Nerve Control in Transplanted Salamander Limbs," by Paul Weiss.
2. "Rearrangement of Neural Connections," by Roger W. Sperry.
3. "Feeding Behavior of the Blowfly," by Vincent G. Dethier.
4. "Homeostatic Control of Food Intake in the Rat," by Bartley G. Hoebel.
5. "Brain Control of Aggression," by José M. R. Delgado.
6. "Brain Localization: The Motor Cortex," by Imperial Chemical Industries.
7. "Cerebral Hemispheres in Man," by Roger W. Sperry.

Divided Brain and Consciousness. Harcourt Brace Jovanovich, 1977. 22 minutes, color. HBJ.

This film focuses on the functioning of the cerbral hemispheres. The four major segments of the film present some of the tests developed by Jane and Norman Mackworth to study brain-damaged patients; demonstrations by Robert Ornstein of experiments that use an electroencephalograph to record the alpha rhythm of brain waves in normal subjects; reenactments of tests developed for use with split-brain patients; and Ernest Hilgard's use of hypnosis to demonstrate what he calls "divided consciousness" and the phenomenon of the "hidden ob-server." The four types of experiments—along with interpretive remarks by Elliot Valenstein—offer a demonstration of the functions of the right and left hemispheres of the brain.

Hard Choices: Behavior Control. KCTS Seattle, 1981. 59 minutes, color. PBS.

This presents ethical issues concerning modern technology in behavior control.

The Hidden Universe: The Brain. ABC News (Closeup), 1977. 45 minutes, color. CRM/MHF.

An overview of the functions of the brain, including motor control, memory, and sensory perceptions, it covers brain surgery, split-brain research, and a patient who controls chronic pain with a portable electric stimulator. A variety of brain malfunctions and possible treatments are discussed.

The Mind of Man. Produced by NET, BBC, and Swedish and Bavarian Television, 1970. Available in four segments. PSU, IU.

The Mind of Man: Part 1
27 minutes, color.

This segment surveys recent research on the brain. How the mind controls body functions is demonstrated by a yogi who limits his body's needs for oxygen. The film also covers the structure of the brain and its electrical activity, mental development in infants, dreams and sleep research, effects of drugs on the brain, and the nature of memory and learning.

The Mind of Man: Part 2
34 minutes, color.

Nobel-Prize-winning scientist Sir John Eccles experiments with brain cells. Dr. Harry Harlow's famous experiments with baby monkeys show how emotions affect behavior. The film covers sexuality and the brain, aggression, and communication. Donald Hebb discusses the way intelligence increases emotional intensity and vulnerability. Actors show how we manipulate emotions. Also shown is Dr. Neal Miller's experiment in which a man lowers his blood pressure by willpower alone.

The Mind of Man: Part 3
28 minutes, color.

This segment includes visual illusions and selective perception, the use of robots to discover how humans recognize and perceive objects, development of reasoning abilities in children, brain damage affecting certain areas of the brain but not necessarily other areas, and the effect of malnutrition on the brain.

The Mind of Man: Part 4
30 minutes, color.

This part includes the region of the brain that controls language, a discussion of human language development by Noam Chomsky, and how autistic children are trained to speak. Sarah, an experimental chimpanzee at the University of California at Santa Barbara, uses written symbols to communicate. Nobel Prize-winning physicist Richard Feinman discusses human imagination and creativity. B. F. Skinner discusses behaviorism. Donald Hebb's approach to the question of man's soul is covered, as are split-brain operations and the discovery of separate functions of the right and left hemispheres.

Mind over Body. BBC, 1972. 35 minutes, color. TLM. PSU.

This shows how routine illnesses and bodily injuries are greatly influenced by the psychological state of the patient. Interviews with doctors and psychologists conducting research are alternated with sequences of experiments in progress. The film goes into the control of involuntary bodily functions: heartbeat, flow of blood, brain waves.

Split Brain. NET, 1967. 13 minutes, b/w. PSU.

A film of historical value demonstrating and explaining experiments performed by Dr. R. W. Sperry, utilizing animals and humans whose two cerebral hemispheres have been surgically separated. The results of the experiments are discussed in terms of their contribution to knowledge of normal brain functioning.

Split Brain. Harper & Row Media, 1980. 17 minutes, color. HARM.

This examines what happens to "split-brain" patients before, during, and after surgery. The experiments question the concept of a global unity of mind, until recently accepted as uncontestable.

What Time Is Your Body? BBC. 1973. 24 minutes, color. TLM.

This demonstrates that the body is a natural clock regulated by circadian rhythms and endogenous movement. It shows isolation experiments performed on humans to ascertain natural rhythms.

CHAPTER 3. MOTIVATION

Autonomic Nervous System. International Film Bureau, 1974. 17 minutes, color. PSU, IFB.

This reviews sympathetic and parasympathetic systems which control involuntary body processes such as breathing, heart rate, blood pressure, digestion, body temperature, contraction and dilation of the iris.

Keep Us Awake. Ciba-Geigy, 1978. 29 minutes, color. AF.

This film explores narcolepsy, a sleep disorder characterized by excessive daytime sleepiness and attacks of muscular weakness brought about by strong emotions. The film demonstrates how sleep and dreaming mechanisms can malfunction in some humans and lower animal species, and it describes possible treatments for the disorder.

A New Look at Motivation. CRM, 1980. 32 minutes, color. CRM/MHF.

This examines affiliation, power, and achievement in the work environment and relates each quality to personality characteristics.

The Psychology of Eating. Harcourt Brace Jovanovich, 1978. 29 minutes, color. HBJ.

Elliot Valenstein explores the psychology of eating by posing several seminal questions: What motivates animals and humans to seek food? Why are some foods preferred over others? What causes obesity? What are some strategies for losing unwanted weight? The film includes Lipsitt's work on taste preferences in newborns, Garcia's research on conditioning taste preferences, Powley's experiments on food intake regulation, Valenstein's investigations of the role of the hypothalamus in eating behavior, Rodin's work on the causes of human obesity, and Stunkard's program for the treatment of obesity.

The Secrets of Sleep. WGBH and BBC, 1976. 52 minutes, color. Time-Life Media.

This discusses the uncertainties of scientific knowledge of sleep, exploring questions involving drug-induced sleep, jet lag, and dreaming.

Sleep and Dreaming in Humans. Houghton Mifflin, 1971. 14 minutes, color. HM.

Dr. William Dement demonstrates the research techniques used to study sleep and dreaming in human subjects. Stages of wakefulness, sleep, and dreaming are specified by polygraphic recordings and behavioral observations made at the Stanford Sleep Clinic. A subject is awakened at various times during the night; the audience observes his dream reports and other mental activity, as well as the physiological indices of sleep and dreaming.

The Sleeping Brain. Houghton Mifflin, 1971. 23 minutes, color. PSU.

This film demonstrates procedures for exploring structures of the brain associated with sleep and dreaming.

To Sleep . . . Perchance to Dream. NET, 1967. 30 minutes, b/w. PSU.

Candid scenes at the Sleep Laboratory of the University of California at Los Angeles document several investigations into the nature of sleep. The recording and interpretation of electrical impulses from a sleeping subject and the rapid eye movements during dreaming are shown. Experiments to determine the relationship of dreams to stomach secretions, the amount of time infants spend dreaming, and the effect of depriving a subject of his dreams are shown and explained.

US. Campus Films, 1971. 28 minutes, color. CAMP.

This examines the lives of a variety of American drug users, including housewives, business people, and youths.

CHAPTER 4. LEARNING

Animal Reasoning. NET and Tulane University, 1967. 9 minutes, b/w. IU, PSU.

This film shows laboratory experiments with rats performing learning tasks that illustrate inductive reasoning and the effects of brain damage on reasoning.

Behavior Modification in the Classroom. University of California, Berkeley, 1970. 24 minutes, color. UC Berkeley.

This demonstrates the use of operant conditioning and modeling by teachers.

Biofeedback and Self-Regulation. Harper & Row, 1980. 21 minutes, color, HARM.

This film describes recent research in the basics of experimental and clinical biofeedback, and it explores prospects for future applications.

Business, Behaviorism, and the Bottom Line. CRM, 1973. 22 minutes, color. CRM/MHF.

B. F. Skinner presents behaviorism, conditioning, reinforcement, and shaping, and he gives a personal interpretation of these in an industrial setting.

Classical and Instrumental Conditioning. Harper & Row, 1978. 20 minutes. HARM.

Principles of conditioning are presented both in the laboratory and graphically, and they are applied to human behavior.

A Conversation with B. F. Skinner. CRM, 1972. 23 minutes, color. CRM/MHF.

In this filmed interview, B. F. Skinner discusses such questions as "Just how free is man?" "What would happen to creativity in a society controlled by operant conditioning?" and "Who is to keep the controllers (i.e., those responsible for modifying others' behaviors) honest or benevolent?"

A Demonstration of Behavioral Processes. Prentice-Hall, 1971. 28 minutes, color, PH.

B. F. Skinner reviews the history of operant conditioning. He describes the apparatus involved, then demonstrates differential reinforcement and shaping. Applications of operant principles to human behavior are discussed.

Involuntary Control? John Wiley & Sons, 1971. 21 minutes. JW.

This shows a variety of experiments in which biofeedback is used to bring about voluntary control of bodily functions.

Learning. CRM, 1971. 30 minutes, color. PSU, CRM/MHF.

This film has laboratory demonstrations of human and animal reactions to various stimuli and basic principles of learning. B. F. Skinner discusses the theory of operant conditioning; Lewis Lipsitt shows infant learning; David McClelland discusses motivation techniques. Silent-film sequence shows classically conditioned fear in a child, operant reinforcement, generalization, and ultimate extinction in the adult.

Pavlov: The Conditioned Reflex. USSR Central Television and Soviet Academy of Sciences, 1975. 23 minutes, b/w. PSU.

This film provides rare documentary footage of Pavlov at work in his Leningrad research center. (It also includes a review of methodology.) It focuses on Pavlov's studies of the conditioned reflex and his famous dog experiment.

Reward and Punishment. CRM, 1974. 14 minutes, color. CRM/MHF.

This shows examples of the influence of reward and punishment in changing the behavior of children.

The Tool Users. National Geographic Society, 1975. 14 minutes, color. PSU.

This film illustrates the wide range of animal species that use tools and in some instances modify objects in the environment into tools. Examples include weaver ants weaving a communal nest, the Galápagos finch using thorns to reach insects, Egyptian vultures hurling rocks at ostrich eggs, and chimpanzees assembling and using simple tools.

A World of Difference: B. F. Skinner and the Good Life (Nova). WGBH, 1979. 57 minutes, color. TLM.

This is an intimate film that traces the life of behavioral psychologist B. F. Skinner. His belief that a better society could be shaped by positive personal reinforcement was put into practice at a rural cooperative, Twin Oaks. A careful examination of Twin Oaks indicates that Skinner's system works better in theory than in practice.

CHAPTERS 5 AND 6. SENSORY PROCESSES & PERCEPTION

Behavior of Animals and Human Infants in Response to a Visual Cliff. R. D. Walk, E. J. Gibson, Pennsylvania State University, 1959. 15 minutes, b/w. PSU.

This is a comparative study of the depth discrimination of animals and human infants. The central platform on top of the glass prevents the use of cues other than visual ones. The pattern is located directly under glass on one side of the platform, and the opposite side has the same pattern located some distance below the glass (appearing as a cliff). Subjects descend to near side and avoid the cliff side. The film shows that as an organism becomes capable of locomotion, it is also capable of depth perception.

An Introduction to Visual Illusions. Pennsylvania State University, 1970. 12 minutes, color. PSU/MHF.

This demonstrates visual illusions involving depth, direction, afterimages, apparent movement, and other facets of visual perception.

Living in a Reversed World. Mauthner and Erismann, 1958. 12 minutes, b/w. PSU.

This film demonstrates a perception experiment in which university students wear devices that invert their fields of vision, and it shows stages of adaptation to new situations. It was filmed at the Institute of Experimental Psychology at Innsbruck.

The Mind of Man. Produced by NET, BBC, and Swedish and Bavarian Television, 1970. Available in four segments. PSU, IU.

> The Mind of Man: Part 3
> 28 minutes, color.
>
> This film shows visual illusions and selective perception, the use of robots to discover how humans recognize and perceive objects, development of reasoning abilities in children, brain damage affecting certain areas of the brain but not necessarily other areas, and the effect of malnutrition on the brain.

Motion Perception 1: 2-Dimensional Motion Perception. Houghton Mifflin, 1971. 10 minutes, color. HM, PSU.

This film asks how stimuli moving in 2-dimensional space are perceived by a viewer, and how motions are seen and analyzed in terms of groups and sub-groups. It provides an example of the Gestalt law of common fate. Both computer-generated stimuli and movements of human subjects are used. The viewer can identify a series of complex motions with few sources of light.

Motion Perception 2: 3-Dimensional Motion Perception. Houghton Mifflin, 1971. 10 minutes, color. HM, PSU.

The film shows the tendency to perceive changing stimulus patterns as 3-dimensional changes. Computer-generated stimuli and movements of human subjects show the information or cues necessary to perceive 3-dimensionality. Motion patterns and changes of size or length are illustrated alone and in combination, and resulting effects are specified.

The Senses and Perception: Links to the Outside World. Indiana University, 1975. 18 minutes, color. IU.

This looks at how information reaches the brain and is interpreted based on its content as well as past experience.

Senses of Man. Indiana University, 1965. 18 minutes, color. IU.

The film briefly explains the structures and functions of the sense organs.

The Sensory World. CRM, 1971. 33 minutes, color. CRM/MHF.

This film demonstrates how sensory information reaches the brain; it also displays several perceptual illusions.

Upright Vision through Inverting Spectacles. E. J. Mauthner and Erismann, and I. Kohler, 1953. 11 minutes, silent, b/w. PSU.

This film shows a perception experiment in which the subject wears a device that inverts his field of vision, and it shows the stages of adaptation to the new situation. It was filmed at the Institute of Experimental Psychology at Innsbruck.

Visual Perception. H. Cantril, Educational Testing Center, 1959. 19 minutes, color. PSU.

Demonstrations used at the Perception Center at Princeton University show the effects of some of our assumptions on what we "see," including the distorted room and the trapezoidal window.

Vision with Spatial Inversion. Pronko and Snyder, 1951. 18 minutes, silent, b/w. PSU.

The film reenacts the classical experiment in which subject wears inverting spectacles continuously for several weeks. Initial difficulties in orientation, walking, eating, writing, and card sorting gradually dissipate as the subject becomes accustomed to "upside-down world."

World to Perceive. NET, 1963. 29 minutes, b/w. PSU.

Herman Witkin, Eleanor Gibson, and Richard Walk demonstrate the role of perception in handling information we receive from our environment and how our personalities affect our perception. The film includes visual cliff and field dependence-independence research.

CHAPTER 7. MEMORY

Fidelity of Report. Wilbert S. Ray, 1946. 6 minutes, silent, b/w. PSU.

Audience participation demonstrates the accuracy of observation and report. A dramatic action sequence concerns a woman robbed while waiting for a bus. The action takes sixty seconds, after which the projector is stopped. A standard set of questions is given to the audience for their answers. The dramatic action is repeated by continuing projection; each observer is then asked to check the accuracy of his observation.

Human Memory. Harcourt Brace Jovanovich, 1980. 28 minutes, color. HBJ.

The film demonstrates the processes of memory, memory aids, and the cognitive distortions created while reconstructing memories. It includes a rumor-chain experiment.

Information Processing. CRM, 1971. 29 minutes, color. CRM/MHF, PSU.

Psychologist Donald A. Norman and comedian David Steinberg use a cocktail party to reveal basic principles and far-reaching ramifications of human information processing. The film covers short- and long-term memory, the Stroop phenomenon, mnemonics, retrieval strategies, and problem solving.

Memory. CRM, 1980. 30 minutes, color. CRM/MHF.

The film discusses long- and short-term memory and gives examples of how to use mnemonics.

CHAPTER 8. THINKING

Decisions . . . McGraw-Hill, 1980. 30 minutes, color. Syracuse Films.

This film examines the decision-making process.

Koestler on Creativity. BBC, 1971. 40 minutes, color. TLM.

This film presents Arthur Koestler's ideas on how the creative mind works, explaining how creativity affects the artist, the scientist, and our daily thoughts. Problem solving, in Koestler's view, is the mental shuffling of existing solutions.

Problem Solving Strategies: The Synthetic Approach. CRM, 1980. 27 minutes, color. CRM/MHF.

This looks at some recent innovations in creative problem solving.

Why Man Creates. Pyramid, 1969. 25 minutes, color. P, UC.

In Saul Bass's highly imaginative exploration of human creativity, eight episodes—all humorous and some surrealistic—present the process and result of inventiveness through the ages, the judgment of artists by the public, the dedication of scientists to solving problems, and the celebration of the individual's power to create.

CHAPTER 9. LANGUAGE

The First Signs of Washoe. WGBH, 1976. 59 minutes, color. TLM.

This film documents the attempts of the Gardners to teach American Sign Language to Washoe, a baby chimpanzee. Lana, another chimp, is taught to communicate with a computer.

The Mind of Man. Produced by NET, BBC, and Swedish and Bavarian Television, 1970. Available in four segments. PSU, IU.

The Mind of Man: Part 4
30 minutes, color.

This film shows the region of the brain that controls language, presents a discussion of human language development by Noam Chomsky, and shows how autistic children are trained to speak. Sarah, an experimental chimpanzee at the University of California at Santa Barbara, uses written symbols to communicate. Nobel Prize-winning physicist Richard Feinman discusses human imagination and creativity. B. F. Skinner discusses behaviorism. Also presented are Donald Hebb's approach to the question of man's soul, a split-brain operation, and the discovery of the separate functions of the right and left hemispheres.

Talk to the Animals. CRM/McGraw-Hill Films, 1978. 12 minutes, color. CRM/MHF.

This film shows the progress being made in teaching communication skills to chimpanzees in experimental labs at Stanford, Oklahoma University, and the Yerkes Primate Center in Atlanta, Georgia. Light, fast-moving sequences show a surprising sophistication of primate responses, and describe how techniques and tools which were used in these experiments are also being modified for use in teaching handicapped humans to develop language skills.

CHAPTER 10. THE BIOLOGICAL BASIS OF SOCIAL BEHAVIOR

Animal Communication. Time-Life, 1971. 30 minutes, color. TLM.

How do animals communicate? This film looks at the variety of signals used by a dozen species—from insects to primates. It focuses on the cricket's special mating song, how some birds and tropical fish use color, and the importance of scent in the life of dogs.

Babymakers. CRM, 1980. 43 minutes, color. CRM/MHF.

The film explores controversies regarding artificial insemination, "test-tube" babies, surrogate motherhood, and related issues.

Bird Brain (Nova). BBC, 1976. 27 minutes, color. TLM.

The film shows that birds migrate to insure a continuing food supply and will travel up to 20,000 miles, returning to exactly the place where their journey began. Investigations reveal that birds navigate through an instinctive knowledge of wind and weather. The homing pigeon also seems to rely on the sun as a compass, while other birds have been found to use the stars, and even the earth's magnetic field, as a guide.

Invisible Walls. Pennsylvania State University, 1969. 12 minutes, color. PSU.

This demonstrates American perceptions of personal space in experiments that violate invisible spatial barriers of unsuspecting subjects.

Research in Animal Behavior. Harper & Row Media, 1978. 18 minutes, color. HARM.

The film shows research footage of six experiments in animal behavior:
1. "Language of the Bees: The Classic Experiment," by Karl von Frisch.
2. "Visual Displays," by Hal Harrison and H. Kitchen.

3. "Courtship Displays in Lesser and Greater Prairie Chickens," by S. D. MacDonald.
4. "Effects of Crowding on Rats," by John B. Calhoun.
5. "Dominance Hierarchy in Jungle Fowl and Cows," by A. M. Guhl and Ernest Banks.
6. "Social Behavior of Baboons," by Stuart Altman.

Sociobiology: The Human Animal. WGBH and BBC, 1977. 57 minutes, color. TLM.

This film looks at the genetic basis of behavior.

To Discover Our Body's Time Clock: Anticipate the Rhythms of Your Ecstasy and Blues. Document Associates. 20 minutes, color.

The film considers biorhythm phenomena and relationships between biorhythmic variation and behavior change.

CHAPTER 11. SOCIAL PSYCHOLOGY

The City and the Self. Milgram, 1973. 52 minutes, color. TLM, PSU.

This is a study of human relations in the city, based on psychological concepts formulated by Stanley Milgram. It examines city dwellers' perception of their city and their behavior in created situations.

Conformity and Independence. Harper & Row Media, 1975. 23 minutes, color. HARM, PSU.

The film presents social psychology's main findings and principles in these areas, using both field and laboratory settings to reinforce the interplay between experience and experiment. Included are Sherif's experiments on norm formation, Asch's work on group pressure and Crutchfield's variation, Milgram's experiment on action conformity, Kelman's three processes of compliance, and Moscovici's recent theoretical views.

Cornell Candid Cameria Collection. A. Funt, 1959 on. 3–10 minute sequences. (Listing of 250 titles available from 215A Uris Hall, Cornell University, Ithaca, NY 14853)

Among the collections are sequences showing conformity behavior ("Face the Rear"), public opinion polling ("Tampa Survey"), and obedience to authority ("Don't Eat Light").

Eye of the Storm. Xerox, 1971. 29 minutes, color. PSU.

This explores the nature of prejudice, how it is learned and developed by dividing a sixth-grade all-white rural class into those with and those without blue eyes. Discrimination is practiced against each group on alternating days.

Academic performance of each group is related to whether they are "top dogs" or "underdogs."

Group Dynamics: Groupthink. CRM, 1973. 22 minutes, color. CRM/MHF, PSU.

Presented here are the eight symptoms of "groupthink" as proposed by Dr. Irving L. Janis in his book *Victims of Groupthink.* The film includes examples of group decision-making processes which influenced such historical events as Pearl Harbor, the Korean War, and the Bay of Pigs. It shows how effective leadership can prevent a decision-making group from falling into "groupthink."

Invitation to Social Psychology. Milgram, 1975. 25 minutes, color. HARM, PSU.

This provides an introduction to social psychology, with emphasis on three questions. What is the subject matter of social psychology? What are its methods of investigation? And what are some of its findings? Examples include interpersonal events in a cafeteria, reactions of bystanders on a city street, Milgram's obedience study, and Zimbardo's prison simulation.

Leadership: Style or Circumstance. CRM, 1975. 30 minutes, color. CRM/MHF.

This film demonstrates how verbal and nonverbal styles of communication can affect leadership qualities.

Obedience. Milgram, 1962. 45 minutes, b/w. NYU.

This is a film on the well-known obedience to authority experiments conducted by Stanley Milgram at Yale University. It describes the experimental procedure and shows the behavior of obedient and defiant subjects.

The Pain of Shyness. ABC-TV, 1984. 18 minutes, color. ABC.

With Dr. Philip Zimbardo, the film explores the social disease of shyness and presents ways to deal with it.

The People of People's Temple. Ruxin-Gottlieb, 1979. 24 minutes, color. Films, Inc.

This examines the attractions and abuses of Jim Jones's People's Temple.

Prejudice: Causes, Consequences, Cures. CRM, 1974. 24 minutes, color. CRM/MHF.

This film examines findings in research on prejudice and the implications for dealing with various minorities.

Social Psychology. CRM, 1972. 33 minutes, color. CRM/MHF.

The first portion of this film is documentary footage of the first busing of black children to previously all-white schools in the middle-class suburbs of Westport, Connecticut. In the second part, basic social psychological concepts are introduced with a discussion of their possible applications to the social problems presented in the documentary portion of the film.

Until I Get Caught. Cornell University, 1980. 30 minutes, color. MTPS, CUCC.

This is a documentary showing the psychological and physiological effects of alcohol on driver attitudes and performance. Designed specifically for college audiences, the film provokes discussion on attitudes, attitude change, and cross-cultural differences.

Violence: Will It Ever End? Document Associates, 1976. 19 minutes, color. DA.

Rollo May, José Delgado, David Cappon, and others discuss various approaches to understanding violence.

When Will People Help? The Social Psychology of Bystander Intervention. Harcourt Brace Jovanovich, 1976. 25 minutes, color. HBJ, PSU.

What makes a bystander decide to help or to ignore a potentially critical situation. Daryl Bem discovers the problem and presents experiments by social psychologists. Tests indicate that the physical danger, legal harassment, need for a quick decision, and embarrassment result in nonintervention. The bystander, who must define this situation as an emergency and must feel the weight of responsibility on himself, is often deterred by the presence of other people.

CHAPTER 12. THE INDIVIDUAL AND SOCIETY: THE CONTRIBUTIONS OF SIGMUND FREUD

Deeper into Hypnosis. Prentice-Hall, 1980. 27 minutes, color. PH.

This film explores hypnosis from a scientific perspective, differentiating between fact and fiction with regard to hypnotic phenomenon. Ernest Hilgard demonstrates how highly hypnotizable subjects can experience distortions of perception, emotion, and memory. Among the phenomena shown are negative and positive hallucinations, age regressions, and posthypnotic suggestions. An experiment involving pain receptivity shows how some individuals can achieve analgesia through hypnosis. Martin Orne discusses the experimental controls necessary to test whether or not a given hypnotic phenomenon is "genuine."

Freud. Universal 16, 1962. 140 minutes, b/w. (Universal 16, 445 Park Avenue, New York, NY 10022)

A theatrical film focusing on the five-year period in which Sigmund Freud established the foundations of psychoanalysis. (Starring Montgomery Cliff, directed by John Huston.)

Ratman. BBC, 1974. 53 minutes, color. TLM.

An enactment of the analytic sessions, between Freud and a young man suffering an obsessional neurosis, that led to the discovery of infantile sexuality.

CHAPTER 13. GENERAL ISSUES IN DEVELOPMENT

Benjamin. BBC, 1977. 42 minutes, color. TLM.

The birth of Benjamin Pile and his development for the next six months were recorded on film. Using slow-motion and frame-by-frame analyses, the film shows that the very young have an astonishing range of abilities.

Child's Play. Harcourt Brace Jovanovich, 1976. 20 minutes.

This film introduces the methods and perspectives of the developmental psychologist. Scenes of children at play reveal changes in cognitive and social levels from infancy to adolescence.

Development of the Child: Infancy. J. Kagan, H. Gardner, 1972. 20 minutes, color. HARM, PSU.

Behavior and cognitive patterns in the first eighteen months of life are shown. The child has an immediate ability to respond to basic sensations. The film shows these motor responses and reflexes, as well as the control exerted by maturational forces on motor and cognitive processes. Also covered are the concept of attachment, stranger and separation anxiety, object permanence, and individual differences in the child's temperament, which may be a function of biological factors.

CHAPTER 14. COGNITIVE DEVELOPMENT: THOUGHT

Cognitive Development. CRM, 1973. 20 minutes, color. CRM/MHF, PSU.

An interpretive overview, this film describes and portrays two major theories of cognitive development—the cognitive development stage approach and the cognitive-behavioral (or learning-based) approach. Jean Piaget's developmental stage approach, with its emphasis on maturational and environmental factors, is first illustrated through animation and then shown applied in an educational setting. Following this is coverage of the cognitive learning or cognitive-behavioral approach, subscribed to by such developmentalists as Jerome Bruner, Jerome Kagan, and Sidney Bijou.

Development of the Child: Cognition. J. Kagan, H. Gardner, 1972. 30 minutes, color. HARM, PSU.

Problem solving is approached in terms of perception, memory evaluation, and reasoning. Also covered are the generation of hypotheses to solve problems and an overview of Piaget's theory of intellectual development—sensory motor, preoperational, concrete operational, and formal operations.

Development of the Child: Cross-Cultural Approach to Cognition. Kagan, 1975. 20 minutes, color. HARM, PSU.

The film examines the effects of environment, particularly modernization, on the rate of psychological development. It focuses on perceptual inference, memory for objects and locations, performance of operation on memory, growth of reflectivity, and appearance of concrete operational thinking.

Playing Together. BBC, 1968. 30 minutes, b/w. PSU.

The film explains that the child of three and four years needs to be surrounded with materials which develop notions of shape, size, weight, distance, speed, color, and texture. It presents children in various play situations.

Three Cognitive Skills: Middle Childhood. CRM/McGraw-Hill, Inc., 1978. 21 minutes, color. CRM/MHF.

This film discusses the development of reading, memory, and creative skills in childhood.

CHAPTER 15. COGNITIVE DEVELOPMENT: LANGUAGE

Development of the Child: Language. Kagan and Gardner, 1972. 20 minutes, color. HARM, PSU.

The film discusses the child's language processes in the first four years; the development of phonemes, syntax, and semantics; the process by which language is acquired and how acquisition can be influenced.

Language Development. CRM/McGraw-Hill Films, 1973. 20 minutes, color. CRM/MHF.

This film shows research experiments involving language acquisition in youngsters. David Premack presents his studies in which chimpanzees use plastic word symbols to perform such functions as word identification and answering questions.

CHAPTER 16. SOCIAL DEVELOPMENT

Adolescence: The Winds of Change. Harper & Row, 1974. 30 minutes, color. HARM.

The film discusses physical, sexual, and cognitive changes in adolescents, and the effects of parental attitudes and other pressures on them.

Aging. CRM, 1973. 22 minutes, color. CRM/MHF.

The film illustrates problems of aging and discusses various theories of adjustment to old age.

Childhood: The Enchanted Years. MGM-Noxon, 1972. 52 minutes, color. Films, Inc.

This explores the path of development from total dependence to independence.

Day Care for a Kibbutz Toddler. Stone, 1976. 23 minutes, color. PSU.

Of the two hundred Israeli Kibbutzim, around 10 percent have their children sleep in the parents' apartments. Shows day care for these children at the Children's Houses and the role of the metaplet. Questions are posed concerning the nature of this family-style day care, and the relevance of the methods to other countries.

Development of the Child: A Cross-Cultural Approach to the Acquisition of Sex Roles and Social Standards. Kagan and Gardner, 1975. 23 minutes, color. HARM, PSU.

Social pressures affect a child's behavior as early as the second year of life. Several different cultures are examined to show how sex roles, aggression, peer-group relationships, and cognitive development are affected. The film shows the influences of biological as well as social factors.

Divorce: For Better or For Worse (Parts I and II). CRM, 1977. 45 minutes, color. CRM/MHF.

This film explores the traumas associated with divorce.

Emotional Development: Aggression. CRM, 1973. 17 minutes, color. CRM/MHF.

This discusses social learning theories of aggression and their relation to anger, frustration, or instinct.

Everybody Rides the Carousel. Hebley and Aubley, 1976. Three 24-minute films, color. P.

This series of three animated films accurately illustrates the eight stages of life as defined by Erik Erikson.

Growing Up Female. Julie Reichert, 1971. 60 minutes, color. New Day Films.

This is an award-winning look at the socialization of the American woman through a personal view of the lives of six females. The film shows the effects of parents, teachers, and media as forces that shape these women's lives.

Happy to Be Me. Arthur Mokin Productions, Inc., 1979. 25 minutes, color. MOK.

The film discusses the importance of perceptions of masculinity and femininity as aspects of social phenomena. It explores young peoples' attitudes toward gender and male and female roles.

Human Aggression. Harper & Row Media, 1976. 24 minutes, color. HARM, PSU.

Spontaneous occurrences of aggression in real life, such as the activities of a youth gang, are depicted and related to scientific principles and laboratory findings. The film includes Bard on the psychological training of police, Bandura and Walters's Bobo doll experiment, Milgram's work with group influences on aggression, Syke and Matza on the legitimization of aggression in delinquent groups, and a statement by former Attorney General Ramsey Clark on aggression among the disadvantaged.

Kids for Sale. Action for Children's Television, 1979. 22 minutes, color. Mass Media Ministries.

The film looks at the effects of commercial television on behavior.

Moral Development. CRM, 1973. 28 minutes, color. CRM/MHF.

This film re-creates Milgram's classic obedience study. Emphasis is placed on the social learning theory of moral development, which emphasizes the influences of social and environmental factors on moral reasoning over an individual's cognitive maturity.

Moral Judgment and Reasoning. CRM, 1978. 17 minutes, color. CRM/MHF.

This film describes the characteristics of moral development from three perspectives. Included are psychoanalytical theory as introduced by Freud, social learning theory which contends that children learn through observation, and cognitive developmental theory, with emphasis on Piaget's work.

Mother Love. CBS, 1960. 26 minutes, b/w. CF.

A colony of newborn rhesus monkeys was tested as to their reaction to a variety of unusual and inanimate mother substitutes (mother surrogates), in order to find the key to the bond between mother and child and the effect of denial of maternal love. Experiments show that the single most important factor is body contact, holding, and nestling; its deprivation can cause deep emotional disturbance, even death.

Need to Achieve. NET, 1963. 30 minutes, b/w. PSU, IU.

The film presents Dr. David McClelland's psychological theory that the economic growth or decline of nations depends upon the entrepreneurs of these nations.

Observational Learning. Harper & Row, 1978. 23 minutes, color. HARM.

The film presents the "Bobo doll" experiment, vicarious emotional conditioning, modeling therapy, and children imitating behavior seen on television.

Parents and Children. Research Press, 1979. 24 minutes, color. RP.

This summarizes reinforcement principles and examines ways to use positive reinforcement with children.

The Pinks and the Blues. WGBH, 1981. 57 minutes, color. TL.

This is an award-winning look at sex-role stereotypes in the process of socialization.

Rock-a-Bye Baby. BBC, 1971. 30 minutes, color. TLM.

This shows the importance of the mother-child relationship in human development from birth to three years and techniques used to measure mothering practices. It goes into how monkeys raised in isolation from mothers develop humanlike schizophrenia; how premature babies, missing the motion inside the mother's body, lag behind in development; and it shows a new method of rocking that has been devised to compensate for this deficiency.

Sex Role Development. CRM, McGraw-Hill Films, 1974. 23 minutes, color. CRM/MHF.

This film examines the influence that sex roles and stereotypes have on almost every facet of people's lives; the ways they are instilled in successive generations of Americans; and the way in which some people are currently trying to find better models for human behavior.

Sexuality: The Human Heritage. MEDCOM, 1975. 60 minutes, color. MED.

This explores questions concerning gender and role identity in light of genetic, physiological, and social factors.

Socialization: Moral Development. Harper & Row Media, 1980. 22 minutes, color. HARM.

Where do our ideas of good and evil come from? Are they learned? Or are they inbred and universal? This film explores theories of morality and moral development, and it dramatizes classic experiments (with brief methodological critiques).

Transitions. CRM, 1979. 29 minutes, color. CRM/MHF.

This examines the process of making major life changes and the personal, emotional, and internal adjustments that are necessary. It focuses primarily on the work setting.

Two Ball Games. Cornell University, 1977. 28 minutes, color. AF.

A documentary comparing spontaneous vs. organized sports for children. Factual and uncontrived, the film compares a child-organized backyard ballgame with an adult-run Little League game. It provokes discussion on several topics in child development and parent-child relationships.

Women: The Hand That Cradles the Rock. Document Associates, 1976. 22 minutes, color. DA.

   This film presents advertisements showing stereotyped images of women. The ads are interspersed with discussions of the women's liberation movement.

CHAPTER 17. INTELLIGENCE: ITS NATURE AND MEASUREMENT

Intelligence: A Complex Concept. CRM/McGraw-Hill Films, 1978. 20 minutes, color. CRM/MHF.

   What is intelligence? When people on the street were asked this question, their filmed answers revealed much confusion between what intelligence is as tests measure it and what intelligence is in everyday life. This film explores some of the varied definitions, including those of Piaget and J. P. Guilford. The problems inherent in testing are also discussed, and a variety of test types are illustrated.

IQ Myth: Parts 1 and 2. CBS News, 1975. 51 minutes, color. CF, PSU.

   This film shows the ways in which the IQ concept has been used. It illustrates the controversy concerning the validity of IQ tests with regard to environment, family mores, and racial background, and it indicates the importance of test results in the child's future education and career.

Whales, Dolphins and Men. BBC, 1973. 52 minutes, color. TLM.

   The film shows the intelligence and grace of whales and dolphins. Experiments and observations show that they are in many ways akin to man. It also considers the effects of the whaling industry and makes a plea for conservation.

CHAPTER 18. PERSONALITY ASSESSMENT

Individual Differences. CRM/McGraw-Hill Films, 1978. 18 minutes, color. CRM/MHF.

   Genetic traits and environment are different for all babies, which means that each one will be an individual; each will vary from all others. This film explores human individuality and the broad range of characteristics that are considered normal. Tests devised to separate personality differences from traits that indicate developmental problems are shown.

Personality. CRM, 1971. 30 minutes, color. CRM, MHF.

   The film studies the personality of a male college student. It demonstrates the use of self-report, rating by others, and standardized tests in personality assessment.

CHAPTER 19. PSYCHOPATHOLOGY

Abnormal Behavior: A Mental Hospital. CRM, 1971. 28 minutes, color. CRM/MHF.

This film explores a modern psychiatric hospital. It includes doctor-patient interviews that expose symptoms of schizophrenia. It also illustrates shock therapy.

Abnormal Psychology: The Psychoses. Harper & Row Media, 1980. 22 minutes, color. HARM.

What exactly are psychotic disorders? Where do they come from? How do psychotic individuals behave? This film takes viewers to a schizophrenia ward in a mental institution and interviews depressive patients. The film provides an introduction to etiology, behavior, treatment, and prognoses.

Alcoholism: A Model of Drug Dependency. CRM, 1972. 20 minutes, color. CRM/MHF.

This is an award-winning presentation of alcoholism and its treatment.

Assessment of Childhood Psychopathology. Pennsylvania State University, 1980. 26 minutes, color. PSU.

This presents psychiatric assessment of children based on DSM-II and DSM-III.

Case Study of Multiple Personality. Pennsylvania State University, 1957. 30 minutes, color. PSU.

This contains excerpts from the film *The Three Faces of Eve*, which depicts multiple personality. It also includes actual interviews with the subject.

The Class That Went to War. CRM, 1978. 35 minutes, color. CRM/MHF.

This film discusses the legacy of the Vietnam war and the veterans who are still facing the stress.

Constructive Use of the Emotions. University of California, 1970. 22 minutes, color. UC.

This reviews different responses to anxiety-causing situations and how suitable these responses are to these situations.

The Cry for Help. Pennsylvania State University, 1962. 28 minutes, color. PSU.

The film presents suicide attempts as a cry for help and as an expression of emotional conflict. It discusses how to handle a suicide attempt.

Death. Filmmakers Library, 1968. 42 minutes, color. FL.

This follows the last days of a terminally ill cancer patient, discussing psychological defenses used to face death and portraying the reactions of family, nurses, and others.

Denise: The Tragedy of Child Abuse. Boston Broadcasters, Inc., 1980. 58 minutes, color. ABC.

This discusses the problem of child abuse. It includes interviews with family and social workers involved in a real-life case.

The Maze. Houghton Mifflin, 1971. 30 minutes, color. PSU, HM.

This is a sensitive documentary on the life of William Kurelek, an artist who struggled with feelings of inadequacy and depression that led to a period of hospitalization. Kurelek's paintings and interviews with his family and the hospital staff provide an unusual glimpse into personality and psychiatry. The film provokes a lively and extensive discussion of mental disorder, its diagnosis and treatment.

One Man's Madness. BBC, 1974. 32 minutes, color. TLM.

This is a documentary of a writer who became a manic-depressive. His swinging moods, from ecstasy to severe depression, and his symptoms of alienation and withdrawal are shown both when he is at home and in the hospital.

R. D. Laing: A Dialog on Mental Illness and Its Treatment. R. D. Laing, 1976. 21 minutes, color. HARM, PSU.

This focuses on Laing's theories of treating the mentally ill. He discusses interuterine memory as one therapeutic technique based on prebirth memory rituals, and its effects on patients. He also relates his position in the antipsychiatrist arguments. The film shows the need for hospitals to be sanctuaries.

Schizophrenia: The Shattered Mirror. NET, 1967. 60 minutes, b/w. PSU.

Experiences of schizophrenics are presented to evoke understanding in the viewer, rather than aversion. The film shows research being conducted to develop a better knowledge of the disorder and better treatments.

Silent Snow, Secret Snow. Macmillan Films, Inc., 1969. 17 minutes, b/w. MAC.

A schizophrenic boy withdraws into a private world of fantasy in a short story by Conrad Aiken.

Titicut Follies (Parts I and II). Grove Press, 1969. 84 minutes, b/w. GRO.

This is a revealing exposé of conditions at a hospital for the criminally insane.

CHAPTER 20. TREATMENT OF PSYCHOPATHOLOGY

Achievement Place. University of Kansas, 1970. 30 minutes, color. UK.

This shows the use of a token economy system to successfully resocialize delinquent boys at a halfway house.

Anyplace But Here. CBS Reports, 1979. 50 minutes, color. CF.

The dilemma facing the mentally ill in America and the people who try to help them are examined in this documentary. This shows three patients as they seek release from the hospital and its bureaucracy.

Behavior Modification: Teaching Language to Psychotic Children. I. Lovaas, 1969. 42 minutes, color. PH, PSU.

Ivar Lovaas shows reinforcement and stimulus-fading techniques in teaching speech to psychotic children. Bizarre echolalic speech, self-destruction, and pervasive failures in acquisition of social and intellectual behaviors are depicted, followed by imitative verbal behavior. Methods and data are presented on the acquisition of certain aspects of meaning, as well as the establishment of relational terms.

Behavior Therapy: An Introduction. Harper & Row Media, 1978. 23 minutes, color. HARM.

Behavior Therapy shows how three models of learning—operant, classical, observational—are used by therapists to eliminate problem behaviors and habits, to remove irrational fears and anxieties, and to promote coping strategies and develop skills where deficiencies exist. The film demonstrates how the three basic processes of contingency management, counterconditioning, and role playing are applied to the problems of three individuals, and how changes in their behavior are effected following these therapy techniques.

Come Out, Come Out, Wherever You Are. Indiana University, 1971. 59 minutes, color. IU.

This portrays psychotherapy sessions and techniques.

Madness and Medicine. CRM, 1977. 49 minutes, color. CRM/MHF.

This two-part sequence investigates patients' feelings about the treatment they receive, administration of drugs, electroshock therapy, and psychosurgery.

Otto: A Study in Abnormal Psychology. Indiana University, 1975. 27 minutes, color. PSU.

This is a dramatized, open-ended case study. It portrays Otto as a middle-aged man suffering from real and imagined pressures at home and at work. Otto suffers from insomnia and becomes increasingly withdrawn and anxious. Interpretations and discussions of the case are provided in four additional films in the Otto Series (psychoanalytic, behavioral, phenomenological, and social perspectives).

Reinforcement Therapy. Smith, Kline, and French, 1966. 45 minutes, b/w. PSU.

This film shows three experimental programs that apply learning theory or operant conditioning to the treatment of autistic children, retarded children, and chronic schizophrenic adults.

Three Approaches to Group Therapy. Psychological Films, 1974. Three films, 30 minutes each, color. PFI.

This three-part series is a sequel to the "Gloria" films (see next entry). Part 1 shows Everett L. Shostrom's theories of actualizing therapy. Part 2 demonstrates the technique of rational emotive therapy, developed by Albert Ellis. Part 3 deals with decision therapy, developed by Harold Greenwald. All three therapists conduct a group of the same members.

Three Approaches to Psychotherapy. Psychological Films, 1968. Three films: 48 minutes, 32 minutes, 36 minutes, color. BU, KSU, UMich, NYU.

The three films cover: client-centered therapy, demonstrated by Carl Rogers; Gestalt therapy, demonstrated by Frederick Perls; and rational emotive therapy, demonstrated by Albert Ellis. All therapists treat the same patient, "Gloria."

APPENDIX. STATISTICS: THE COLLECTION , ORGANIZATION, AND INTERPRETATION OF DATA

Statistics at a Glance. Wiley, 1970. 26 minutes, color. JW.

Using animated cartoons and film opticals, the film provides a graphic presentation of elementary descriptive statistics. Measures of central tendency are especially well illustrated.

Catalogs

The following list includes film companies and university film libraries that have considerable holdings in psychology. Each publishes a catalog of films for rent and sale. It would be helpful to the instructor to request catalogs and thus become better informed about the multitude of available materials and their sources. Although each instructor will have to evaluate films for his or her specific requirements, the *Journal of the Teaching of Psychology* and *Contemporary Psychology* both have media reviews that alert teachers to outstanding materials. The most comprehensive listing of audiovisuals in psychology is the *Index to Psychology: Multimedia*, 3rd ed., 1977, available from the National Information Center for Educational Media, University of Southern California, University Park, Los Angeles, CA 90007. Although there are hundreds of film libraries, companies, and catalogs not mentioned here, the list provided encompasses the majority of large suppliers. Specific addresses of all sources mentioned appear at the end of the section on audiovisual materials (see pp. 266–68).

Agency for Instructional Television
AIMS: Films and Videocassettes for Better Health
Anti-Defamation League of B'nai Brith
Association Films
Boston University, Krasker Memorial Film Library
Carousel Films

Corinth Films
Cornell University Candid Camera Collection
CRM/McGraw-Hill Films
Document Associates
Film Programmer's Guide to 16mm Rentals, prepared by Kathleen Weaver and
    published by Reel Research, 1975. This book lists practically every film made
    by Hollywood and foreign producers. It includes a film's specific topics and
    where the film can be rented.
Films by and/or about Women, published by Women's History Research Center,
    1972.
Florida State University Film Library
Guidance Associates
Harcourt Brace Jovanovich
Harper & Row Media
Human Relations Media
IBIS Media
Indiana University Audio-Visual Center
International Film Bureau
Kent State University Audio-Visual Services
Modern Talking Picture Service
National Audiovisual Center
National Film Board of Canada
National Geographic Educational Services Catalog
New York University Film Library
PBS Video Program Catalog
Pennsylvania State University Audio-Visual Department (Publishers of the *Psy-
    chological Cinema Register*, a comprehensive annotated listing of most psy-
    chology-oriented films)
Professional Research
Pyramid Films
A Selective Guide to Materials for Mental Health and Family Life Education
    (3rd ed., published by the Mental Health Materials Center, 1976).
Sunburst Communications
Time-Life Multimedia (U.S. distributor for the British Broadcasting Corporation,
    including the NOVA titles)
University of California (Berkeley), Extension Media Center
University of Illinois Visual Aids Service
University of Michigan Audio-Visual Education Center

Film Series

The following are specialized series or collections that might be of interest to
instructors who wish to focus on a specific topic in depth. The abbreviations at

the end of the entries refer to distributors of the materials described in the entries. At the end of the section on audiovisual materials, full names and addresses of the distributors are given (see pp. 266–68).

The Actualization Group. This seven-film series shows actual psychological group therapy. The viewer is able to observe and study the group's progress through the seven therapy sesssions. PFI and PSU.

Albert Ellis: Rational Emotive Psychotherapy. Albert Ellis, founder of rational emotive therapy, explains and demonstrates his approach in five films: *Rational Emotive Psychotherapy; Rational Emotive Psychotherapy Applied to Groups; A Demonstration with an Elementary School Age Child; A Demonstration with a Young Divorced Woman;* and *A Demonstration with a Woman Fearful of Expressing Emotion.* APGA.

Animal Behavior. Five films produced by the National Geographic Society investigate animal learning and its relationship to animal behavior. Titles are *Do Animals Reason?; The Function of Beauty in Nature; Invertebrates: Conditioning or Learning?; Konrad Lorenz: Science of Animal Behavior;* and *The Tool Users.* CM.

Behavior in Business. This series shows how the science of human behavior stimulates an organization's productivity and efficiency. The seven films are *Business, Behaviorism and the Bottom Line; Communication: The Nonverbal Agenda; Group Dynamics: "Groupthink"; Leadership: Style or Circumstance?; Productivity and the Self-Fulfilling Prophecy; Transactional Analysis;* and *Women in Management: Threat or Opportunity?* BU, UC, CRM/MHF, UI, and KSU.

Behavior Theory in Practice. The series is a set of four films that present basic concepts of conditioning, both classical and operant, and illustrate the usefulness of the principles in a wide variety of settings. Titles include *Respondent and Operant Behavior* (the first in the set); *Shaping Various Operants, Various Species* (including work on programmed learning with humans); *Generalization, Discrimination, and Motivation* (with some material on intracranial self-stimulation); and *Sequences of Behavior* (including a demonstration of the training of Seeing Eye dogs). Produced in 1966. UI, IU, KSU, UMich, PSU, and PH.

The Brain. Produced in 1984 by WNET/TV, this eight-part series of hour-long, color films examines the intricacies and mystique of the human brain. The titles are *The Enlightened Machine; Vision and Movement; Rhythms and Drives; Stress and Emotion; Learning and Memory; The Two Brains; Madness;* and *States of Mind.* Annenberg/CPB Collection.

Carl Rogers on Marriage. In these five films, Carl Rogers shares his views on the relationship between men and women. Film titles are *Persons as Partners; An Interview with Hal and Jane; An Interview with Bob and Carol; An Interview with Nancy and John;* and *An Interview with Jane and Jerry.* APGA.

Character Formation in Different Cultures. This classic set of films relating to cultural differences and their effects was prepared in the early 1950s, at least in part under the direction of both Margaret Mead and Gregory Bateson. Titles include *A Balinese Family; Bathing Babies in Three Cultures; Childhood Rivalry in Bali and New Guinea; First Days in the Life of a New Guinea Baby; Karba's First Years;* and *Trance and Dance in Bali.*

Concepts in Transactional Analysis. The five films in the series are *Stroke Seeking Behavior: Therapeutic Traps and Pitfalls; Patsy; Mary; Charlotte;* and *Bruce.* The names are those of participants in group therapy sessions, who present different problems to illustrate concepts of transactional analysis. APGA.

Conflict and Awareness. Subjects in this thirteen-film series include suicide, homosexuality, parent-child relationships, parental divorce, job interviewing, group conformity and rejection, self-identity/sex roles, and others. CRM/ MHF and KSU.

Cornell Candid Camera Collection. Over 200 sequences from yesteryear's *Candid Camera* television series have been selected by psychologists at Cornell University for educational use. A catalog of titles, with annotations, is available. Films are for purchase only and range from $10 to $70. For a description of the nature of the collection, see J. B. Maas and K. M. Toivanen, "*Candid Camera* and the Behavioral Science," *Audio-Visual Communication Review*, 1969, *17*, 307–14. CUCC.

Focus on Behavior. Produced in 1963 with the cooperation of the American Psychological Association, this set of ten films has been widely acclaimed. The films vary somewhat in quality and in the speed with which they are becoming outdated. Titles are *Brain and Behavior; Chemistry of Behavior; Computers and Human Behavior; Conscience of a Child; Learning About Learning; The Need to Achieve; No Two Alike; Of Men and Machines; Social Animal;* and *A World to Perceive.* BU, UC, UI, IU, KSU, UMich, and PSU.

Frontiers of Psychological Inquiry. This is a widely acclaimed series of experiential films designed to demonstrate psychological phenomena and stimulate students to pursue psychological issues on their own. The films serve as thought-provoking supplements to lectures and are accompanied by teacher's guides for holding intensive discussions. The specific titles are *The Maze,* an award-winning documentary on the life and works of an artist who was hospitalized for a time with schizophrenia; *Sleep and Dreaming in Humans,* showing the procedures used for recording all-night sleep and dreaming behavior (with W. Dement); *The Sleeping Brain,* demonstrating techniques for ascertaining the structures and functions of sleep and dreaming mechanisms (with M. Jouvet); and *2-Dimensional Motion Perception* and *3-Dimensional Motion Perception,* illustrating cues for perception of motion (with G. Johansson). HM and PSU.

Great Scientists Speak Again. This series of six 16mm color films features impersonation lectures by Professor Richard Eakin. The scientists portrayed are Louis Pasteur, William Harvey, Charles Darwin, Gregor Mendel, William Beaumont, and Hans Spemann. UC.

Harcourt Brace Jovanovich series. The six films in the series provide an in-depth study of major topics in psychology. Titles are *Child's Play: Window on Development; Divided Brain and Consciousness; Human Memory; The Psychology of Eating; Schizophrenia;* and *When Will People Help? The Social Psychology of Bystander Intervention.* HBJ.

Harper & Row College Media series. A large series of films and videotapes primarily in social psychology, developmental psychology, experimental psychology, abnormal psychology, and psychotherapy. Titles include *Socialization: Moral Development; Biology and Behavior; The Psychoses; Child Development: The Adolescent Boy, The Adolescent Girl; A Cross-cultural Approach to the Acquisition of Sex Roles and Social Standards; Language Development; Cognition; Conformity and Independence; Classical and Instrumental Conditioning; Behavior Therapy; R. D. Laing on R. D. Laing.*

The Human Senses. Produced by the National Geographic Educational Services in 1982, this is a series of five parts, in color, each of which is fifteen minutes long. The films are *In Touch With the World; A Matter of Taste; Learning to See; Listen! Hear!;* and *On the Nose.* NGES.

Mental Health Association films. The Mental Health Media Center distributes about thirty films that were either produced or approved by the Mental Health Association. A few titles are *Depression: A Study in Abnormal Behavior; The Fragile Mind; Journey;* and *Only Human.* MHMC.

National Broadcasting Company films. The National Broadcasting Company has produced a number of films of relevance focusing on contemporary problems of society. Some currently available titles include *A Chance to Learn* (issues and possible solutions for central-city schools); *In the Name of Law* (violence and the breakdown of law and order); *A Little Younger/A Little Older* (the generation gap, drugs, and the problems of affluence); *Oh, Woodstock!* (the festival viewed both by young participants and by adults, including two psychologists); and *The Orange and the Green* (prejudice and culture conflict in Northern Ireland). FI.

Notable Contributors to the Psychology of Personality. The series is a set of seventeen films consisting of interviews conducted by Richard I. Evans with notable psychologists. Subjects are Gordon Allport, Raymond Cattell, Erik Erikson, Hans Eysenck, Erich Fromm, Ernest Hilgard, Carl Jung, R. D. Laing, Konrad Lorenz, Arthur Miller, Gardner Murphy, Henry Murray, Jean Piaget and Barbel Inhelder, J. B. Rhine, Carl Rogers, Nevitt Sanford, and B. F. Skinner. MAC and PSU.

Ordinal Scales of Infant Psychological Development. The series was prepared by Ina C. Uzgiris and J. McVicker Hunt in 1966 to illustrate behavioral phenomena of early sensory-motor development as described by Piaget. There are six films in the series, including *Development of Means; Development of Schemata; Imitation; Object Permanence; Object Relations in Space;* and *Operational Causality.* UC and UI.

Otto. This series of five films deals with abnormal behavior. Four perspectives are involved: psychoanalytic, behavioral, phenomenological, and social. The films are available in 16mm and video casette. IU.

Project Head Start films. Project Head Start in the Office of Child Development of Health, Education, and Welfare, has produced thirty-five films relating to cultural deprivation and its effect, and illustrating training procedures. MTPS.

Psychic phenomena. Three films record the latest scientific psychic phenomena. They are *To Solve the ESP Mystery: Extra-Sensory Perception Is No Dream; To Discover a New Psychic Force—P. K.: Even Healing May Be Possible with Psychokinesis;* and *The Occult: X Factor or Fraud?* The films present both scientifically and sensibly the points of view of practitioners. DA and NYU.

Psychology Today. The series consists of eight films: *Abnormal Behavior; Aspects of Behavior; Development; Information Processing; Learning; Personality; The Sensory World;* and *Social Psychology.* The *Learning* film is truly outstanding. BU, CRM/MHF, UI, and KSU.

Social psychology. These six films on social psychology are titled *Taking Care of Business; Max Out; Nonverbal Communication; Human Aggression; Invitation to Social Psychology;* and *Conformity and Independence.* HARM.

Studies of Normal Personality Development. This is a very well-known and highly regarded set of films made over a period of years at the Child Development Laboratory School at Vassar College. Some have to do with the use of play techniques in studying child personality (*Balloons: Aggression and Destruction Games; Finger Painting;* etc.); others deal with the behavior of essentially normal children at various age levels (*Abby's First Two Years: A Backward Look; This Is Robert; When Should Grownups Help?;* etc.). All have a focus on childhood behavior. UC and NYU.

Understanding Human Behavior. This thirty-part color series was produced in 1980. It is an introduction to psychology that encourages an understanding and appreciation of the scientific approach to the study of human behavior. An integrated learning system, this television course surveys the physiological, intra-psychic, and social-behavioral perspectives on human thought and behavior; sensation and perception; motivation; learning and memory; maturation and development; personality theory and psychotherapy; and social psychology. Each part is thirty minutes long. The titles are (1) *Human Psychology,* (2) *The Brain,* (3) *Consciousness and Sleep,* (4) *Altered States of Consciousness,* (5) *Functions of the Brain,* (6) *Sensory Psychology,* (7) *Taste, Smell, Hearing,* (8) *Vision,* (9) *Sensory Deprivation,* (10) *Visual Perception,* (11) *Subliminal Perception,* (12) *Motivation and*

Hunger, (13) *Sexual Motivation*, (14) *Stress*, (15) *Conditioning*, (16) *Operant Conditioning*, (17) *Memory*, (18) *Pain and Hypnosis*, (19) *Genetic Psychology*, (20) *Emotional Development*, (21) *Cognitive Development*, (22) *Personality Theory*, (23) *Personality Tests*, (24) *Abnormal Psychology*, (25) *Psychotherapy, Part I*, (26) *Psychotherapy, Part II*, (27) *Interpersonal Attraction*, (28) *Social Groups*, (29) *Persuasion*, and (30) *Applied Psychology*. PBS (Adult Learning Service).

Wide World of Learning: 20/20 Series.   This ABC Video Enterprises series of six 20-minute, color films includes *Heroin Alley* (drugs and the middle class, 1983); *They're Murdering Our Children* (child abuse, 1984); *A Triumph of Love* (Pheobe Snow and her brain-damaged daughter, 1983); *Who Am I . . . Who I Am* (Gay ex-congressman Robert Bauman, 1984); *The People Inside Me* (schizophrenia, 1983); and *Bulimia* (an eating disorder, 1982; produced and distributed by CRM). All but the last distributed by ABC.

Slide Sets and Overhead Transparencies

There are many slide and overhead transparency sets useful in illustrating psychological apparatus, major concepts and paradigms, psychological tests, physiological systems, perceptual phenomena, and results of classic experiments. These slides and transparencies, often coupled with the teacher's own visual aids, increase student understanding, shorten the time needed to clarify concepts, and provide for greater student participation through demonstrations and visual experiments. Semi-darkness is not required when teachers use overhead projectors, rear-screen projection methods, or the Kodak Ektalite Daylight Projection Screen.

The most comprehensive set of 35-mm slides (300, in color) is the *Slide Group for General Psychology*, covering all areas of the introductory course. The slide set includes an instructor's guide and student study guide. It is available from McGraw-Hill Book Company. A second set, including 200 additional color slides, is also available. MHB. Several excellent slide or transparency sets, somewhat narrower in scope are:

Anatomical Transparencies for Neurobiology.   R. King, M. Glickstein, and E. LaBossiere, 1972, 72 transparencies. MHB.

General Psychology, Parts 1-5. Research Media, 36 transparencies, color; Part 1—*Statistics*; Part 2—*Perception*; Part 3—*Physiology*; Part 4—*Heredity*; and Part 5—*Learning*. RM.

Introduction to Psychology: A View of Behavior, Parts 1-11 (rev. ed.) (slide-tape program with administration manual, instructor's guide, student workbook, and tests). Paul L. Brown, 1977; Part 1—*Psychology as a Science*; Part 2 —*Classical Conditioning*; Part 3—*Operant Conditioning*; Part 4—*Human Learn-*

ing; Part 5—*Physiological Psychology*; Part 6—*Motivation*; Part 7—*Feeling and Emotion*; Part 8—*Sensation and Perception*; Part 9—*Child Development and Intelligence*; Part 10—*Social Influences on Behavior*; and Part 11—*Development of Personality*. RM.

Perception and Problem Solving, Parts 1–5. Research Media, 51 transparencies, color; Part 1—*Visual Perception*; Part 2—*Mirror-Tracing Kit*; Part 3—*Problem Solving*; Part 4—*Stereo and Binocular Perception*; and Part 5—*Experiments in Perception*. RM.

Slide Set for Introductory Psychology. W. B. Saunders, 1977, 151 slides. WBS.

Transparencies for General Psychology. H. Slucki, 1968, 64 transparencies (36 color). SF.

Slide or transparency sets on a range of very specific topics are available from the following sources:

Lansford Publishing Company.

Life Science Associates.

Zimbardo, P. G. *Stanford Prison Experiment* (a 50-minute slide-cassette presentation, with script; available from P. G. Zimbardo, P.O. Box 4395, Stanford, CA 94305).

Audio Catalogs and Programs

American Academy of Psychotherapists, Tape Library.

American Association for the Advancement of Science.

Audio Colloquies. The colloquies are interviews with eminent behavioral and social scientists. HARM, 1977.

Audio-Forum.

Audiotapes on the Health and Behavioral Sciences, distributed by the University of California (Berkeley), Extension Media Center.

BMA Audio Cassette Programs.

Center for the Study of Democratic Institutions. The Center's holdings include over 600 tapes, many dealing with the topics of race and culture.

Florida, University of, College of Education, Institute for Development of Human Resources.

Instructional Dynamics. This group publishes a series of cassette tapes that can be called "Mental Health Seminars" (e.g., *Personal Adjustment* by Carl Rogers).

Lansford Publishing Company.

Listening Library.

Michigan, University of, Audio-Visual Education Center. The University publishes a separate catalog for its audio tape recordings.

National Center for Audio Tapes.

Pacifica Tape Library.

Psychology Today cassettes. *Psychology Today* Tapes, Box Number 059061, Brooklyn, N.Y. 11205-9061. Over 100 audio cassettes covering a wide range of topics in psychology and mental health.

Psychotherapy Tape Review.

Sound Seminars in Psychology. Over 300 cassettes make up this collection, distributed by Jeffrey Norton Publishers. Most feature very well-known psychologists, who speak on a wide variety of subjects.

Addresses of Distributors

ABC-TV—American Broadcasting Company, TV, 1330 Avenue of the Americas, New York, NY 10019

ABC Merchandising, Inc., Film Library, 267 W. 25th Street, New York, NY 10001

Action for Children's Television, 46 Austin Street, Newtonville, MA 02160

AIMS Films and Videocassettes, 626 Justin Avenue, Glendale, CA 91201-2398

American Academy of Psychotherapists, Tape Library, c/o Dr. Herbert Roth, 2175 N.W. 86th Street, Suite 7, Des Moines, IA 50322

American Association for the Advancement of Science, 1515 Massachusetts Avenue, N.W., Washington, D.C. 20005

American Personnel & Guidance Assoc., 1607 New Hampshire Ave., N.W., Washinton, D.C. 20009

Annenberg/CPB Collection, 1213 Wilmette Avenue, Wilmette, IL 60091

Anti-Defamation League of B'nai B'rith, 315 Lexington Avenue, New York, NY 10016

Aspect IV Educational Films, 41 Riverside Avenue, Westport, CT 06880

Association Films, 600 Grand Avenue, Ridgefield, NJ 07657

Audio-Forum, 901 North Washington Street, Suite 200, Alexandria, VA 22314

BFA Educational Media, 2211 Michigan Avenue, P. O. Box 1795, Santa Monica, CA 90406

BMA Audio Cassette Programs, 270 Madison Avenue, New York, NY 10016

Boston University, Krasker Memorial Film Library, School of Education, 765 Commonwealth Avenue, Boston, MA 02215

British Broadcasting Corporation (BBC), c/o Films Incorporated, 773 Green Bay Road, Wilmette, IL 60091

California, University of, Extension Media Center, Berkeley, CA 94720

Campus Films, 20 E. 46th Street, New York, NY 10017

Carol Media, East 36A Midland Avenue, Paramus, NJ 07652

Carousel Films, 1501 Broadway, New York, NY 10036

Center for Advanced Study of Human Communication, P.O. Box 14461, Columbus OH 43214

Center for the Study of Democratic Institutions, P.O. Box 4068, Santa Barbara, CA 93103

Churchill Films, 662 North Robertson Boulevard, Los Angeles, CA 90069

Corinth Films, 410 East 62nd Street, New York, NY 10021

Cornell University Candid Camera Collection, 215A Uris Hall, Cornell University, Ithaca, NY 14853

Coronet Films, 65 E. South Water Street, Chicago, IL 60601

CRM/McGraw-Hill Films, 110 Fifteenth Street, Del Mar, CA 92014

Document Associates, 211 East 43rd Street, New York, NY 10022

Filmmakers Library, 290 West End Avenue, New York, NY 10023

Films Incorporated, 1144 Wilmette Avenue, Wilmette, IL 60091

Florida State University, Film Library, Tallahassee, FL 32306

Florida, University of, College of Education, Institute for Development of Human Resources, 513 Weil Hall, Gainesville, FL 32601

Grove Press, 53 E. 11th Street, New York, NY 10003

Harcourt Brace Jovanovich, 1250 Sixth Avenue, San Diego, CA 92101

Harper & Row Media, 10 East 53rd Street, New York, NY 10022

Houghton Mifflin Co., New Media, One Beacon Street, Boston, MA 02107

Human Relations Media, 175 Tompkins Avenue, Pleasantville, NY 10570

IBIS Media, P.O. Box 308, Pleasantville, NY 10570

Illinois, University of, Visual Aids Service, Champaign, IL 61820

Indiana University, Audio-Visual Center, Bloomington, IN 47401

International Film Bureau, 323 South Michigan Avenue, Chicago, IL 60604

Jeffrey Norton Publishers, Audio Division, 145 East 49th Street, New York, NY 10017

Kent State University, Audio Visual Services, Kent, OH 44242

Lansford Publishing Co., P.O. Box 8711, Department QQ, San Jose, CA 95155

Learning Corporation of America, 1350 Avenue of the Americas, New York, NY 10019

Life Science Associates, One Fenimore Road, P.O. Box 500, Bayport, NY 11705

Listening Library, Inc., One Park Avenue, Old Greenwich, CT 06870

Macmillan Films, 34 MacQuesten Parkway South, Mt. Vernon, NY 10550

McGraw-Hill Films, 1221 Avenue of the Americas, New York, NY 10020 (for purchase information) or Princeton Road, Hightstown, NJ 08520 (for rental information)

McGraw-Hill Book Co., Trade Order Services, College Division, Princeton Road, Hightstown, NJ 08520

MEDCOM, 1633 Broadway, New York, NY 10019

Mass Media Ministries, 2116 North Charles Street, Baltimore, MD 21218

Mental Health Materials Center, 419 Park Avenue South, New York, NY 10016

Mental Health Media Center, 4907 Cordell Avenue, Bethesda, MD 20014

Michigan, University of, Audio-Visual Education Center, 416 Fourth Street, Ann Arbor MI 48109

Modern Talking Picture Service, 2323 New Hyde Park Road, New Hyde Park, NY 11040

Arthur Mokin Productions, 2900 McBride Lane, Santa Rosa, CA 95401

National Audiovisual Center, National Archives and Records Service, General Services Administration, Washington, D.C. 20409

National Center for Audio Tapes, Stadium 348, University of Colorado, Boulder, CO 80309

National Film Board of Canada, 1251 Avenue of the Americas, New York, NY 10020

National Geographic Educational Services, Department 82, Washington, D.C. 20036

National Information Center for Educational Media, University of Southern California, University Park, Los Angeles, CA 90007

National Medical Audiovisual Center (Annex), Station K, Atlanta, GA 30324

New Day Films, 22 Riverview Drive, Wayne NJ 07470-3191

New York University, Film Library, 26 Washington Place, New York, NY 10003

PBS Video Program, 475 L'Enfant Plaza, S. W., Washington, D.C. 20024

Pacifica Tape Library, Department P. 5316 Venice Boulevard, Los Angeles, CA 90019

Pennsylvania State University, Audio-Visual Department, Special Services Building, University Park, PA 16802

Prentice-Hall Film Library, Englewood Cliffs, NJ 07632

Psychological Films, 205 West 20th Street, Santa Ana, CA 92706

Psychotherapy Tape Library, 59 Fourth Avenue, New York, NY 10003

Pyramid Films, Division of Adams Productions, P.O. Box 1048, Santa Monica, CA 90406

Reel Research, Box 6037, Albany, CA 94706

Research Media, 96 Mount Auburn Street, Cambridge, MA 02138

Research Press, 2612 North Mattis Avenue, Champaign, IL 61820

Roundtable Films, 113 North San Vicente Boulevard, Beverly Hills, CA 90211

W. B. Saunders Company, West Washington Square, Philadelphia, PA 19105

Schloat Productions of Prentice-Hall Media, 150 White Plains Road, Tarrytown, NY 10591

Scott, Foresman, and Co., 1900 East Lake Avenue, Glenview, IL 60025

Sunburst Communications, 41 Washington Avenue, Pleasantville, NY 10570

Time-Life Films, 43 West 16th Street, New York, NY 10011

Time-Life Multimedia, Time & Life Building, New York, NY 10020

University of Kansas, 746 Massachusetts, Lawrence, KS 66044

John Wiley & Sons, 605 Third Avenue, New York, NY 10016 and/or 512 Burlington Avenue, LaGrange, IL 60525

WGBH-TV, 125 Western Avenue, Boston, MA 02134

Women's History Research Center, 2325 Oak Street, Berkeley, CA 94708

Ziff-Davis Publishing Co., Consumer Products Division, 595 Broadway, New York, NY 10012

Index of Abbreviations

ABC	ABC-TV
AF	Association Films
APGA	American Personnel and Guidance Association
BFA	BFA Educational Media
BU	Boston University
CAMP	Campus Films
CF	Carousel Films
CHF	Churchill Films
CM	Carol Media
CRM/MHF	CRM/McGraw-Hill Films
CUCC	Cornell University Candid Camera Collection
DA	Document Associates
DF	Dimension Films
FI	Films Incorporated
FL	Filmmakers Library
GA	Guidance Associates
GRO	Grove Press
HARM	Harper & Row Media
HBJ	Harcourt Brace Jovanovich
HM	Houghton Mifflin
IFB	International Film Bureau
IU	Indiana University
JW	John Wiley and Sons
KSU	Kent State University
LCA	Learning Corporation of America
MAC	Macmillan Films, Inc.
MED	MEDCOM
MHF	McGraw-Hill Films
MHMC	Mental Health Media Center
MOK	Arthur Mokin Productions, Inc.
MTPS	Modern Talking Picture Service
NAC	National Audiovisual Center
NGES	National Geographic Educational Services
NMAC	National Medical Audiovisual Center
NYU	New York University
P	Pyramid
PFI	Psychological Films, Inc.
PH	Prentice-Hall Film Library
PSU	Pennsylvania State University
RM	Research Media
RP	Research Press
SC	Sunburst Communications

SF	Scott, Foresman, and Co.
TLM	Time-Life Multimedia
UC	California, University of
UI	Illinois, University of
UK	University of Kansas
UMich	Michigan, University of
WBS	W. B. Saunders

Computer Simulations

We are beginning to see software developed as supplemental instruction aids in introductory psychology. The following is a list of some available software series.

Psychworld. McGraw-Hill Book Company, College Division, 1221 Avenue of the Americas, New York, NY 10020

Psychworld is an original, user-friendly program that shows students fourteen important psychological experiments. It consists of seven disks with documentation that can be used by students in labs or by instructors in classroom demonstrations.

Program 1: Split-Brain Syndrome
Program 2: Split-Brain Model
Program 3: Brain Localization
Program 4: Sleep and Dreams
Program 5: Classical Conditioning
Program 6: Operant Conditioning
Program 7: Short-Term Memory and Chunking
Program 8: Color Sensation
Program 9: Perception of Space and Motion
Program 10: Feature-Detecting Neurons
Program 11: Development in Infancy
Program 12: Psychoanalysis of a Dream
Program 13: Abnormal Behavior
Program 14: Statistical Microworld

Software for Psychology. David M. Lane, Department of Psychology, Rice University, Houston, TX 77251-1892; 713-527-8101

1. Geometrically Rotated Text
2. Machine Language Library for Use in Psychology Experiments
3. Analysis of Variance Program
4. Demonstration Experiments in Psychology

Stimuli for Recognition Memory Experiments.   John Brooks, Department of Psychology, Rice University, Houston TX 77251-1892; 713-527-8101

Snodgrass and Vanderwart in 1980 published norms for 260 line drawings. Each drawing is rated on name agreement, image agreement, familiarity, and visual complexity. These stimuli have been digitized and stored in MacPaint format for easy use in memory experiments.

Software for Psychology.   Doug Chute, Department of Psychology and Sociology, Drexel University; 215-895-1722

1. Perceptual and Motor Skills. Mirror tracing and pursuit rotor experiments for an introductory psychology course.
2. Central Nervous System. Introduction to the structure and function of the central nervous system.